Ethics and Digital Transition

Ethics and Digital Transition

Edited by

Marie-Hélène Abel
Nada Matta
Hedi Karray
Inès Saad

iSTE

WILEY

First published 2025 in Great Britain and the United States by ISTE Ltd and John Wiley & Sons, Inc.

ISTE Ltd
27-37 St George's Road
London SW19 4EU
UK

www.iste.co.uk

John Wiley & Sons, Inc.
111 River Street
Hoboken, NJ 07030
USA

www.wiley.com

Library of Congress Control Number: 2025930136

British Library Cataloguing-in-Publication Data
A CIP record for this book is available from the British Library
ISBN 978-1-78630-957-0

Contents

Foreword

Ethics is a branch of philosophy that determines the rules to which we should all adhere with regard to our behavior. What should we do? How should we behave in society? What maxims should we adopt to guide us through the world? What do we mean by doing the right thing? Ethics helps – or so it claims – to answer these questions. Originally, ethics were based on lessons learned from old habits and precepts, or on people's desire for perfection, their aspiration to virtue. From the Age of Enlightenment onward, there was a desire to find broad, general principles, on a par with those of the physical sciences, to which all recommendations could be reduced. Such is the case with "deontic", which commands respect for a set of rules acceptable to all, or "utilitarianism", which proposes maximizing a measure of utility. In the course of the 20th century, these principles entered a crisis: the complexity of the issues at stake meant that individuals were no longer able to assess the consequences or the very meaning of their actions, and were thus no longer able to guide themselves. Philosophers began to think about a wide range of issues in order to define ethics. Such was the case with Jurgen Habermas' work on the sincere, disinterested deliberation view to agreeing on standards of acceptable behaviors, or Hans Jonas' reflections on the "heuristics of fear" and responsibility toward future generations.

In the age of digital technology, social networks and targeted advertising, the way people live and interact with each other is challenged. The ties that weave the fabric of society – friendship, trust, reputation – are being rewritten. Globalization also means we need to refer to shared values on a planetary scale. In this context, agreeing on a common moral code is even more delicate than in the past. Nevertheless, even if it is still difficult today to establish the basis of our ideas of what is good and right, from which we decide to regulate our behavior, we remain free and therefore responsible for our actions. Unless we are deprived of the means to act, or lose the use of reason, we always assume the consequences of our actions.

With devices programmed using artificial intelligence techniques, in particular machine learning algorithms trained on large masses of data, we are now confronted with unprecedented situations: automata seem to decide for us, or at least whisper decisions to us, without being able to understand what drives them. These devices are sometimes referred to as “agents”, or even “autonomous agents”, to mean that they act on their own. However, this is a misnomer for two reasons. On the one hand, they are not agents in that they do not initiate action, even if they contribute to automatic decision-making; in other words, there is no human intervention between the acquisition of information and action. On the other hand, they are not autonomous in the strict sense of the word, as they have no will of their own. There are times when we strive to preserve a human presence in the decision-making process, but when this happens, the human presence is all too often mere tokenism. This is particularly true when the machine’s verdict remains as unclear as that of an oracle. We then have no choice but to submit to it or reject it outright. The fact remains, however, that we are increasingly acting through such devices, either by delegation or under their control. In this context, we are no longer always in a position to answer for our actions.

Therefore, if we are to assume our responsibilities, we need to take steps at an early stage in the design, production and monitoring of machines. For example, we need to check that they preserve individuals’ freedom of choice and protect privacy by not leaking personal data, that they are free from the weight of prejudices or what we now call biases, that they indicate the information elements that lead to the decision in each particular case so that human operators can exercise their judgment without being subject to the dictates of the machine, etc. Such “autonomous agents”, subject to all of these requirements, cannot be qualified as moral or ethical. To use the old Kantian distinction, they do not act “out of duty”, but “according to the rules of duty” that we impose on them.

If properly designed, however, they will help us to behave as moral agents ourselves. The various decisions we make through them will conform to our self-imposed moral prescriptions. The stakes are accordingly high. This book focuses on just that: how do we go about designing such devices in practice?

Also, what ethical criteria should be applied to their design? We are thinking here of compliance with laws and regulations, the biases we have mentioned, the resolution of conflicts of norms and changes in professions and in working life.

Jean-Gabriel GANASCIA
February 2025

Introduction

Ethics and Digital Transition Challenges and Investigations

Ethics was originally defined in antiquity as "moral principles" (Singer 1986; Aristotle 2019; Frey and Wellman 2008) dictating the virtues of behavior (Hursthouse 1999). Today, it is increasingly identified with principles of deontology and social rules linked to the consequences of actions (Bonhoeffer 2012; Siau et al. 2020). The dimension of evaluating activity and systems has therefore become important in order to respond to these principles.

Furthermore, society's digital transition is tending to exploit systems emanating from artificial intelligence (AI) and data processing. AI techniques tend to simulate behavior and, above all, reproduce thoughts and actions. The consequences of these actions must then be assessed in the light of social rules and ethics. In fact, AI techniques are mainly based on sampling and data analysis, on the one hand, and cognitive rules and procedures, on the other hand. The results of these approaches modify our everyday behavior by introducing new elements generated by the connections of massive knowledge processing and algorithms. Deep and machine learning, as well as ChatGPT[1], are among the main examples of this invasion of our activity.

The main question debated in this book is: "what are the different aspects to be considered when assessing ethical principles in approaches to digital

---

Introduction written by Nada MATTA, Marie-Hélène ABEL, Hedi KARRAY and Inès SAAD.

1 See: https://openai.com/blog/chatgpt?utm_source=bdmtools&utm_medium=siteweb&utm_campaign=chatgpt.

transition and intelligent systems in particular?". To answer this question, we first explain the main technologies, techniques and uses of intelligent systems. We then explore the works addressing ethics in digital transition to highlight the ethical dimensions to be taken into account in the development of these systems. These are extracted from a survey of digital researchers. Finally, we introduce a summary of the seven chapters of this book that address these issues.

These investigations are being carried out as part of the activities of the French chapter of IEEE SMC[2], where a number of initiatives focus on studying the relationship between digital technology and human activity.

I.1. The digital transition and its challenges

Information technologies increasingly offer processing approaches that enable us to understand the internal and external socio-economic ecosystem. On the one hand, these techniques make it possible to capture and exploit data and information produced by an activity and/or existing in the environment, and, on the other, to provide decision-support tools. Socio-economic players are therefore called upon to grasp these technologies and integrate them into their organizations (Hesse 2018).

The digital transition is defined as the integration of information processing technologies, while conveying a profound change in habits, to enable an understanding of the ecosystem, thereby leading to better organizational performance (Hesse 2018; Zacklad 2020). We can cite, as an example, the massive exploitation of teleworking support tools (Zoom®, Microsoft Teams®, Webex®), notably during the Covid-19 health crisis. Similarly, our understanding of the environment is currently raising social awareness, leading to more sustainable action.

Advances in information processing technologies are bringing about radical changes in activities and behavior, particularly in communication and decision-making (Figure I.1) (Zacklad 2020; Vial 2021).

These technologies are largely based on AI approaches that have proven their worth in supporting ecosystem understanding and decision-making.

2 See: https://r8.ieee.org/france-smc/.

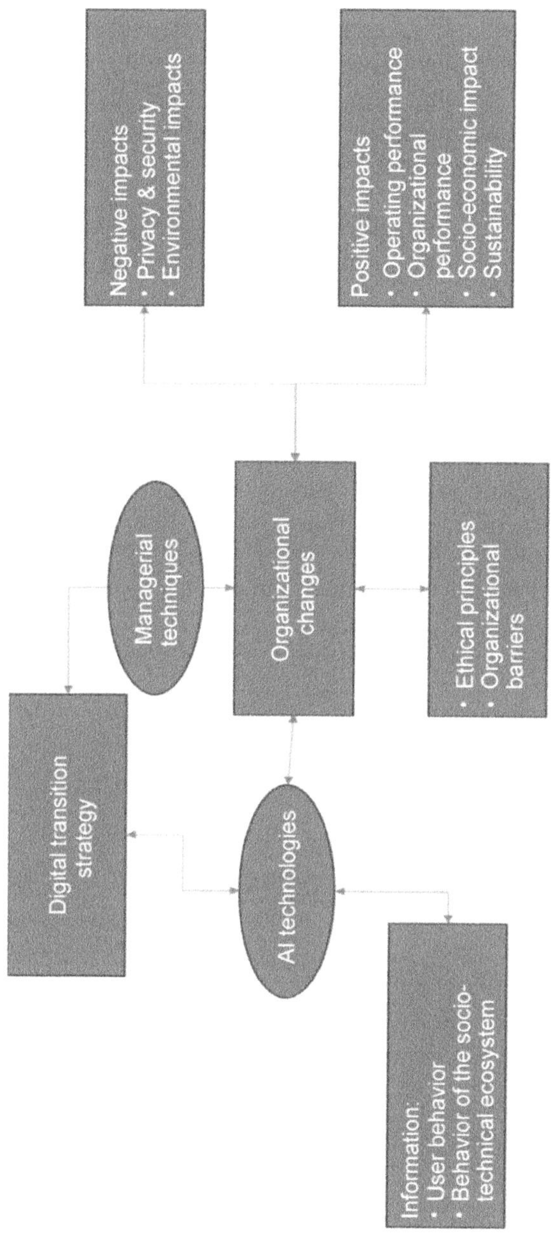

Figure I.1. *The digital transition of organizations (Vial 2021)*

I.1.1. *Artificial intelligence techniques*

The basic principles of AI approaches are to represent human reasoning and behavior in computational techniques (Fetzer et al. 1990; Dick 2019). For instance, rule-based systems tend to illustrate mainly deduction, case-based reasoning stands for inferences by analogy, while machine learning algorithms tend to simulate induction.

We also mention multi-agent systems that represent the cooperation of bees and ant communities. This similarity in the behavior of living organisms is leading to real collaborations between humans and AI algorithms, and not just to help with decision-making and assistance.

Some AI approaches use cognitive dimensions and propose logical reasoning based on experience feedback knowledge (ontologies, rule-based and case-based systems). Other techniques use statistical data processing, based on data lakes to aggregate features and generate rules and reasoning models (neural networks, deep learning) (Hunt 2014).

These two approaches interconnect through supervised learning, currently referred to as hybrid AI (Figure I.2).

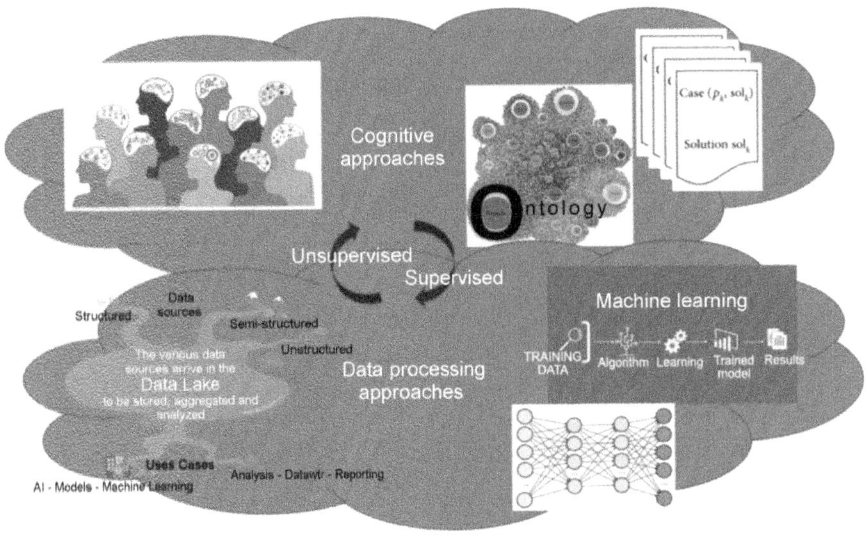

Figure I.2. *Main artificial intelligence techniques. For a color version of this figure, see www.iste.co.uk/abel/ethics.zip*

Important questions arise concerning the influence and relevance of these techniques for understanding the ecosystem:

– Are the expertise and data used in these techniques enough complete to suggest models for reasoning and effective decision-making? Are the data global enough to represent real-life situations?

– Can these models be so complete as to claim to represent different aspects of human reasoning?

– Can these approaches recognize and avoid erroneous data and incomplete experiments?

I.1.2. *The main applications of AI*

From 1955 (the birth of the notion of AI and the Turing test) to the present day, the application of AI has grown exponentially, especially with the increasing computational capabilities of machines. In terms of applications, AI was initially used in healthcare and industry as knowledge- and case-based systems (Dick 2019). Other techniques, such as fuzzy logic and neural networks, are used in image and speech processing (Hunt 2014) and robotics. Similarly, multi-agent systems are used in networking and Cloud Computing.

We can cite a number of applications for these systems in certain fields (Figure I.3):

– natural language processing: translation, information retrieval and text generation for medical, industrial, marketing and legal applications;

– image processing: supervision, cultural and archaeological recognition, facial recognition, medical diagnosis, climate change, augmented reality, digital twins, etc.;

– digital data processing: problem prediction, maintenance, behavior prediction, supervision, customer-market relations, recommendation, etc.;

– the Semantic web: data web, information retrieval, text generation, chatbot, social networks and mutual aid, e-learning, etc.

These tools lead to a transformation in user behavior and a major organizational change while considering the influence of data characterization and the prediction on the ecosystem behavior. These approaches not only represent human behavior, but also emphasize their mutual influences with the environment. We can even mention the possibility of self-evolution of AI systems, just like the reasoning they represent. The apprehension of these techniques increasingly raises ethical questions, which are essential to the integration of these approaches in the socio-economic environment.

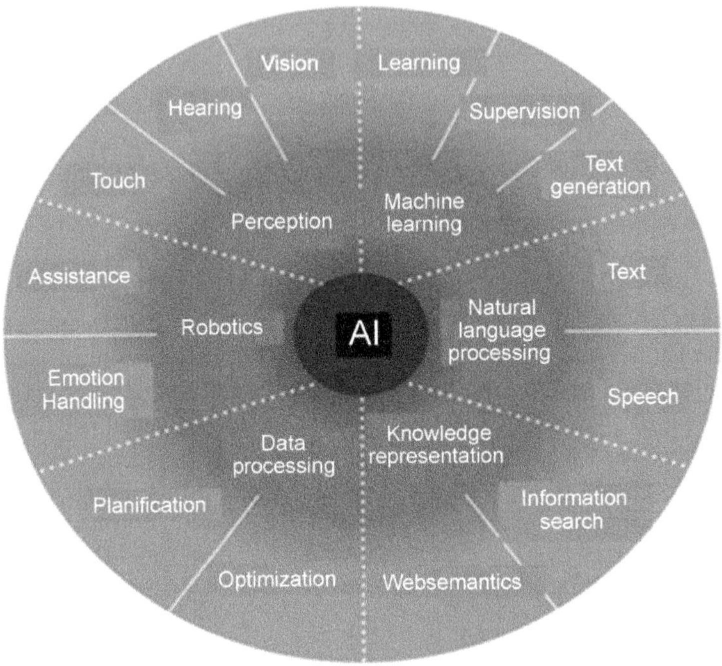

Figure I.3. *Examples of AI application fields. For a color version of this figure, see www.iste.co.uk/abel/ethics.zip*

I.2. Ethical principles

Ethics, by definition, is related to morality, virtues of behavior and social rules (Hursthouse 1999). The issue of applying theories of morality and virtues as principles of ethics (Siau et al. 2020) is addressed in several sciences, including law, medicine, business and engineering (Frey and Wellman 2008). As a result, principles were then defined, wherein the consequences of these sciences in society are mainly studied. We can note, for example, that in the medical sciences, certain principles have been prescribed such as common goals, fiduciary duties, legal and professional standards and responsibility, as well as methods for transforming these principles into practice. Similarly, the notion of environmental ethics and the sustainable behavior of human in their ecosystem are studied in the engineering sciences (Palmer et al. 2014). In this science, ethical concepts are introduced as responsibility, autonomy, virtue, right and moral status (Powers and Ganascia 2020).

I.3. Ethics and artificial intelligence

The application of theoretical ethical definitions in the digital transition primarily points to the analysis of the nature and social impact of this transition and the justification of this impact (Newell and Marabelli 2015; Majchrzak et al. 2016; Mittelstadt et al. 2016). Companies are invited to manage a trade-off between their performance and ethical principles (Vial 2021). These trade-offs should be at the operational and strategic levels (Zacklad 2020; Vial 2021). The application of ethical principles in the digital transition is strongly linked to the integration of data processing applications and AI technologies.

Currently, several scientific organizations such as the ACM and IEEE have defined certain ethical principles for the digital transition and AI. The OECD (2019) and the European Commission's Artificial Intelligence Expert Group (AI HLEG 2019) have proposed four principles concerning human autonomy, harm avoidance, fairness and explicability. These principles are derived from those defined in certain sciences and especially in the medical sciences (Mittelstadt et al. 2016). Mittelstadt et al. (2016) argue that these principles cannot be applied directly in the digital transition. Indeed, confusion exists in the definition of the responsibility that must be shared between the multiple developers of AI technologies and the behaviors of these technologies users. Therefore, there are major challenges ahead in defining the standards and ethical rules for these technologies, particularly in order to ensure sustainable development and use. It will be essential to develop AI systems that interact ethically with humans and society. In his paper, Hagendorff (2020) presents a survey of various guidelines on AI ethics. Key principles are highlighted in this study such as accountability for explainable AI, fairness, privacy and discrimination related to data mining, and bias and robustness in machine learning.

Similarly, AI techniques can influence research and discovery in science, especially when data mining and machine learning are used. Powers and Ganascia (2020) mention "the expansion of knowledge due to AI seems to be a resource for epistemic study, and at the same time, we cannot fully understand what we are actually getting". Ethical principles such as justice and morality are therefore necessary to deal with this exploration, in order to avoid discrimination and prejudice. The autonomy and dynamic evolution of AI agents and algorithms tend to simulate behavior. Fairness, robustness and explicability must play an important role in the evolution of these techniques to take account of social rules, sustainability and environmental impacts (Palmer et al. 2014).

We can note that studies on the application of ethics in the digital transition, and AI approaches in particular, still raise a number of challenges. In our study, we conducted a survey of the French AI research community on these issues. Some results of this survey are explored in the following section.

I.4. Research surveys in France

Surveys on ethics in AI have been carried out among French researchers in AI and digital systems, organized by the French chapter of the IEEE SMC scientific community.

A number of questions were asked on these subjects via the mailing list of the CNRS I3 research group "Modeling and interoperability of companies and information systems"[3]:

1) What ethical aspects do you think intelligent systems should take into account?

2) How can these aspects be modeled?

3) Can machine learning be considered ethical, and under what constraints?

4) Ethics can be considered at various stages: audit, knowledge acquisition and needs identification, data collection, processing of this knowledge and/or data, development of rules and decision support systems, operation and use of these systems. How can we ensure compliance?

5) Could the identification of a trusted third-party organization be one of the solutions to identify responsibilities? Which organizations could play this role?

---

3 See: http://crinfo.univ-paris1.fr/ModESI/index.htm.

6) Which disciplines do you think should take part in ethics research in the digital transition?

A group of 26 researchers answered these questions. Their answers are summarized below.

I.4.1. *Ethical considerations for digital systems*

Various aspects of ethics have been identified in intelligent systems. Some of these aspects are linked to the philosophical definition of ethics, such as morality and value, but others correspond to social rules and behaviors.

Examples include prudence, loyalty, group ethics and responsibilities (Figure I.4).

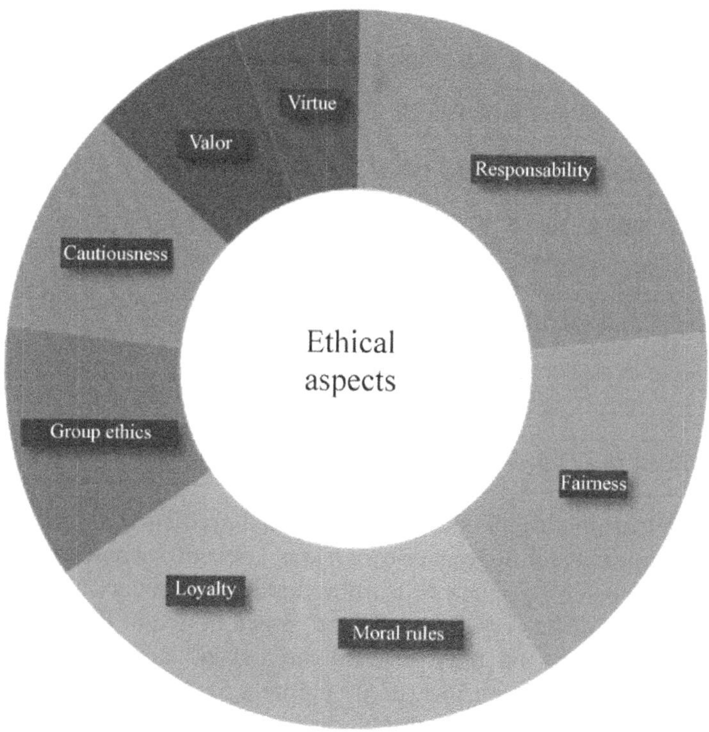

Figure I.4. *Ethical dimensions to consider in AI. For a color version of this figure, see: www.iste.co.uk/abel/ethics.zip*

I.4.2. *How do we consider ethics in digital technologies?*

The development of decision support systems is linked to the explicability and transparency of these techniques that are mentioned as guides for the following.

– Modeling approaches:

- design and modeling rules;
- expression of model constraints and limits;
- author and institution metadata search;
- reaching compromises on standards and techniques;
- reduction errors due to bias and abstractions.

– Development of decision support systems:

- sharing of responsibilities between human actors and digital systems;
- the final decision will be made by a human;
- specification and explanation of rules.

– Actors who need to be involved:

- legislators;
- end users;
- human and social scientists;
- system designers and developers.

I.4.3. *Ethical machine learning*

Machine learning offers decision-making and prediction algorithms based on the recognition and aggregation of data. Lack of completeness of data sources and representativeness of learning models, discovery and search can largely influence the results, whether prediction or decision-making. Awareness and alerts on bias, discriminated data, lack of resources and uncontrolled use have been identified (Figure I.5). Recommendations have been formulated to reduce these dimensions, in particular on the expressiveness and explanation of machine learning algorithms using semantic representations, in order to highlight the transparency of such processing and ethical validation.

	Semiotic data status
	1.1. Decision support tools
	1.2. User-friendly tools
	1.3. Ethical uses
Positive	A fair and open approach (Open Source)
	Properties of fairness, loyalty, transparency and explicability
	Validation by an independent expert
	1.4. Validation by the public
	1.5. Supervision under principles

	Bias
	1.6. Discrimination bias
	1.7. Incomplete resources
Negative	1.8. Subjectivity
	1.9. Uncontrolled uses
	Social context not taken into account
	1.10 Automatic decision

Figure I.5. *Recommendations for ethical machine learning. For a color version of this figure, see: www.iste.co.uk/abel/ethics.zip*

I.4.4. *How can we ensure that ethical principles are respected in intelligent systems?*

Two main dimensions were noted in response to this question:

– The people involved in developing these systems should have integrity and show complete transparency in their processing. Similarly, there should be a clear separation of concerns and purposes, to reduce the financial interests underlying these developments.

– Social and democratic debates are necessary, to validate the potential uses of these systems regarding privacy, intellectual property, certifications and legal regulations.

I.4.5. *Trusted organizations*

As a guarantee of compliance with such knowledge and recommendations, researchers propose the definition of trusted organizations with legal, governmental and scientific experts (Figure I.6).

1.11.	CNIL, CSA
Scientific and legal committees (by branch)	
1.12.	Trusted third parties
1.13.	Expert and citizen committees
1.14.	States, European Union
1.15.	The whole world
1.16.	Audit platforms

Figure I.6. *Trusted organizations. For a color version of this figure, see: www.iste.co.uk/abel/ethics.zip*

I.4.6. *Disciplines to mobilize*

As shown in Figure I.6, developers of digital systems cannot apply ethical principles by themselves. They need to collaborate with researchers from other disciplines to introduce these aspects into their products, especially when we consider the significant impact of these products on the society.

Figure I.7 shows that law, social sciences and philosophy are needed to identify the rules and principles of evaluation, in collaboration with the engineering sciences that mainly develop and use these systems.

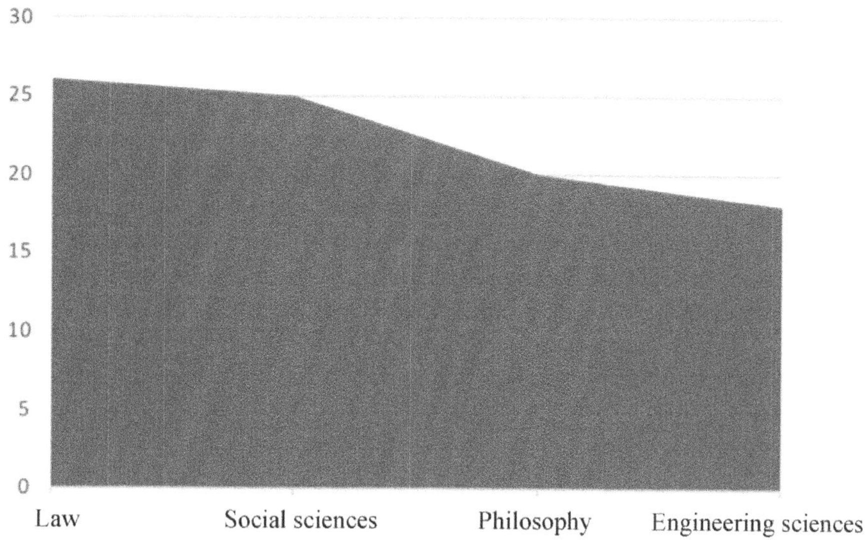

Figure I.7. *Disciplines involved in the ethical validation of digital systems*

I.5. The book's layout

This book is organized into seven chapters that address a number of ethical issues in the digital transition. First, in Chapter 1, Bruno Bachimont discusses the philosophical dimension of ethics in technology, highlighting the notion of the non-neutrality of technology and ethical design. In Chapter 2, Florence Sèdes highlights the voluntary and involuntary biases in clustering algorithms and approaches that support decision-making, in particular the machine learning currently widely used and influencing decision-making strategies. Transparency and sustainability are discussed in this context. Chapter 3 by Alain Mille examines the use of digital techniques, particularly AI approaches. A number of characteristics are set out to guide the designers of digital tools in responding to ethical notions. In Chapter 4, Grégory Bonnet, Nadjet Bourdache, Abdel-Illah Mouaddib and Mihail Stojanovski discuss the integration of ethics in the design of autonomous systems, arguing the difficulty of providing these agents with the ability to judge their own actions. The applicability of digital approaches in the industry of the future is then presented in Chapter 5 by Emmanuel Caillaud and Lou Grimal. They underline the stakes of these approaches to face sustainability and ecological challenges in production systems. Some principles are then defined to guide industry actors facing these challenges. Chapter 6 by Damien Trentesaux, Lamia Berrah and Karine Samuel completes these reflections with a discussion of the ethical risks associated with the various uses of digital techniques in industry. The link between these risks and industrial performance is highlighted in order to propose an operational framework to integrate ethical concepts into the future industry. In Chapter 7, Anne Dourgnon, Eunika Mercier Laurent and Alain Antoine present an application of digital techniques within industry, illustrating the transformation brought by the digital transition in the daily actions in several organizations such as EDF, FRAMATOME, SPIE Nucléaire and TECHNICATOME, Boost Conseil and ASSYSTEM. The book concludes with a discussion of the future challenges of ethics in the digital transition by Hedi Karray.

I.6. Acknowledgments

This book is the fruit of the efforts of the French IEEE SMC chapter. We would particularly like to thank Jean-Paul Barthès, Jean-Paul Jamont, Mickaël Coustaty and François Rauscher for their help.

I.7. References

AI HLEG (2019). Ethics guidelines for trustworthy AI. Document, European Commission, Brussels.

Aristotle, A. (2019). *The Ethics of Aristotle*. BoD – Books on Demand, Norderstedt.

Boden, M.A. (1996). *Artificial Intelligence*. Elsevier, Amsterdam.

Bonhoeffer, D. (2012). *Ethics*. Simon and Schuster, New York.

Dick, S. (2019). Artificial intelligence. *Harvard Data Science Review*, 1(1), 1–8.

European Commission (2019). High level expert group on Artificial Intelligence. Ethics guidelines for trustworthy AI. Report, Brussels.

Fetzer, J.H. (1990). *What is Artificial Intelligence?* Springer, Amsterdam.

Frey, R.G. and Wellman, C.H. (2008). *A Companion to Applied Ethics*. Wiley-Blackwell, Oxford.

Hagendorff, T. (2020). The ethics of AI ethics: An evaluation of guidelines. *Minds and Machines*, 30(1), 99–120.

Hesse, A. (2018). Digitalization and leadership – How experienced leaders interpret daily realities in a digital world. In *Hawaii International Conference on System Sciences*, Waikoloa Beach, 1854–1863.

Hunt, E.B. (2014). *Artificial Intelligence*. Academic Press, Cambridge.

Hursthouse, R. (1999). *On Virtue Ethics*. Oxford University Press, Oxford.

Majchrzak, A., Markus, M.L., Wareham, J. (2016). Designing for digital transformation. *MIS Quarterly*, 40(2), 267–278.

Mittelstadt, B.D., Allo, P., Taddeo, M., Wachter, S., Floridi, L. (2016). The ethics of algorithms: Mapping the debate. *Big Data & Society*, 3(2). doi: 10.1177/2053951716679679.

Newell, S. and Marabelli, M. (2015). Strategic opportunities (and challenges) of algorithmic decision-making: A call for action on the long-term societal effects of 'datification'. *Journal of Strategic Information Systems*, 24(1), 3–14.

OECD (2019). Forty-two countries adopt new OECD Principles on Artificial Intelligence. Document, Paris [Online]. Available at: http://www.oecd.org/science/forty-two-countries-adopt-new-oecdprinciples-on-artificial-intelligence.htm.

Palmer, C., McShane, K., Sandler, R. (2014). Environmental ethics. *Annual Review of Environment and Resources*, 39, 419–442. doi: 10.1146/annurev-environ-121112-094434.

Powers, T.M. and Ganascia, J.G. (2020). The ethics of the ethics of AI. In *The Oxford Handbook of Ethics of AI*, Dubber, M.D., Pasquale, F., Das, S. (eds). Oxford University Press, Oxford.

Siau, K. and Wang, W. (2020). Artificial intelligence (AI) ethics: Ethics of AI and ethical AI. *Journal of Database Management (JDM)*, 31(2), 74–87.

Singer, P. (1986). *Applied Ethics*. Oxford University Press, Oxford.

Vial, G. (2021). Understanding digital transformation: A review and a research agenda. In *Managing Digital Transformation*, Hinterhuber, A., Vescovi, T., Checchinato, F. (eds). Routledge, Oxford.

Zacklad, M. (2020). Les enjeux de la transition numérique et de l'innovation collaborative dans les mutations du travail et du management dans le secteur public. In *Les transformations du travail dans les services publics*, Gillet, A. (ed.). Presses de l'EHESP, Paris.

1

Digital Ethics: Empowering Agents and Taking Care of Systems

1.1. Introduction

Ethics has become a commonplace question in the context of technical design. However, technology has long been ignored in debates on ethics or moral philosophy on the grounds that it serves only as a tool in the service of an intention and an action, and that only the latter can possess an ethical or moral dimension: the possible mobilization of techniques is not involved in the moral scope of the action.

Indeed, technology suffers from a double deficit, between logos and ethos. The epistemic values of technology have fallen back on the science of which it is the application: the intellectual values of technology are those of the science from which it derives and which it equips. In the context of technology, moral values, which are specific to action and come under the heading of philosophy or practical reason, according to traditional terminology, are related to their use, to the actor, to implementation, but never to technology itself, which remains neutral in relation to its use.

It could be argued that this stance is still very much in evidence, for if technology is invited into debates on ethics, and if the latter asks about technology, it is often through the questioning of use, in particular via the challenge of design, which aims to translate practical goals into technical structure. The engineer should therefore be accountable for their inventions

---

Chapter written by Bruno BACHIMONT.

through the intentions of use materialized in the functionalities programmed or inscribed in the technical object.

If this posture persists, it is because it conceals a part of the truth that we do not wish to renounce, even if it does not allow us to deal satisfactorily with the question of the ethics of our systems. If we are to believe, Kranzberg (1986) and the six laws he enunciates about technology, particularly the first one, technology is neither good nor bad; nor is it neutral. In other words, while it is certainly difficult to associate an ethical value with a technical object in itself – a knife can slice my neighbor's neck or a slice of bread – this object can nevertheless play a role and influence on the ethical behavior of agents, and thus have an ethical dimension. This raises, on the one hand, a legitimate question concerning contemporary digital systems and how they modify or reconfigure the ethical aspects of technology, and, on the other hand, the stakes of their use.

To this end, we will approach the issue gradually. First, we will clarify and deepen the thesis of the ethical non-neutrality of technology, and how the notion of ethical design can be misleading as a watered-down, modernized form of the neutrality of technology and its objects, with the ethical question arising only when humans intervene, in use and, to appear modern and responsible, in design.

In this context of the essential non-neutrality of technology, we will address the question of the digital and the algorithm: what role does computation play in the ethical functioning or otherwise of the artifacts it animates or instrumentalizes? We must first clarify what we mean by ethics here in order understand that ethics boils down to the question of moral imputation and responsibility. We propose an ethical typology that distinguishes between ethical agent, patient and witness. An ethical agent is someone who can answer for their actions. An ethical patient is someone for whom we must answer, because they are not in a position to assume ethical responsibility, although they could do so in certain circumstances. The ethical witness is our witness of morality: our behavior towards it is the mirror of our morality. The preferred ethical witnesses are nonhuman living beings, artifacts and the environment.

While digital systems are never ethical agents or patients as such, we will address their ethical dimension from several angles.

On the one hand, digital technology provides a universal computational medium which, on the sole condition that data is available and can be manipulated, regardless of its heterogeneity, enables the most diverse realities to be processed in a single movement for variable purposes. For example, correlating diets and health to define insurance premiums, or recruitment profiles based on these same diets, gives rise to a decision-making principle that appears arbitrary and unjustified when it comes to allocating or not allocating an insurance premium or a job. Numerical systems then become tyrannical instruments, as they import hierarchies from other, heterogeneous domains, thereby introducing arbitrariness. The principle of the independence of different spheres of practice, knowledge and power is at stake here.

On the other hand, digital systems address users by positioning them in various ways: the instrumentation of practical situations by digital systems should enable users to exercise their role as moral agents. These tools must enable users to behave in a way that develops the qualities needed to exercise their ethical commitments. When, for reasons specific to the situation, the system has to decide a priori on the decisions to be taken (response time, complexity of processing, etc.) in place of the users, the design that determines these decisions must consider the consequences entailed by these decisions. Ultimately, however, the decision taken by the tool must never concern people's lives, and must be referred back to a human decision-maker.

In terms of the classic postures of contemporary ethics, our conclusions are clear: a system must enable users to assume an ethics of virtues, or else the design must assume a consequentialist perspective to decide in the best interests of the stakeholders, while respecting prohibitions, thereby adhering to a deontological perspective. This brings us to the conclusion that we must take care of these systems, which are now the mediators of our actions and the constituents of our environment, like an already existing thing to be inscribed in its own order and maintained in harmony with its environment.

1.2. Technology and ethical neutrality

The non-neutrality of technology has often been argued in the sense that it is ambivalent:

> It is in this context, which can't help but be passionate, that I'd like to draw attention to one of the most important

> characteristics of technical progress: its ambivalence. By this I mean that the development of technology is neither good, nor bad, nor neutral – but is made up of a complex mix of positive and negative elements – "good" and "bad" if we want to adopt a moral vocabulary. By this I also mean that it is impossible to dissociate these factors in such a way as to obtain a purely good technique, and that it does not depend at all on the use we make of technical tools to obtain exclusively good results. In fact, in this very use we are in turn modified. In the technical phenomenon as a whole, we do not remain untouched; we are not only indirectly oriented by the equipment itself, but also adapted with a view to making better use of the technique, thanks to the psychological means of adaptation… (Ellul 1965).

Technology is not neutral, because it modifies us through the use we make of it, through the adaptation it imposes on us. While it is impossible to limit the use of a tool to situations where it would be good, and to exclude those where it is bad, the moral question concerning which use of technology is desirable or which should be avoided is not limited to the use of the tool itself. The moral question of technology directly affects human beings, and not just the use they make of their artifacts. To use a traditional vocabulary, the ethical question arises in the context of an ontological division between being and ought-to-be. If the former corresponds to what is, with knowledge and science aiming to give an account of what is, thus positing the value of truth as what must be attained, the latter concerns what ought to exist, to be, even if this is not the case, as this would be a world conforming to what ought to be. The human agent pursues truth by describing the world as it is, and pursues happiness or goodness by contributing to and acting in accordance with what the world ought to be and not as it is.

Technology has no place in this great sharing, other than as a possible means of helping to bring about what ought-to-be. However, technology shows that this great sharing is incomplete, because it is not situated in either of the two terms, but rather refers to the power-to-be. Technology is the invention of the possible: that which is not yet defined as being, whether as effective being (being) or desirable being (ought-to-be). Technology is not simply what makes it possible to realize what is possible, i.e. what is already identified and defined in ontology, but what makes it possible to invent it. Technology transforms ontology into a dynamic of invention (Stiegler 1998). By creating the possible, technology reconfigures both being and ought-to-be, and consequently the stakes of human action. Ethics is a question that arises not in the abstract, but in the conditions of our instrumented action, an action made possible by this instrumentation, and in the conditions of our identity reconfigured or reinvented by this instrumentation. Ethics is a technical question.

1.3. What are the ethics of technology?

1.3.1. *Contemporary ethics*

The ethical questions raised by technology are not new, but they have become increasingly important since the industrial era, when the consequences of technology on people's lives meant that technology became part of the ethical debate. However, although the tradition has been considerably renewed, it is not easy to know how to integrate the technical question into the ethical debate. The contemporary tradition considers ethical issues from three complementary angles.

– Meta-ethics, which would be to ethics what metaphysics is to physics (Desmons et al. 2019): whereas for the latter, the question is not so much to know what are the given properties of a physical object, but to determine what it is to be a physical object. Meta-ethics does not seek to know what should be done, but rather wants to determine whether this question makes sense and whether it has one answer or several, and finally how it is appropriate to proceed to reach them. This questioning is usually divided into four parts:

- moral semantics, where we want to know what is the appropriate vocabulary (if any) and what are the modes of signification of moral judgments (for example, whether or not moral judgments have a truth value);

- moral epistemology, which is concerned with the question of whether moral judgments are a form of knowledge;

- moral ontology, which links moral judgments to moral facts whose modes of existence must be established;

- moral psychology, which deals with the motivations that drive people to act morally or not.

– Normative ethics, which adopt a point of view to determine a way of acting, which it then standardizes. Three normative ethics are distinguished:

- deontologism, inspired by the Kantian imperative (Kant 2015): according to the latter, an action is moral if its rule can be universalized without contradiction (we do not have the right to lie, because if everyone lies, then lying no longer has any impact: it is because people usually tell the truth that disguising it allows us to be believed nonetheless). Deontology is the abstract formalism of conformity to a rule or law. What is moral is what is right because it conforms to a universal rule, often a negative one ("thou shalt not lie");

- consequentialism, which is inspired by Mill's utilitarianism (Mill 2015) and determines moral action as that which maximizes the good: whereas deontologism looks more for the just than the good, which seems indeterminable according to this approach, consequentialism is based on a conception of the good that should be maximized;

- virtue ethics, more Aristotelian in inspiration (Aristotle 1965), determines moral action as that which the virtuous agent would do; in other words, moral is that which conforms to the virtues and honors them by conforming to them (courage, probity, loyalty, honesty, etc.).

– Applied ethics, which are concerned with the application of normative ethics in a practical, organizational or social context. Examples include medical ethics and business ethics.

In this architectonics of ethics, technology could be seen as an applied ethic. This is often the point of view adopted by various professional circles. For example, Cigref and Syntec Numérique have published a digital reference framework in which it is clearly explained that:

> There are several families of ethics, all stemming from moral philosophy: normative ethics, meta-ethics and applied ethics. The latter is what we're concerned with here. Indeed, we can consider that digital technology opens up a new space for action, which is not neutral and must therefore be able to apply a certain number of ethical principles. Some of these considerations may be novel, as each technology raises its own issues. Digital ethics is therefore above all an applied ethics, which will have to adapt or reinvent itself, depending on the contexts and technologies in place (Duplan et al. 2018).

However, this evidence does not seem to be relevant to an object such as technology, whether it be specialized to one type of technology, in this case digital technology, particularly in view of its non-neutrality. Indeed, as we have seen, if technology deserves special ethical consideration, it is above all because of its constitutive and constituting dimension (Steiner 2010), or insofar as it transforms us (Ellul 1967; Kranzberg 1986). The ethical question can therefore only be posed in the context of the system formed by humans and technology, rather than considering one independently of the other. Indeed, it is not a question of determining the moral actions of a human equipped with tools by considering only the human, which would be a way of reconducting the thesis of the indifference or neutrality of technology, or only the tool or instrument, which would be a way of introducing a technical determinism into ethics. What we therefore need is an approach that thematizes the position or posture of the equipped moral agent, taking into account the overall human-technical complex.

We realize, however, that the traditional approaches mentioned above, despite their immense interest and relevance, do not directly address the question of the moral agent, the one for whom there is a moral judgment and a decision to be made. For this, we turn to a different tradition, one that is more complementary than opposed to those already mentioned, inspired by Paul Ricœur's phenomenology. Nonetheless, the different approaches mentioned here will be used to thematize the different relationships we can have with a digital system.

1.3.2. *The ethics of moral agents*

Following Paul Ricœur's proposals in "Oneself as Another" ("Soi-même comme un autre") (Ricœur 1992), the moral agent is the subject of moral imputation, the one who assumes their past and commits themselves to their future. Being responsible for what has happened (take responsibility for) and for what will happen (make a commitment) is the key to an agent's morality. If agents, on the basis of these assumed or claimed responsibilities, make judgments whose semantics must be elucidated, concerning facts whose ontology must be clarified and, lastly, concerning reasoning and knowledge whose status and nature must be studied, this merely declines the fundamental fact of the human agent's inscription in a time that they make their own, a past that becomes theirs because they assume and claim it, a future that they appropriate because they project themselves into it. The meta-ethics and normative ethics we have mentioned are all ways of studying and describing this anthropological and phenomenological fact of being thrown into a world that we must make our own: subject and world are co-constituted, the "world" becoming my world only as "I" become a subject within it.

The key here is temporality. Following Husserl's (1964) *Lessons on the Phenomenology of the Intimate Consciousness of Time*, the human individual is constituted in their personality, their consciousness or self-presence, as a duration that is gradually enriched and transformed by past and future experiences. The flow of time becomes a constituted time when present moments, instants or punctual impressions are maintained in consciousness in the form of retention, of being held back as just past. Likewise, the present moment is animated by protentions, which aim at or anticipate moments to come. The present moment is no longer an isolated point between a bygone past and an as-yet unrealized future, but a tension between a retained past and an anticipated future. Consciousness is then a duration, a temporal phenomenon existing only as an unfolding, a temporal flow. A moral conscience is necessarily built on this temporal phenomenology: the past that becomes mine because I retain it, and the future that is promised to me because I anticipate it (protention).

If we add to this temporal structuring the symbolic play of the linguistic sign, of language, it becomes clear that consciousness retains not just what has just happened, but what has happened elsewhere, via the representation of language. This past that has happened elsewhere takes a variety of forms: the historical past (it really happened), the lived past (I really experienced it), the imagined or fictitious past (it could or may have happened, beyond any particular temporal anchorage). The temporal structure of consciousness and the symbolic dimension of language give the personality a narrative identity, retaining what has happened and recounting what has happened to it, what it recognizes as its own or as something else, what it can recognize as its responsibility or not. Narrative identity is thus the reverse of the moral agent, whose obverse is the action taken, understanding by action what political philosophy (Manent 2010) means, namely behavior accompanied by a discourse capable of arguing and justifying it.

Action is that which can be accounted for, that which is the consequence of the behavior of an agent endowed with reason, who is rational in principle if not in all of their actions. However, the fact of being rational or endowed with reason does not mean that the agent thinks about all of their actions in the sense that cognitive or economic sciences assume (often in an idealized, even naïve way), but that they must be able to do so, a priori or a posteriori, because it is always possible and justified to ask them to justify their actions. The moral agent is rational in the sense that they must be able to justify everything they do, and will be judged or considered in human society on this basis. To give reason, to produce a discourse, consists of adopting a narrative perspective, mobilizing the threads of the past to put the action under consideration into perspective, and to consider its consequences.

This theme of narrative identity lies at the heart of Time and Narrative (Ricœur 1984), where the central thesis is that time only becomes human when it is narrated, and that humans only become temporalized – or humanized, we should say, since human consciousness is only temporal – through narrative. The moral agent is the one who, through the telling of their story – what has happened to them, as well as to others – determines their identity, and therefore what they claim to be and what they are prepared to assume, in responsibility for what has happened and what is going to happen.

The ethical dimension of narrative identity is by no means self-evident. In fact, it has been strongly contested (Strawson 2004) by an episodic model of personal identity: the individual is not constituted in a narrative and recapitulative identity, but as a succession of episodes that are more or less discontinuous and foreign to one another. This is how I remember having lived through this or that event, without seeing them as snippets of my narrative, but as events that are not particularly mine, except that I was present, but an "I" that I consider to be someone else. My past is thus a soap opera whose episodes are discontinuous, with the only coherence being their chronological organization and the presence of actors who were as many distinct "I"s. This model is very convincing, but it operates at a psychological, not phenomenological, level. Narrative identity does not mean that I recognize myself as myself in the past self, but that I assume it in the narrative of my life. A narrative can be the integration of interwoven stories, actors and narrators, creating a narrative polyphony. The most enlightening figure for understanding how narrative identity is not a hypothesis of continuity and coherence is that of metalepsis (Genette 2004), where the narrator plays on the thresholds of discourse (the author intervenes in the story, the secondary narratives they articulate, etc.) to interweave different statements and different voices. Episodic identity can then be understood as so many metalepses of narrative identity.

This is why Paul Ricœur articulates the notion of narrative identity with that of "ipseity" and not "sameness". While the latter indicates equality, equivalence, numerical or physical identity between terms, the former indicates evolution, transformation through continuity that persists and endures. If the stone in the garden remains the same according to sameness, biological and human individuals do not remain the same while retaining their identity, their ipseity. Yet, this identity is not so much that which is constituted by the recurrence of the same traits or characteristics, as that which is assumed because it is recounted in a story that recapitulates, situates and articulates these traits. This is how we can think of our shared identity with what is no longer (our genetic, family, social and cultural heritage, etc.) or with others who are not us.

However, if the moral agent is the one who appropriates the time in which they are immersed as their own through the narrative, this is because they know how to relate to the situations in which they are immersed, with the context that surrounds them, by taking the appropriate actions. The moral agent makes decisions and performs actions based on the narrative recapitulation, which will prompt them to integrate these actions and decisions into what they are ready to assume and justify.

Narrative identity is not an abstraction or a retrospective vision, but rather a dynamic of construction and integration that enables the agent to account for what they do, according to what they have recognized as having done, is ready to assume and claims as their own (heritage or history). Reciprocally, it is also a principle of demarcation from what they reject as their own, from what they consider foreign or indifferent.

This dynamic of construction is a logic of inscription in context and of projection into the here and now as it is perceived and apprehended, on the one hand, and as it is formalized and understood in terms of narrative identity, on the other.

Thus, a moral agent can only be an entity for which there is context and history, contextual inscription in situations and historical identity, of which narrative is the principle. When we approach the question of technology, we need to understand how the agent equipped with tools becomes or remains a moral agent, and to what extent the tools used to transform us modify the conditions of action and decision.

1.4. Calculation, algorithm

The notion of ethics has now been clarified through the concept of a moral agent elaborated in a narrative identity, but we need to understand how technology modifies or reconfigures this concept, particularly in the case of digital technology. To begin with, we need to remember that a digital technical system is not a moral agent, and that it does not act as such. In other words, it does not behave in a way for which it can give a reason, and which it can support with reasons. A moral agent is one who can discuss their behavior.

While this may seem self-evident, the boundary between the human agent and the technological system sometimes seems to blur insofar as these systems make decisions and implement principles of rationality that are considered to be the source of morality. For example, from a consequentialist perspective, the machine is undoubtedly better equipped than most humans, from a formal point of view, to calculate the consequences of an action and maximize the resulting good.

However, since all of this ultimately depends on the apprehension of the situation in which we must engage and decide on an action, the issue is to know whether calculus can provide projection into the context, on the one hand, and historical construction, on the other. Here again, we must not jump to conclusions, for calculus, as has been widely argued and discussed (Lassègue 2013; De Glas and Lassègue 2020), is a form of writing. From writing to textuality, and from the latter to narration, the chain is easily established even if, as we will show, there is no implication.

According to Herrenschmidt (2007), calculation is one of the three fundamental forms of writing: counting (numbers), communicating (letters or signs) and exchanging (currency). These activities involve the mediation and manipulation of objects that, depending on the case, take the place of numbers, letters or currency. What matters is their structure, which enables them to be recognized and assembled according to rules of handling. The underlying universal is that of the ability to handle: to grasp with the hand objects that can be moved in a space where objects of the same type are already present. These are the letters on an inscription surface, the balls on an abacus, the knots on a cord or the pieces on a trebuchet. Whatever the case, we need elements that we can recognize by their type (a drawn letter referring to the type of letter "a", for example, or a ball representing a 10, or a coin representing a given metallic value with its weight in silver or gold) and by the actions we can perform with them. In other words, all of these activities are ultimately calculations, if we remember that this term designates little pebbles (calculi) that take the place of whatever we want.

This conceptual understanding of the nature of the activity and object that is a calculation is reflected in contemporary works that characterize calculation formally and mathematically (Turing 1937; Wagner 1998). Since the logical works of the 20th century, a calculation can be described and understood as the *blind manipulation of meaningless symbols*. It is these two fundamental notions that enable us to understand what a calculus is: on the one hand, we are concerned with symbols that have no meaning, and, on the other, we manipulate them according to rules that have no meaning either.

To speak of symbols devoid of meaning, or signs that have no meaning, sounds like an oxymoron, because a sign is first and foremost a signifier referring to a signified. A sign being only a signifier, without a signified, is literally not a signifier, and therefore not a sign. It is more appropriate to speak (Bachimont 2010, 2017a, 2017b) of *tokens*, or even *calculus* in the sense of small pebbles, as recalled above. To count is to manipulate small pebbles. These pebbles – let us call them calculi from now on – are not signs: all we ask of them is that they be graspable, manipulable, on the one hand, and distinguishable, on the other. These calculi must therefore be discrete (etymologically, discrete means separate), and their separation must enable us to distinguish them: to know that we are dealing with, that we are seizing, one pebble and not another. In contemporary terms, by way of pebbles, we consider 0s and 1s, and what is required of the 0 is to be distinguishable from the 1 and manipulable independently of the 1. In particular, to avoid confusion, the 0s and 1s of numerics are not those of arithmetic, the latter being rather an interpretation that can be made of the 0s and 1s manipulated at the numerical level. We could have called these calculi something else: Tic and Tac, Castor and Pollux, Bonnie and Clyde, or # and @. The key is to distinguish and manipulate them. But if in the end 0 and 1 were the names given, it is because the arithmetical interpretation, in this case binary, took precedence.

Moreover, what we do with these pebbles is nothing more than grab them and move them into a space, a manipulation space where what matters is the position of the pebbles being moved. More formally and theoretically, the Turing machine (Turing 1937) is where these characterizations are implemented. Its principles are well known: an infinite memory strip constitutes the manipulation space, where the position is given by the memory strip's squares, and where a single symbol at most, say 0 or 1, is inscribed. An internally stated read head, positioned on a cell of the memory strip, can read and write a symbol and move one cell to the left or right. Finally, rules specify what is to be done according to what is read from the memory strip and the internal state of the read head: read, write, move. The Turing machine is therefore a principle of manipulating meaningless symbols according to arbitrary writing and moving rules.

In these terms, we understand that symbols are not considered in terms of context, nor is their manipulation. The computational process is non-contextual and asemantic. Nevertheless, in order to do something with it, it is necessary to interpret and associate it with external entities. This is where the notion of code and coding comes in. Indeed, when we speak of a calculation code, we mean that this code will give rise to a manipulation, a calculation in other words, as well as that it represents a reality that it codes. When the target reality is a particular domain, we tend to speak of a format: for example, a character format for calculations on writing (word processing), or formats for images and sounds. Applications, which are designed to respond to given tasks, rely on formats to capture the realities needed to carry out the task.

Code, format and application are the three levels that structure digital tools. None of them function in a contextual way: the code's own nature is to execute only according to the calculi present. The local determines the global behavior and ensures that the algorithm terminates safely and effectively. The fact that the calculi represent external entities does not alter this observation. Once interpreted, these calculi become data that is understood thanks to the formats mobilized. Data, even if it originates from a context (e.g. produced by sensors), is a manipulable entity independent of the context from which it originates, and no longer belongs to it. Extracted from the context, data is a decontextualized representation. This decontextualization is not a defect, or rather is a necessary defect. It is only by this means that data, having become autonomous, can be enrolled[1] in an algorithm and can participate in obtaining a result whose certainty is that associated with the algorithm's rules (e.g. probabilistic, deterministic algorithms, etc.).

This contextual independence means that the algorithm does not operate on the basis of a situation, but on the basis of its coded representation. This representation guarantees that, when a data configuration is obtained, the algorithm applied gives the response as the designers intended, without actually being in the operating situation but simply anticipating it. It could be argued that data are generated dynamically, according to the sensors coupled

1 Let us recall the etymology: enrolled means reproduced on parchment or rolled-up support. In other words, like the letter which is not in the world of what it designates, it belongs to the page on which it is inscribed, not to the world designated by this page. The data is no longer of the captured world, but now belongs to a space of manipulation.

to the situations, but this generation is always a separation. The sensor must be activated according to the expected physical form, the data must be generated according to the adopted logical format and the algorithm must then be applied. Data always corresponds to an expected form and format. In principle, there is no room for the unforeseen as such, in other words, that which escapes sensors and formats. Yet, living beings, and humans in particular, are sensitive (in the sense of perception) to unforeseen events, to what makes an event (Romano 1998), to the unheard of (what we did not expect to hear).

In conclusion, the calculating machine cannot be a moral agent because, even if it can mobilize principles modeling moral behavior, it does not apply them like a moral agent, meaning judging them *in context* and being ready to *justify and argue* through the reasons associated with this behavior.

1.5. The ethical challenges of digital technology

This section characterizes how a calculating machine, out of context, even if used in a given context, can give rise to an ethics presiding over its use.

1.5.1. *Complexity and technology: temporal alienation*

To address this delicate issue, we will follow the phenomenological approach we have already taken, according to which an agent's consciousness is a temporal phenomenon, on the one hand, and that their ethics correspond to a narrative identity that is constantly elaborated and discussed, on the other. If we ask ourselves about the conditions of the possibility of such an ethic, they can only consist of the temporal possibility of telling a story and constituting a narrative that manages the adjustments and arguments with the actions performed and their consequences. In other words, the challenge is to remain synchronized, i.e. to share a common temporal framework, with the world resulting from our decisions and behavior.

Technology can pose a problem in this respect, as it desynchronizes the human agent from their environment through systems that act on their behalf, leaving no time for adjustment. Technology does not always allow for the construction of a common time between machines and the humans who are their actors, users or elements. As has been argued recently, technology becomes an instrument of alienation, as humans become strangers to the world constructed by technology. This exclusion from the world is based essentially on the acceleration of socio-technical processes and the resulting desynchronization (Rosa 2009).

If we take up the characterization of technology we proposed (Bachimont 2010), technology is any device that organizes elements in space to determine the temporal unfolding of their interaction. In other words, technology is the programming of an unfolding in time through organization in space. This programming ensures both the necessity of the result obtained from the initial conditions and the repeatability of the process. From the internal-engine, with its cycle organized by the arrangement of engine parts, to the computer, where the organization of files within and between them determines execution sequences, every device is the material formalization of a mechanism, whose implementation executes a sequence of actions enabling a programmed result to be obtained.

However, if technology programs time by means of a material arrangement, its objective is to make the future result as immediately available as possible once execution has been completed. One tendency of technology is therefore to accelerate the achievement of the desired result, via the materialization of the device. Digital technology, for its part, has made it possible to abstract this principle from the material conditions of the device: not only is technology always a device, but the latter can be characterized solely by the interactions between its constituent elements, regardless of their actual nature.

In other words, any device programming a time sequence can be represented as an algorithm whose combinatorial efficiency, or complexity, must be optimized. This optimization, however, is arbitrary in relation to the actual physical time, which depends on the physical substrate adopted. Digital time is indifferent to physical time, and abstracts from it. The challenge is simply to do things faster in terms of complexity (Perifel 2014), and to adopt a physical substrate that brings accelerated execution speed.

In so doing, technology can cause difficulties, because it short-circuits the time needed to manage the consequences and to come to terms with the environment modified by the irruption of technology. The time imposed by the technical device falls out of sync with the time of the environment, whether social or natural. Resynchronization requires adaptation. A classic example of this is church time being replaced by factory time (Elias 1984). More recently, genetic manipulations can be seen as problematic insofar as they are out of sync with associated environmental changes. The domestication of species consisted simply of optimizing a genetic heritage according to certain criteria, but this optimization took place at the pace of animal generations and reproductions, immersed in co-evolving environments. Genetic manipulation would be problematic not so much insofar as it is genetic, but insofar as it desynchronizes the evolution of genomes from associated environments. Similarly, algo-trading is also problematic to the extent that it imposes decision-making in sub-human time, implying possible disturbances that cannot be managed in the time of the decision, but only in that of the crisis caused by the desynchronization (Laumonier 2013).

We must therefore give priority to allowing nature's time and agents' time to adjust to technological decisions. Any acceleration thus becomes a source of alienation. However, in saying this, it is important to define an ethics that leaves room for ethical or moral agents, on the one hand, and the environments associated with them, on the other. Several authors have already insisted on this dimension, including Ruha (2019), who formulates the injunction to "move slower and empower people", and Columbia University's *Logic(s)* magazine, which states, as the title of its issue 19: "move slow and heal things".

1.5.2. *Data, algorithms: alienation of property*

In the universality of encoding heterogeneous realities in the same, usually binary, alphabet, digital technology makes it possible to apprehend entities and representations that belong to separate spheres of practice in the same computational space. This is undoubtedly the greatest strength of number as a principle of enumeration and calculation as a principle of manipulation. The rules for using the entities calculated or manipulated do not depend on what is represented. They are comanipulable, via coding, just as entities become commensurable (measurable together) through measurement.

This possibility opens up unprecedented perspectives: it becomes possible to establish correlations between realities that were previously independent. This makes it possible to take account of considerations that were previously ignored when deducing a decision. However, this possibility is precisely what is problematic from an ethical point of view. The calculation of a decision in one domain can exploit data from another, imposing its own order and bringing them under its own standard. Why, for example, should the automatic sorting of resumes take into account a person's height, sex, eating habits or sporting activities? How do these parameters relate to professional quality, and if they do, how is it legitimate to use them?

This is the question of spheres of power or justice[2]. It has been explored by the seminal work of Michael Walzer (1983). This author draws on an old observation already noted by Pascal in *Pensées* (Pascal 2015): "tyranny consists in the desire for universal domination and beyond its order". He continues:

> Various chambers, of strong, beautiful, good spirits, pious, each of which reigns at home, not elsewhere, and sometimes they meet. And the strong and the beautiful fight foolishly to see who will be each other's master, for their mastery is of various kinds. They fail to agree. And their fault is to want to rule everywhere. Nothing can, not even force. It achieves nothing in the realm of the wise. It is master only of external actions (Pascal 2015, 92–58).

In the contemporary digital and AI context, data is collected and exploited according to its availability and manipulability, not its representativeness. The absence of real data curation in contemporary practices, as well as the possibility of co-manipulating all kinds of data independently of their meaning (the blind symbolism we mentioned earlier), leads to a tyranny of algorithms relying on the epistemological nothingness of data.

On the one hand, this leads to decisions that can rarely be explained, and, on the other, are difficult to justify. What right does an algorithm have to make a decision concerning the life of a human being? How could this right, which we recognize with difficulty to our peers, via institutions elaborated in complex and debated traditions, belong to algorithms (Lassègue and Garapon 2018)?

---

2 We owe this to the work of Rémy Demichelis in his doctoral research: Demichelis (2023). Ethical issues of machine learning and Big Data: a hermeneutic perspective.

1.5.3. *Moral agents and their acolytes*

The reason that ethics is based on responsibility and commitment, and on the possibility of giving reasons and arguments for past actions and future decisions, is that it is based in principle on the possibility of recognizing that there are other moral agents. Personal ethics are constituted and limited by the very fact that there are other moral agents, who assume in principle, if not in practice, the same requirements. Ethics must therefore be formulated in terms of this first imperative, categorical if you like, according to which the moral agent always acts in consideration of other moral agents.

From our point of view, the entities to be considered in an ethical context are those for which we can be held accountable. What we have to answer for, and what we have to take care of, has ethical status. We will therefore distinguish between ethical agents, patients and witnesses, and among the latter living witnesses, environmental witnesses and technical witnesses.

Ethical or moral agents are those who, like us, are capable of assuming (the past), committing (to the future) and giving an account of their actions. These are the primary agents for ethical action, insofar as humans are first exposed, in their phylogenesis and ontogenesis, to encounters with such agents: the child and its mother, the early human with its partners, especially sexual partners, since every bisexual species is first and foremost driven by reproduction. The human being is above all a social animal, becoming human only in society, as Aristotle (1993) teaches us.

However, we can also distinguish between moral agents who are prevented from fulfilling their ethical responsibilities: those who are able to assume their ethical responsibilities but are unable to do so, for reasons inherent to their constitution (early childhood, old age, illness, disability, etc.), or more contingent (situations where they find themselves deprived of their abilities). These are *ethical patients.*

Then, there are the entities that are not capable of having an ethical position or commitment, but whose attitude towards us defines our ethical condition and value. These entities are the witnesses of our ethical condition, the mirror of our morality. This is why we call them *ethical witnesses*, our witnesses to morality, not because they answer to us, but because our behavior towards them reveals something about us and our ethical commitments.

The privileged ethical witness is the living being, in other words, an entity that possesses its own logic of development, and therefore an intrinsic temporality. The behavior of the latter is not merely the physical consequence of its environment, but is based on an autonomous decision-making principle (whether we call it instinct or consciousness). According to our considerations, any entity possessing intrinsic temporality has an ethical status, whether or not it is a moral agent in the full sense of the term. We could then speak of *ethical animates*, in the ancient sense that they have a principle of movement and action in themselves, without being capable of assuming it as a moral agent. This means that we must integrate the *ethical animate* into the realm of responsibilities to be assumed, and refer it to its behavior in order to judge it. This is how a particular animal can be judged dangerous in its behavior and suffer the consequences (muzzling, euthanasia, etc.), or how in the Middle Ages it was possible to put animals on trial (Baratay 2023).

Finally, we can consider entities that are neither agents, nor patients, nor living witnesses. These are *inert, environmental and technical witnesses*. These are objects in general: their ethical status derives from the fact that they belong to an already existing situation, shared with other agents, which comes from a past that is certainly bygone, but which carries the transmission of vanished agents, and which is promised to have a future if given the opportunity. While the object itself is not the source of its ethical status, it is the bearer of values whose conservation and transmission we are responsible for. This is obviously heritage (Poulot 2006) in its contemporary sense (as an object of memory or mnemonic (Bachimont 2021a)), as well as respect for and loyalty to what surrounds us and what we have built: what, although made by us, is no longer ourselves, but an otherness to which and towards which we have committed ourselves. We must take care of it.

1.5.4. *Ethical situations*

As ethical agents, we encounter ethical entities in situations. However, not all situations are the same, and not all our decisions and behaviors are on the same level. Still taking as our guide the notion of commitment and responsibility, on the one hand, and the mediation of a technical system in resolving the situation, on the other, three situations emerge:

– Firstly, the situation in which we intervene is shared with other ethical agents who have the possibility of adjusting their behavior according to their own commitments and responsibilities. In this case, we do not have to decide for them, but rather respect the autonomy of their decision: the challenge is to ethically empower the agents so that, with full knowledge of the facts, they act and then answer for their actions.

– Secondly, the situation does not allow the other agents concerned to adjust: either they do not have the time, they do not have the means to act or they do not have the necessary knowledge. In this case, we are obliged to decide for them, on their behalf.

– Finally, in a situation where a system has to make decisions in real time, short-circuiting the time of both designers and users, it is essential that the system does not make decisions affecting the lives of the agents involved. The system must preserve the purest possibilities of the entities concerned.

– The ethical attitude that may be appropriate in each of these situations is set out below.

1.5.5. *Empowering agents*

Empowerment is a traditional topic in the design of digital systems, especially those interacting directly with users (and not just with other digital systems), because a dilemma needs to be resolved. Concerning all of the manipulation possibilities offered (on content, in a transaction, in interaction with other users), some need to be selected, some aggregated into services, and others hidden. This compromise between what is made visible to enable use, and what is hidden to make it effective and efficient, is always a delicate one, since we have to decide for the user what will be useful when the time comes.

This tension has recently reached a paroxysm with recommendation algorithms in online platforms, or search engines, as the near-infinite mass of possible choices is reduced or structured according to users' supposed recommendations or preferences. The following excerpt from a report on a Business Ethics Circle conference devoted to artificial intelligence in business aptly evokes this dilemma:

> According to Professor Balagué, in the cultural field and with regard to the principle of fairness, recommendation algorithms should be required to make fair proposals, meaning decorrelated from user preferences (Cercle d'éthique des affaires 2019).

If we understand the underlying intention, which is to promote cultural diversity, we may well ask why we should force users to see what they are not interested in, rather than what is close to what they have already seen? How can we avoid drowning cultural diversity in the insignificance of a plurality of proposals with no connection to what we are looking for? If this recommendation is nonetheless relevant, and certainly worth implementing, it is because it leaves the final decision to the user to make an informed choice. In other words, while the recommendation decides for the user, the so-called fair proposals let the user sort according to their own preferences: in other words, the user has the right to change their mind and look for elements that are unlikely to interest them!

Another aspect frequently noted in the use of digital systems is the opacity of processing and the inability of users to understand what they are seeing, what is being proposed and what is being achieved by the system. The sheer volume of data mobilized and the complexity of the calculations involved mean that, even for the designer, it is impossible to understand why a given result is proposed in a given situation. As we have already proposed elsewhere, this interpretative opacity (Bachimont 2018) must call upon other hermeneutic tools where users make sense of and give meaning to what is computationally produced. For our part, we have proposed (Bachimont 2024) the narrative approach, where the challenge is to make interaction with a system intelligible through a narrative that, on the one hand, abstracts the essential and, on the other, structures it in a coherent and comprehensible logic, namely a logic of actors enrolled in a temporal unfolding. The user then becomes the narrator of their use, and the system must integrate itself into the story they tell, rather than imposing its own arbitrary interpretation.

In this type of situation, we can see that it is not a question of being ethical on behalf of others, but of guaranteeing that they can be ethical according to their own commitments and responsibilities, in an enlightened way, in their own autonomy. The designer must therefore have an attitude and posture that reflect values that can be described as virtuous. Loyalty, honesty and transparency in design are what enable an agent to make a decision based on the attitude of others, giving them the means to behave as a moral agent if they can or wish to do so. Virtue ethics addresses moral agents, and enables the society of agents to be constituted in the principle of individual freedom. It is also the only way to overcome hermeneutic complexity (Bachimont 2021b), a phenomenon resulting from situations where agents take into account others' interpretation of them in their own interpretation. As MacIntyre (2013) points out, this complexity prohibits rational anticipation and predictability of events. It implies that users must be trusted, in their virtues, by allowing them to exercise them and therefore having a system that also materializes them according to adequate design principles. This is what ethical *design*[3] is all about.

1.5.6. *Taking care of patients*

However, when agents are prevented from exercising their judgment for a variety of reasons, linked to the agents themselves or to the situation, they find themselves the ethical patients of the situation. The system must be able to decide for them, because it must do so without them. The design must therefore take into account the possible consequences of the decisions the system may have to make in the situation. This calls for a consequentialist attitude, in the sense described above: the overall benefit of the situation must be maximized. The difficulties of such an exercise are easy to see: consequences are not always calculable. If we escape from hermeneutic complexity, we find ourselves back in synthetic or systemic complexity (Bachimont 2021b), where we have to manage the heterogeneity of the components of the system and the situation, while no model or theory provides a global intelligibility.

Furthermore, this situational consequentialism is bound to come up against the alienation of property mentioned earlier. Consequently, it can only reasonably be implemented in contexts or situations where variability is controlled or contained, and the consequences of decisions are predictable and calculable. This singularly limits the cases in which such approaches can be implemented, and implies that we should instead be looking at ways of bringing human beings back into the loop, and integrating their ability to manage the unexpected and adapt to the context.

System design too often thinks of human beings as the weak link, when in fact they are the only ones who can deal with the hazards of a situation intelligently and ethically. In other words, a situation in which only ethical patients are involved is likely to be poorly designed, and should be rethought to broaden the range of players involved and enable them to adapt to the constraints of the situation.

3 See: https://beta.designersethiques.org.

1.5.7. *Taking care of witnesses*

Actors' empowerment implies that a digital system, beyond the mass of data and the complexity of processing, should be able to submit to a narrative intelligibility and a suspension of decision-making so that it can be delegated to the user's judgment. This translates into a necessary knowledge and familiarity with the systems that become the partners of our actions, and the environment in and on which they act.

This familiarity translates not only into knowledge, but also into systems maintenance and administration. In other words, in the same way that each and every one of us becomes the administrator of our own domestic installation, adopting an ethical approach to the use of a digital system means taking care of it, and maintaining it so as to be aware of its possibilities and limits. This is not so much a question of becoming a system specialist but rather of having a culture of use: a motorist overtaking on a country road, unaware of their vehicle's braking and acceleration capacities, endangers their passengers and other road users. They do not need to be mechanics, but they do need to be aware of their vehicle's condition, and know how it works in real-life situations.

In the digital context, we can see the difficulty of striking a balance between expertise and care for a device in the use of so-called smartphones. Indeed, most users have acquired a certain expertise in handling them, but at the same time regularly change their phone, rather than remaining attached to tools that have already rendered good and loyal service.

While the offer of additional services and programmed obsolescence may encourage this frenzy of change, the fact remains that the object's time is abused by a use that evolves according to promises (performance that in no way affects use, such as the number of pixels, the associated AI process, etc., parameters that no longer have anything to do with the targeted services).

While digital systems often aspire to operate like black boxes, where users no longer have to worry about so-called technical complexities, technical knowledge of operating principles is nonetheless required to appreciate (in the sense of evaluating, as well as liking) the system's behavior. This is a theme particularly championed by Gilbert Simondon (2020) and more recently by Xavier Guchet (2010, 2021).

1.6. Conclusion

Digital technology and artificial intelligence may present new challenges for ethical reflection, but they are nonetheless part of a long tradition in which the contributions of technology have been addressed from the perspective of moral philosophy. This debate is inescapable, insofar as technology is neither good nor bad, and even less neutral, and so it enters the ethical debate neither as an object in itself, whose intrinsic conformity to ethical requirements must be established, nor as an object that is external to them, since it is independent of them. Technology transforms us, and we act through it and the possibilities it invents and offers us. It is therefore in the context of modified situations, configured by technology as a principle of new possibilities and a tool for implementing them, that we need to determine the principles of ethical reflection.

The latter can be based, as we have done here, on the notion of a moral agent who assumes responsibility for the past and commitment for the future through a narrative identity constantly elaborated to account for and argue what has happened and what has been done. The moral agent is the one who accompanies their actions with a discourse, before, during or after, specifying the conditions of their action and stipulating what they assume or intend to give reasons for. The moral agent as such is not alone: they exist as such only in a human society, facing alter egos with whom to argue, discuss and assume responsibility. In addition to the other moral agents they encounter, however, the moral agent must also engage with agents whose moral autonomy is impeded, as well as those we have called ethical patients, and finally objects that bear witness, entities possessing their own temporal dynamics as well as those inscribed in a history shared with human societies.

An ethically mobilized technical system must enable the agents concerned to exercise their ethical reflection, without assuming or directing it on behalf of the agents. To do this, it must be part of the agents' own temporality, as well as that of the associated animate and ethical objects. When applying this approach to the digital world, we come up against the fact that systems based on massive amounts of data possess both an interpretative opacity and a complexity that makes their behavior unintelligible, and thus prevents users from exercising their judgment. In other words, digital systems tend to "decapacitate" human agents. The challenge, then, is to introduce principles into the design process whereby agents are always empowered, giving them the freedom and opportunity to judge, in context, what they are prepared to assume morally or not. Thus, the challenge is not to prohibit humans from being able to do this or that, but to ensure that they can do so with full knowledge of the facts, and can therefore be called to account.

However, asking agents to take on such responsibility means rethinking the alliance between humans and technology: developing a technical culture in which we take care of the objects with which we interact, and cultivate a familiarity and complicity with them. For we must answer with them for what we do, and answer for them. Although we are not putting technical systems on trial as we once did animals, it becomes clear that it is a human-technical entity that becomes the agent. As artificial intelligence asserts itself as a technical paradigm, it becomes necessary for users to familiarize themselves with its principles, to adopt a culture of its use, so that they can assume the consequences of its use. Taking care of our artifacts is a prerequisite for our ethical empowerment in their use.

1.7. References

Aristotle (1965). *Éthique de nicomaque*. Garnier-Flammarion, Paris.

Aristotle (1993). *Les politiques*. Garnier-Flammarion, Paris.

Bachimont, B. (2010). *Le sens de la technique : le numérique et le calcul*. Encres Marines, Paris.

Bachimont, B. (2017a). Numérique et manipulation : la constitution technique des connaissances. In *Le numérique en débat : des nombres, des machines et des hommes*, Chazal, G. (ed.). Éditions universitaires de Dijon, Dijon.

Bachimont, B. (2017b). *Patrimoine et numérique : technique et politique de la mémoire*. Ina Éditions, Bry-sur-Marne.

Bachimont, B. (2018). Formats : transparence manipulatoire et opacité interprétative ; la question du sens dans les dispositifs techniques. In *Le sens au cœur des dispositifs et des environnements*, Mitropoulo, E. and Pignier, N. (eds). Connaissances et Savoirs, Saint-Denis.

Bachimont, B. (2021a). Archive et mémoire : le numérique et les mnémophores. *Sémiotique de l'archive*, 12, 1–19. doi: 10.4000/signata.2980.

Bachimont, B. (2021b). La complexité herméneutique à l'épreuve du calcul. *Interfaces numériques*, 10(3), 1–19.

Bachimont, B. (2024). The code paradigm: Trace amnesia and arbitrary interpretation. In *Philosophies of Technologies: Theory as Practice*, Charolles, V. and Lamy-Rested, E. (eds). ISTE Ltd, London and John Wiley & Sons, New York.

Baratay, E. (2023). *Les animaux dans l'histoire*. Tallandier, Paris.

Cercle d'éthique des affaires (2019). Compte rendu de la conférence : les enjeux éthiques de l'intelligence artificielle en entreprise. Report, Paris.

De Glas, M. and Lassègue, J. (2020). Turing, du paradigme de l'écriture formelle à l'émergence non-écrite des formes. *Intellectica*, 72, 5–30.

Demichelis, R. (2023). Enjeux éthiques de l'apprentissage automatique et du Big Data : une perspective herméneutique. PhD Thesis, Université Paris-Nanterre, Paris.

Desmons, O., Lemaire, S., Turmel, P. (2019). *Manuel de métaéthique*. Hermann, Paris.

Duplan, S., Fischer, F., Frija, R. (2018). Éthique et numérique : un référentiel pratique pour les acteurs du numérique. Report, Cigref and Syntec Numérique, Paris [Online]. Available at: https://www.cigref.fr/ethique-numerique-un-referentiel-pratique-pour-les-acteurs-du-numerique [Accessed 13 September 2023].

Elias, N. (1984). *Über die Zeit*. Suhrkamp Verlag, Berlin.

Ellul, J. (1965). Réflexions sur l'ambivalence du progrès technique. *La revue administrative*, 18(106), 380–391.

Ellul, J. (1967). *The Technological Society*. Vintage Books, New York.

Genette, G. (2004). *Métalepse : de la figure à la fiction*. Le Seuil, Paris.

Guchet, X. (2010). *Pour un humanisme technologique : culture, technique et société dans la philosophie de Gilbert Simondon*. Presses Universitaires de France, Paris.

Guchet, X. (2021). *Care in Technology*. ISTE Ltd, London and John Wiley & Sons, New York.

Herrenschmidt, C. (2007). *Les trois écritures : langue, nombre, code*. Gallimard, Paris.

Husserl, E. (1964). *The Phenomenology of Internal Time-Consciousness*. Indiana University Press, Bloomington.

Kant, E. (2015). *Critique of Practical Reason*. Cambridge University Press, Cambridge.

Kranzberg, M. (1986). Technology and history: "Kranzberg's Laws". *Technology and Culture*, 27(3), 544–560.

Lassègue, J. (2013). Quelques remarques historiques et anthropologiques sur l'écriture informatique. In *Les mutations de l'écriture*, Nicolas, F. and Tonneau, A. (eds). Éditions de la Sorbonne, Paris.

Lassègue, J. and Garapon, A. (2018). *Justice digitale : révolution graphique et rupture anthropologique*. Presses Universitaires de France, Paris.

Laumonier, A. (2013). *6 : le soulèvement des machines*. Points, Paris.

Macintyre, A. (2013). *After Virtue: A Study in Moral Theory*. Bloomsbury, London.

Manent, P. (2010). *Les métamorphoses de la cité : essai sur la dynamique de l'Occident*. Flammarion, Paris.

Mill, J.S. (2015). *On Liberty, Utilitarianism and Other Essays*. Oxford University Press, Oxford.

Pascal, B. (2015). *Pensées*. Garnier-Flammarion, Paris.

Perifel, S. (2014). *Complexité algorithmique*. Éditions Ellipses, Paris.

Poulot, D. (2006). *Une histoire du patrimoine en Occident XVIIIe–XXIe siècle : du monument aux valeurs*. Presses Universitaires de France, Paris.

Ricœur, P. (1984). *Time and Narrative, 1*. University of Chicago Press, Chicago.

Ricœur, P. (1992). *Oneself as Another*. University of Chicago Press, Chicago.

Romano, C. (1998). *L'événement et le monde*. Presses Universitaires de France, Paris.

Rosa, H. (2009). *High-Speed Society: Social Acceleration, Power, and Modernity*. Pennsylvania State University Press, University Park.

Ruha, B. (2019). *Race After Technology: Abolitionist Tools for the New Jim Code*. Polity Press, Medford.

Simondon, G. (2020). *Individuation in Light of Notions of Form and Information*. University of Minnesota Press, Minneapolis.

Steiner, P. (2010). Philosophie, technologie et cognition : état des lieux et perspectives. *Intellectica*, 1/2(53/54), 7–40.

Stiegler, B. (1998). *Technics and Time, 1: The Fault of Epimetheus*. Stanford University Press, Redwood City.

Strawson, G. (2004). Against narrativity. *Ratio*, 17(4), 428–452.

Turing, A. (1937). On computable numbers, with an application to the Entscheidungsproblem. *Proceedings of the London Mathematical Society*, s2-42(1), 230–265.

Wagner, P. (1998). *La machine en logique*. Presses Universitaires de France, Paris.

Walzer, M. (1983). *Spheres of Justice. A Defense of Pluralism and Equality*. Basic Books, New York.

2

Bias, Discrimination and Decision-Making: Fate or Responsibility?

2.1. Why this question?

The word *bias* can take on several meanings depending on the context[1]. The basic notion is that of cognitive bias, a misleading and falsely logical thought pattern, a "facility", a cognitive shortcut that enables the individual to make a judgment or a decision quickly without mobilizing any reflection. This term is widely used in statistics, designating a difference between the true value of an unobservable variable and the value estimated statistically or econometrically. In scientific methodology, a bias is an error in the method, or a failure to comply with the rules of protocol, which leads to erroneous results, or at least results that can be questioned.

Evoking biases, whether conscious or unconscious (pleonasm), voluntary or involuntary (re-pleonasm), cognitive or statistical, marks a new era of fair, ethical, transparent and loyal decision-making, revealed by the citizen's concern for societal responsibility and sustainability.

Gender inequalities, discrimination, invisibilization in data, subjectivity of algorithms or difficulty in "encoding" rules or laws are all obstacles that undermine confidence in decision support (Huttner 2020).

Chapter written by Florence SÈDES.

1 See: https://en.wikipedia.org/wiki/Bias.

Explicability is at the heart of current discussions on AI[2]: XAI and court rulings, as illustrated by the recent hackathon at the Government Committee “Conseil d’État”, where five competing teams defined a program able to synthesize decisions of the administrative judge to make them understandable to audiences with no legal knowledge.

The new, fully automated tool used by weather organization “Météo-France” to produce forecasts for the general public has been the subject of controversy, with bugs in the system generating inconsistencies in forecasts (28°C forecast in Strasbourg in December, snow forecast at 10°C in Savoie), due to a lack of validation by “human” forecasters.

The many bugs and malfunctions in critical software (social benefits, salaries, recruitment) illustrate the notion of the algorithm as a “socio-technical object” that can be understood in a technical, organizational and human context.

As Mérigoux (2023) demonstrates, “translating the law into code requires a validation method complementary to that of tests, which is too costly to achieve a maximum level of trust on the software”. Legal and IT logic are inversely built on process genericity and exception management: Lawsky (2017), comparing his methodology to the principles of logic programming (McCarthy 1997b), highlights the dichotomy between base cases and exceptions in the U.S. tax law texts.

Now, based on continuous machine learning, generated by “an” AI or at least aided or dictated by generative AIs, decision-making becomes a process based not only on programmed processing, but also on more or less qualified data, which can become opaque because it is non-deterministic, non-explainable, untraceable and therefore potentially unfair.

Recent popularization attempts, speeches, podcasts and videos have popularized the limits and dangers of AI – limits linked to the contingencies of learning data and/or processing, algorithms, neural networks, etc. – at the risk of encouraging mistrust in these models, engines, systems or platforms.

This excerpt from an article in *Binaire*[3] was quoted as the title of Aude Bernheim and Flora Vincent’s book: *L’intelligence artificielle, pas sans*

2 See: https://www.ibm.com/topics/explainable-ai.

3 See: https://www.lemonde.fr/blog/binaire/2017/04/17/des-nanas-pour-les-data/.

elles ![4] ("The artificial intelligence, not without them!") (please note the absence of capital letters and acronyms):

> The desertification of our lecture halls and the deliberate policy of quotas for women are blatant and vain evidence of the lack of interest among girls in our scientific fields of study (Sèdes).

With this in mind, in 2015, we organized a national conference on the theme "femmes&Informatique" (Women&Computing) in Orléans, France. Aware of the division that is taking place in this predominantly male environment, we are advocating awareness of the need for diversity, balance and harmony between the genders, in anticipation of the current abyssal gender gap. Isabelle Collet, a young colleague from the University of Geneva, researcher in educational sciences and author of the *L'informatique a-t-elle un sexe?*[5], was guest speaker.

The lack of a potential pool of female students already precluded any prospect of "rebalancing": the question (Sèdes 2017), long before the advent of deeptech and the popularization of the notion of bias, was "how to break the deadlock?!"[6].

In their book, Aude Bernheim and Flora Vincent, from their point of view as biologists, thus alerted us in 2019 to the now-denounced limits of the invisibilization and absence of women in artificial intelligence.

The observation, now widely shared and "publicized", of this failed coalition between data science and (in)visibilization opens a real societal and scientific challenge. Once this "inevitability" (which turns out not to be the case) has been evoked, we can move on from awareness and observations to action, and the assumption of collective responsibility.

2.2. Bias, history and typology

It is on the basis of this gender imbalance and its consequences in terms of diversity and inclusivity that we examine below the confirmation of biases in the digital transition we are experiencing and leading, their consequences

4 See: https://www.laboratoiredelegalite.org/2220-2/.

5 Collet, I. (2006). *L'informatique a-t-elle un sexe? Hackers, mythes et réalités*. L'Harmattan, Paris.

6 See: https://1024.societe-informatique-de-france.fr/1024/2017/02/1024_HS2_2017_3.html.

in terms of ethics and beyond, in the environmental transition that guides our scientific approaches as well as the need for sustainable decision-making and the "sustainability" of decision-making processes.

The notion of bias in information technology is not new: the information systems community has been interested in it since the 1990s.

Based on the analysis of contemporary information systems, Friedman et al. (1996) categorize biases as preexisting, technical and emergent. Preexisting biases, linked to prejudices, are rooted in social institutions, practices and attitudes. Technical biases stem from technical constraints or considerations (hardware, software, peripherals, etc.). The third type emerges from the context of use.

The article by Friedman et al. (1996) defines and illustrates each category with a use case. A preexisting bias is individual or collective (societal). A technical bias stems from computer tools, decontextualized algorithms, the random generation of numbers or the more or less accurate formalization of human constructs. Emerging biases arise from new societal knowledge, incompatibility between system use and design, non-alignment of expertise or different value systems.

The sources of technical bias lie in many aspects of the design process, including the limits of computer tools such as human–machine interfaces, or the attempt to make human reasoning accessible to computers, forcing us to quantify the qualitative, discretize the continuous, or formalize the nonformal, the intuitive and the implicit.

Information systems sometimes help to implement social policies on which "reasonable" people may disagree as to whether the policies are fair or unfair. The presence of bias is not so much an inherent feature of the system independent of the context of use, as a profile of the system within an operating framework. Although the technical bias is built into the program, it is a phenomenon of the system in use, in a context where users produce a judgment about the system's capability.

Addressing bias from a practical point of view involves at least two types of activity: being able to identify or "diagnose" bias in a given system, and developing methods for avoiding bias in systems and correcting/compensating for it when it is identified.

To minimize preexisting biases, designers must not only review specifications and requirements, but also combine this review with an understanding of relevant potential biases. This consideration is necessary from the earliest stages of the design process, when system specifications are negotiated.

Biases common to all populations may arise as a function of cultural identity, socio-professional category, gender, level of literacy or digital proficiency, (in)visible disabilities, etc.

One example is the Women/Wife Acceptance Factor[7] (1983). This factor, which derives from the *stereotype* that men are attracted by gadgets, cars, hi-fi, computers or digital cameras, and women by the aesthetics and visual appeal of objects and living spaces, designates the compatibility between the usefulness of an object stereotypically described as "masculine" (typically computer, hi-fi or video equipment), and its constraints of appearance, noise or clutter (cables, noise pollution), which are "feminine". Reflecting a technological and emerging bias, this factor is quantifiable (number of sliders, potentiometers, settings, etc.) according to a strong sexism towards a potential "feminine" aversion.

In the academic world, we observe that expectations of "genius" (Storage et al. 2020) underpin the gender distribution between academic disciplines[8]. Similarly, in a seemingly objective and impartial evaluation system, the emphasis on ranking and grading can foster inequity by harming women[9].

Actions to minimize bias in computing can be implemented, such as:

– *Developing awareness of common biases*: becoming aware of common biases to help minimize potential biases in system design. Common bases of bias, such as physical characteristics (age, height), physical disabilities (colorblindness, visual impairment, hearing impairment, sensory motor impairment, dyslexia), cultural perspective (language, gender, occupation, literacy level, background knowledge), level of digital or technological appropriation, etc., are identified.

– *Setting up a forum for exchange*: establishing a forum for dialogue early on in the design process highlights potential biases that may otherwise

7 See: https://en.wikipedia.org/wiki/Wife_acceptance_factor.

8 See: https://www.nyu.edu/about/news-publications/news/2023/june/academic-fields-valuing--brilliance--less-welcoming-to-women--ne.html.

9 See: https://hbr.org/2021/12/research-how-ranking-performance-can-hurt-women.

be overlooked. The forum must bring together all of the players involved, whether individually or in a quality capacity: decision-makers, users, operators, user relations managers, etc.

– *Explicitly targeting potential users*: most systems assume, explicitly or otherwise, target users in particular contexts. An emerging bias occurs when populations not originally targeted by the design use the system in contexts not foreseen ((trans)portability of systems, applications, adaptability, customization, etc.). If target user characteristics and contexts of use are made explicit, then, as users and contexts evolve synchronously or not, new users can be alerted to potential biases in the system. Designers will also be in a better position to make adjustments to the design in order to further compensate for them.

– *Designing for diversity*: designing specifically for diversity can help to minimize unintentional bias, especially preexisting bias. Diversity can be incorporated into the design process in several ways, such as (i) including people with diverse backgrounds and profiles on the development team, (ii) including people who represent the diversity of stakeholders and potential users in the datasets and real grounds.

– *Designing for flexibility*: greater flexibility seems at first sight a desirable design goal, as more flexible systems can be tailored to accommodate specific users. As users and contexts of use evolve, the system can be easily adapted to the characteristics of new users and contexts. However, several difficult questions arise: which features are relevant for the flexibility needed here? What methods should be used to determine the default parameters for these flexible functions? How can we balance increased system control with other indicators such as efficiency, simplicity, portability and ease of use?

– *Tracking biases throughout the design process*: just as we keep experience feedback records of bugs identified and corrected in the design process, we can keep "records" of biases as they are identified and corrected. In the case of a technical bias, certain types of technical decisions may be considered to lead to elicited biases during the design process. In the case of emergent bias, biases may not be identified until the system is in operation. Thus, some biases identified in early versions of the system will have to be fixed in later versions.

– *Setting standards to avoid bias in IT systems*: the absence of bias should be part of the standards by which we judge the quality of the systems used in society (ISO standardization, IEC, ITIL, etc.). A standard requires that companies (1) have a defined and documented process for the gathering of requirements, project planning and testing (among other things), (2) employees follow and document the defined processes, (3) measure and improve processes over time (traceability, impact analysis), and (4) that companies provide the necessary training. As companies are now compliant with these standards and reference frameworks, implementing systematic means of minimizing bias has become part of the industrial culture, provided that the said bias can be identified, measured and corrected.

2.3. Types of bias

Commonly identified data biases fall into several categories:

– *Systemic biases*: some social groups are favored, others devalued.

– *Automation* bias: a fully automated decision is applied without checking its relevance.

– *Selection* bias: data are not properly randomized and thus samples are not representative. It does not really reflect the population being analyzed (e.g. samples of health data focusing only on white, male patients, etc., because it does not take other patients into account). This case also overlaps with racial bias: when data favor a particular group of people from specific demographic groups.

– Data *over-fitting* and under-fitting: a model is trained with so much data that it begins to learn from noise and inaccurate data entries in the dataset.

– *Reporting* bias: consideration of only a subset of results in an analysis, covering only a fraction of the evidence.

– *Generalization* bias: when an observation on one dataset is generalized to others.

– *Group attribution* bias: assuming that an individual's characteristics are always determined by the group's beliefs, or that a group's decisions are influenced by the feelings of all its members. Group attribution bias manifests itself when preference is given to the group (in-group bias) or by stereotyping members of other groups (out-group bias). For example, engineers may be predisposed to believe that applicants who attended the same school as them are better qualified for a job when screening resumes for software developers.

– *Implicit* bias: similar to confirmation bias, which consists of continuing to test machine learning models until results confirm the expected hypothesis (looking for information that supports beliefs and hypotheses, and ignoring information that does not).

When there is not enough data, or when the data is not representative, *sample* biases can lead to erroneous conclusions (the classic example of the system that concludes that all doctors are male because the training data only includes male doctors).

Other biases fall into two broad categories: *cognitive biases*, which relate to errors of judgment or reasoning caused by psychological factors, often linked to emotions, beliefs or past experiences, and *methodological biases*, caused by factors such as the way in which data is collected, processed or analyzed, the statistical methods used or the objectives of the study.

Cognitive biases include these well-known "reflexes":

– confirmation bias: the tendency to look for information that confirms existing beliefs and to ignore information that contradicts them;

– anchoring bias: the tendency to rely on the first piece of information received, even if it is inaccurate;

– self-indulgence bias: the tendency to overestimate ourselves and underestimate others;

– representativeness bias: the tendency to believe that past events are more likely than future ones;

– desire bias: the tendency to believe that things that are wanted or expected are more likely to happen.

Methodological bias is illustrated in:

– selection bias: the data are not representative of the target population;

– measurement bias: data are inaccurate or biased;

– publication bias: studies with positive results are more likely to be published;

– analysis bias: data are analyzed to obtain the desired results.

Since bias can have a negative impact on the validity and reliability of a study's conclusions, it is essential to identify and mitigate it in order to guarantee the quality of the results.

2.4. Bias and fairness – a measure of ethics?

2.4.1. *A mixed picture*

The acceptability of a system is based on a number of criteria: explicability, transparency, fairness, etc. These are qualitative, even subjective notions, which underlie the criteria of reliability and fairness mentioned above. In order to make an informed decision, ethical and technical feasibility must be ensured. However, the existence of stereotypes is more often than not accompanied by a self-fulfilling prophecy ("girls are like that, boys are like that"), due to a lack of awareness and implementation of appropriate compensation mechanisms.

The 17 Sustainable Development Goals (SDGs), the global priorities for 2030 adopted by the United Nations General Assembly, concern the fight against poverty and hunger, education and health, as well as decent work, climate change, biodiversity and sustainable consumption and production. They aim to promote gender equality, reduce the impact of business activities on biodiversity and the climate, and develop products and services that help achieve these goals. In this way, corporate social responsibility, which challenge the strategies of companies, institutions and organizations, constitutes a lever for transforming the business model in order to promote the achievement of the SDGs and, therefore, implement these compensation mechanisms.

Machine learning techniques are being increasingly used in decision-making contexts with important societal implications. These automated decision-making mechanisms operate on the basis of explicit or implicit conceptions of fairness. Sometimes, this fairness is difficult to define and implement, or is not even taken into account in the development of an artificial intelligence solution.

There are numerous examples of applications that illustrate the reproduction of biases in a striking, even caricatural way: Amazon's recruitment application, translation models based on *word embedding*,

Apple Card credit, racist image search engines or household assistants that learn the unpolished language of the home all too well.

One of the best-known cases demonstrating the importance and complexity of this issue is COMPAS (Correctional Management Profiling for Alternative Sanctions). It is a decision support software used in the United States that determines the probability that a defendant may become a recidivist (Benbouzid 2018).

In an article published in 2016, ProPublica demonstrated a blatant bias in COMPAS decision-making towards certain populations by systematically assigning them with a substantially higher risk[10].

Discontinued in 2020, and widely criticized for stigmatizing black and Latin American minorities, PredPol (Predictive Police[11]) was a program designed to allegedly predict the place and time of a crime “up to 12 hours” before it was committed, based on a history of police reports.

The following two figures illustrate the bias in the prediction of recidivism risk: Figure 2.1 shows the risk prediction, potentially associated with a racial or even gender bias, and Figure 2.2 shows the actual facts.

Figure 2.1. *Risk assessment. For a color version of this figure, see www.iste.co.uk/abel/ethics.zip*

10 See: https://www.propublica.org/article/machine-bias-risk-assessments-in-criminal-sentencing.
11 See: https://www.usine-digitale.fr/article/la-police-de-los-angeles-abandonne-predpol-le-logiciel-qui-predit-les-crimes.N956926.

Algorithmic fairness is a real issue that is driving research efforts, with more papers being published on the subject every year. These abuses have led the European Union to address the issue of trust in AI algorithms, and to publish a white paper based essentially on seven requirements for new legislation on the use of such algorithms.

Among these requirements, one in particular is of interest to us for this chapter: "diversity, non-discrimination and fairness". This requirement points at the biases that exist in the training data of an AI algorithm.

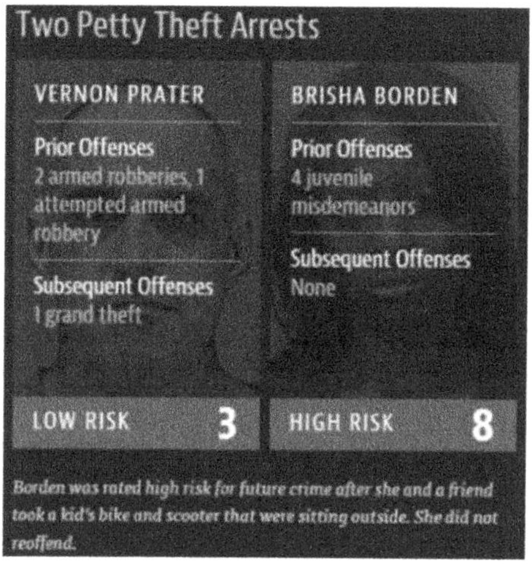

Figure 2.2. *The facts. For a color version of this figure, see www.iste.co.uk/abel/ethics.zip*

This desire to establish a regulatory framework encourages companies to take the necessary steps to develop fair algorithms, especially those in sectors most prone to discrimination, such as medical, banking, legal and human resources.

A single model audit methodology addressing these concerns should aim to:

– limit bias and better integrate ethical concerns into model design;

– meet key business requirements for the adoption of AI algorithms, as part of the new European legislation concerning the regulation of artificial intelligence signed on Friday December 8, 2023, the "AI Act", an agreement regulating their uses and developments.

The primary aim of this chapter is to introduce and raise awareness of the complexity of the fairness issue in artificial intelligence: how can algorithmic biases be defined and quantified? How can they be corrected to ensure a fairer solution? How can we assess the risk associated with this phenomenon (Chassang et al. 2021)?

2.4.2. *How can we define algorithmic fairness?*

Today, there is no universal definition of fairness. In the algorithmic framework of decision-making, Mehrabi et al. (2019) give the following very general definition, which includes two essential elements, discrimination and group distinction:

> Algorithmic fairness corresponds to the absence of any favoritism or discrimination towards an individual or a group formed by innate or acquired characteristics.

The aim is therefore to verify and evaluate the absence of discrimination (neutrality?) that could result from decisions made by an algorithm[12]. The challenge is then to precisely define the biases we wish to avoid, in order to set up metrics to measure and correct them (Charpentier et al. 2022). Protected or sensitive variables are those which, based on the socio-cultural context, may generate biases, or on the contrary be suppressed, in which case the decision could be distorted: ethnic origin, sexual orientation, religious or political beliefs, explicitly and legally defined as sensitive, in compliance with national or international laws and regulations. Deleting variables that are directly or indirectly sensitive when training can lead to a worse bias, with an algorithmic bias remaining in the model output. Cross-referencing sensitive variables with model decisions is necessary in order to identify potential existing biases corresponding to discriminatory decisions made by the model.

2.4.2.1. *Measures of algorithmic fairness*

There are many different definitions of fairness, and therefore many different measures of algorithmic fairness.

12 See: https://journals.openedition.org/statsoc/550?lang=en#tocto2n3.

There are a number of business-oriented proposals based on ad hoc tools[13]. We could imagine a set of metrics forming a universal framework for determining the decision-making biases introduced by an algorithm, but in reality, combining some of these metrics often proves difficult or even impossible. Calibration, i.e. the comparison of data obtained through different biases, is difficult to reconcile, with metrics seeking to balance the classes of the target (the one the algorithm seeks to predict). Thus, in COMPAS, a particular fairness criterion has been chosen, and the discriminations identified are due to its incompatibility with other fairness measures.

Binary classification is the simplest and most widely studied method in the literature, and has a wide range of applications (bank credit, recruitment, customer scoring, testing, etc.). When considering the loan demand, it involves calculating the risk associated with credit default, meaning predicting the probability that a loaned sum will be repaid by the individual.

2.4.2.2. *Independence*

Metrics that seek to meet the independence criterion measure the influence of the groups defined by the sensitive variable on the predicted class. One such metric is the notion of statistical parity. This metric assesses whether each group has the same probability of belonging to the positive predicted class. In the case of loan applications, for example, the probabilities of being able to repay a loan (given by the model) are compared according to whether the applicant is a man or a woman. If four men and twelve women apply for a loan, and the algorithm decides to grant eight loans, we expect two men and six women to be selected (2/4 = 6/12).

2.4.2.3. *Separation*

Independence criteria do not take into account the target class that the algorithm seeks to predict. Definitions based on the separation criterion take it into account in order to measure the independence between the score obtained by the algorithm and the sensitive class (the one for which we seek to evaluate bias) conditioned by the target class.

These definitions allow the former to explain the latter, unlike the previous definitions, which assume that they are independent, thus taking into account the potential influence of one on the other. The equal

---

13 See: https://www.quantmetry.com/blog/intelligence-artificielle-et-ethique-comment-definir-et-mesurer-lequite-algorithmique/.

opportunity metric compares the rates of true positives belonging to the different groups: we thus observe the probabilities that the model predicts the repayment of the loan, depending on whether it is a man or a woman, knowing that the person has actually repaid the sum borrowed.

Consider a sample of 100 people containing 50 women and 50 men. Of the 50 women, 40 have repaid their loans, and of the 50 men, only 20. If, of the people selected by the algorithm, 30 have actually repaid their loans (the other people selected are therefore errors in the algorithm), the algorithm satisfies the metric introduced if, of these 30 people, 20 are women and 10 are men (20/40 = 10/20).

This metric therefore takes into account the information provided by the sensitive class on the target class, meaning in this example that men are less reliable than women when granting credit.

2.4.2.4. *Sufficiency*

The metrics grouped around the sufficiency criterion seek to measure the independence of the target class from the sensitive class conditioned by the score variable (score associated with the algorithm's prediction, between 0 and 1). These metrics are incompatible with positive/negative class balance metrics. Test fairness ensures that the probability of belonging to the positive class is the same for a given score. Considering a score given by the model, and for all persons having obtained this score, we compare the probabilities that this person has effectively repaid the loan according to whether they are men or women.

2.4.3. *And in practice… how can these biases be corrected?*

The analysis and correction of algorithmic biases can be integrated at different levels of a process, upstream, internally or downstream: *preprocessing*, *in-processing*, *post-processing*, in line with ethical metrics.

Thus, the possible interventions to correct a biased model are *preprocessing* on the training data, *in-processing* on the model generation or *post-processing* on the predictions:

– *Preprocessing (data)*: this stage enables us to analyze and process the distribution of the model's training data (sensitive discriminatory variables, class imbalance). The aim is to apply transformations to the input data in order to mitigate bias and make them fairer, but this kind of transformation is likely to have a major impact on the model's interpretability. For example, by projecting the data onto a space orthogonal to the sensitive variable, we may gain in fairness but lose the meaning of the independent variables.

– *In-processing (modeling/optimization)*: the main task at this stage is to define fairness metrics to be optimized in conjunction with performance metrics during model training. The implementation and operation of these methods must therefore be carried out by data scientists.

– *Post-processing (results)*: the aim of this stage is to analyze and transform the model results to identify and deal with potential biases linked to protected variables or to sub-groups linked to these variables. Like *preprocessing*, *post-processing* methods do not require the model to be transparent, and can treat it as a black box. This allows libraries to be used directly without explicit modification. On the other hand, it can make the model less interpretable.

The commonly used correction methods include:

– *Adversarial learning*: an adversary is trained to determine whether the model is fair, and if not, the feedback obtained is used to improve the model (preprocessing and in-processing).

– *Reweighing*: this approach does not alter the data, but only assigns different weights to the training data (preprocessing and in-processing).

– *Transformation*: by applying transformations to the training data, these approaches aim to develop a new representation with better fairness guarantees (preprocessing and post-processing).

– *Regularization/constrained optimization*: this involves adding penalties or constraints to the learning process to penalize inequities (in-processing and post-processing).

– *Calibration*: consists of ensuring balance between the distribution of data and the distribution of predictions (the proportion of positive predictions is equal to the proportion of positive examples), and in the context of fairness, the same principle is applied equally to all subgroups in the data (post-processing).

– *Thresholding*: seeks decision thresholds for the classifier that guarantee a balance between true and false positive rates for all subgroups (post-processing).

2.4.4. *Fairness and interpretability: finding the right balance?*

The study of methods, metrics and experiments tends to demonstrate that making a model fair risks "smoothing out" the samples and, depending on the context and the subject of study, particularly for sensitive variables, degrades its interpretability. It is sometimes necessary or justified to preserve nuances, weak signals, outliers and marginals, to preserve value balances and to face up to even "politically incorrect" ground truth.

Machine learning techniques are increasingly used in important decision-making contexts. Ensuring that they do not generate unforeseen impacts with negative societal implications is one of the best practices that should be specified during the project, in order to identify existing biases in the data and deduce the "right", relevant and informative indicators.

Numerous methods exist to correct these biases and can be integrated into the various stages of a project. The choice of these methods depends, among other things, on the metrics chosen and interpretability constraints. These metrics and correction methods are available on the shelf or via open-source libraries, for example.

However, no scientific or technological consensus exists as to which correction algorithm is best suited to a given business use case to ensure a fairness/performance trade-off.

2.5. "We are open, the door is just very heavy"

This title of a keynote given at RCIS 2022 (Sèdes 2022) illustrates the metaphor of the stranded encounter between women and science: nothing is forbidden to anyone; it is just more or less difficult.

Matilda effect, impostor syndrome, toothpaste tube effect, leaky pipe, glass cliff, etc. Whether it be the disaffection for scientific specialties as part of the high school diploma reform, or the recent phenomenon of opting out ("no thanks") in high-level careers, whether in academia or industry, SME managers or CEOs of major groups, the observation is shared and damning, particularly in the tech and digital professions: where are the women?

As in most fields of activity or sections of society, the representation of women in science is deficient. Even in fields such as life sciences, where female students are in the majority, glass ceilings and sticky floors are the rules when it comes to projecting ourselves into academic careers. What can we say about computer science, which caps at approximately 10% of female students?

Whatever the causes cited to explain this imbalance, and despite the still timid but concrete injunctions and measures taken in an attempt to remedy it, the situation triggers strong alarms, for example, from industrialists willing to give priority to recruiting girls, with equal skills. Strategic fields such as cybersecurity are in dire straits, with the plethora of demand partially met by the implementation of policies to retrain women.

Many studies have been carried out: for example, the "gender paradox" observes that the under-representation of women in STEM fields of science, and more particularly in the "digital world", is a feature of so-called "developed" countries. A number of initiatives have been taken, in Norway (NTNU) and the USA (Carnegie Mellon University), to close the gender gap and balance the number of female and male students.

"We are open. The door is just very heavy". The door is not closed, but it is much heavier for the women who have to invest to get "one foot in" in order to be invited, integrated, accepted, hired, promoted, etc. Is it a lack of interest in a field considered unattractive by the majority of girls, or the hostility of studies and structures in the field?

Just as inclusiveness and accessibility enable everyone to benefit from accommodations initially intended to compensate for or remedy situations of disadvantage, whether visible or not, measures must be taken to achieve balance through diversity, inclusion and equitable cohabitation without discrimination.

The immediate effect of this situation is the generation of biases in the representation data for these sectors, underlining the paradox of gender equality (Amer-Yahia et al. 2022).

Laws, regulations and other administrative circulars govern the legal obligations relating to disability and accessibility. Quotas, penalties and financial sanctions are applied. In the same spirit, the "Parcoursup" platform manages admission lists by applying a 10% interclassification of applications benefiting from a scholarship.

Taking social criteria into account, these official measures enable minorities and other discriminated groups to be represented. As half of humanity is not a minority, a few quota policies are backed up by gender balance and gender diversity. This imbalance is indeed a potential problem, ranging from the disaffection of high-school specialty choices to the under-representation of more mature women in positions of responsibility or with technical skills, not to mention applications to Bachelor programs, university, "CPGE MP2I", engineering schools, etc.

In science itself, and not just in terms of population or scientometrics, a new phenomenon also arises with the evolution of subjects, techniques and tools. This is illustrated by the striking example of the risk of gender and minority invisibilization evoked throughout this chapter. Social representation biases are highlighted (few Wikipedia entries, Matilda effect, lack of historical figures and illustrations, rare "models" in science, etc.) with unbalanced, unrepresentative, poor quality learning data (garbage in, garbage out, etc.). The double question is that of the "fairness" of algorithms and decision (aid) systems, in other words, how the systems are based, on what rules and by whom, with the risk of "encoded" biases, whether conscious or not, of all of the diversity that every decision implies.

This imbalance is dramatic in the medical field, where the absence of certain classes (e.g. the symptoms of a female heart attack) can entail a vital risk. The symptoms, which are radically different, have long been ignored because female risk factors have not been taken into account at the same level as their male counterparts, resulting in the invisibilization of victims.

2.6. Biases: fatality or responsibility? Fatality and responsibility...

A fatality because it is inherent to human nature, since we are all biased, due to our experiences, beliefs and emotions. Stereotypes often imply a self-fulfilling prophecy, which would require a compensation mechanism (a parallel can be drawn with efforts to promote inclusiveness and quotas for staff or students with disabilities), which consists of playing on fairness to reestablish equality. Cognitive biases can prevent us from making objective decisions: for example, confirmation bias prevents us from considering information that contradicts our existing beliefs. Methodological biases can lead us to erroneous conclusions: selection bias, for example, can give a biased picture of a population.

A responsibility, since we have a duty to recognize our own biases, to mitigate and compensate for them. We can do this by being aware of our prejudices, the stereotypes on which we have built ourselves, by reflecting on the factors that could bias our judgments, and by using appropriate methods to conduct and supervise software development, data collection and analysis. Biases can lead to discrimination, for example, self-indulgence bias can lead us to underestimate the abilities of others. Biases can lead to erroneous decisions: desire bias, for example, can lead us to take unnecessary risks.

2.6.1. *Synthetic data for a qualified bias correction approach*

Existing stereotypes and incomplete or flawed measures can influence the stage of data collection. Diversity and representativeness of datasets are crucial. In the absence of original, representative or diverse training data, which is often the case, synthetic data can be used to supplement them, which can help correct data bias. The quality of raw synthetic data is affected by the quality of raw real data. However, the potential of synthetic data is the ability to have control over the output, which can produce a more balanced, clean and useful synthetic dataset. Unlike synthetic data, real datasets do not provide this level of control. Generating synthetic data must incorporate the detection of errors in real data and suggest how to correct them.

Synthetic data can help mitigate bias by complementing/compensating/ diversifying it. When data is biased because it is insufficient, too costly or there is no consent for use in projects, synthetic data helps to fill the gap. Furthermore, if the dataset is unbalanced – for example, the sample is predominantly made up of people from a specific social group – synthetic data can help to balance this data while preserving General Data Protection Regulation (GDPR), privacy and confidentiality of sensitive variables.

Having access to enough high-quality data is essential as the team may be unaware of the initial need for data modeling. In an agile, incremental approach, synthetic data can then provide insight into the type of data used. Such transparency reduces the possibility of introducing bias into machine learning models.

It is essential to ensure that any bias in the original dataset is reduced. By labeling, annotating, cleaning and supplementing the data, this risk of bias is reduced. Including bias testing in the development process is a practice that will help prepare the original datasets that will serve as a model for the generation of synthetic data.

2.7. Debiasing machines

It is important to recognize and realize that biases are a reality, thus we must take steps to mitigate or even compensate for them. By doing so, we can help improve the quality of our judgments and decisions, making them explicable and acceptable. The observation of how women view the digital world, and how the digital world views women, already made, needs to be formalized. If the metaverse is a replica of today's world, like digital twins, will these shortcomings be at best reproduced, at worst accentuated, in an unequal, unbalanced representation of the world that will become our future?

The same recruitment model, the same algorithm, should be applied to claim egalitarian "unbiased" treatment. However, it has now been established, for example, that female curriculum "CVs" are more oriented towards soft skills, which are not explicitly weighted or ranked by the algorithm, illustrating the sensitivity of variables and the need to adapt it to a social, cultural and temporal context.

Work in cybersecurity, cybercrime and social engineering (de Casanove 2022a) analyzes behavioral stereotypes and biases to generate targeted "social" attacks (de Casanove 2022b) in a large-scale applied field dimension.

Initial bias is propagated throughout all applications and cognitive bias has become statistical bias. If algorithms are time-bombs (of social discrimination or otherwise), the time has come to debias the machines: algorithmic decisions are no more objective than human decisions. We need to develop "fair machine learning", the basis of trusted AI.

In a fast-moving context, marked by the unbridled pace of technological advances and a multiplicity of actions to address their ethical and social challenges, keeping a watchful eye on the means put in place to tie AI in with the value of equality between women and men must be an absolute rule.

AI systems can only be as good as their input data. It is important to recognize that bias is a reality and to take action to mitigate it. Based on unrepresentative, unbalanced, biased data, will the AI of the future be inclusive, responsible and sustainable?

2.8. References

Amer-Yahia, S., Bonifati, A., Favre, C., Fromont, E., Labroche, N., Sèdes, F. (2022). Diversity and inclusion activities in EGC, SIGKDD explorations. *Newsletter SIG on Knowledge Discovery & Data Mining*, 24(1), 52–56. doi: 10.1145/3544903.3544911.

Benbouzid, B. (2018). Quand prédire, c'est gérer. La police prédictive aux États-Unis. *Réseaux*, 5(211), 221–256.

de Casanove, O. and Sèdes, F. (2022). Malicious human behaviour in information system security: Contribution to a threat model for event detection algorithms. In *Foundations and Practice of Security*, 13877, 208–220. Springer, Cham.

de Casanove, O., Leleu, N., Sèdes, F. (2022). Applying PDCA to security, education, training and awareness programs. *HAISA*, 658, 39–48. Springer, Cham.

Charpentier, A. and Barry, L. (2022). L'équité de l'apprentissage machine en assurance. *Statistique et société*, 10(3/1), 47–68.

Chassang, G., Thomsen, M., Rumeau, P., Sèdes, F., Delfin, A. (2021). An interdisciplinary conceptual study of Artificial Intelligence (AI) for helping benefit-risk assessment practices. *AI Communications*, 34(2), 121–146.

Friedman, B. and Nissenbaum, H. (1996). Bias in computer systems. *ACM Transactions on Information Systems*, 14(3), 330–347 [Online]. Available at: https://dl.acm.org/doi/pdf/10.1145/230538.230561.

Huttner, L. and Merigoux, D. (2020). Traduire la loi en code grâce au langage Catala. In *Intelligence artificielle et finances publiques*, Nice [Online]. Available at: https://inria.hal.science/hal-03128248.

Lawsky, S.B. (2017). Formalizing the code. *Tax Law Review*, 70(377). doi: 10.2139/ssrn.2987065.

McCarthy, M.A. (1997a). The Allee effect, finding mates and theoretical models. *Ecological Modelling*, 103(1), 99–102.

McCarty, L.T. (1997b). Some arguments about legal arguments. In *Proceedings of the 6th International Conference on Artificial Intelligence and Law*, 215–224. ACM, New York.

Mehrabi, N., Morstatter, F., Saxena, N., Lerman, K., Galstyan, A. (2019). A survey on bias and fairness in machine learning. *ACM Computing Surveys*, 54(6), 1–35. doi: 10.1145/3457607.

Mérigoux, D. (2023). Catala : formaliser la loi grâce à un langage de programmation dédié. *Bulletin de la Société informatique de France*, 1024(20), 77–84 [Online]. Available at: https://www.researchgate.net/publication/365363649_Catala_formaliser_la_loi_grace_a_un_langage_de_programmation_dedie [Accessed 26 November 2023].

Sèdes, F. (2017). Femmes & informatique : le grand Bond en avant ? *Bulletin de la Société Informatique de France*, 1024(HS2), 3–5 [Online]. Available at: https://ut3-toulouseinp.hal.science/hal-03286587.

Sèdes, F. (2022). We are open. The door is just very heavy. In *16th International Conference on Research Challenges in Information Science (RCIS 2022)*, Barcelona [Online]. Available at: https://hal.science/hal-03686718.

Storage, D., Charlesworth, T.E.S., Banaji, M.R., Cimpian, A. (2020). Adults and children implicitly associate brilliance with men more than women. *Journal of Experimental Social Psychology*, 90, 104020. doi: 10.1016/j.jesp.2020.104020.

3

Digital Technology and Artificial Intelligence: How Can We Facilitate the Ethical Control of their Use?

3.1. Introduction[1]

The debate on the mastery of artificial intelligence was reignited with the launch of ChatGPT. This was seen as a clear demonstration of the possibility of human cognitive dependence on the power of AI. ChatGPT and many other variations on the exploitation of LLMs (Large Language Models) were presented as a revolution, capable of generating texts, scenarios, images and films from simple queries, with a quality exceeding the capabilities of the authors of these queries. This latest episode merely rekindles a debate already underway on autonomous vehicles, decision-making systems based on facial recognition, decision-making systems in the legal, insurance and banking sectors, automated industrial production management systems controlling actions delegated to human operators, etc.

In society, there is a polarization of views between those who see digital technical innovation as a solution to society's challenges and those who, on the contrary, believe that these innovations only exacerbate the ethical issues raised.

The users of these technological innovations are excluded from the debate by disembodied technical and scientific discourse and also by

---

Chapter written by Alain MILLE.

1 Disclaimer: this chapter is a rewrite and update of a French article published in *Intellectica* magazine, late 2018 (Mille 2019).

injunctions to adapt to new uses. In this chapter, we take a closer look at digital technical devices that deploy these self-proclaimed innovations. The notion of technical device is borrowed from Bruno Bachimont:

> Technique operates through different structures: the tool, the instrument, the content and finally the machine. Overall, however, technique boils down to the notion of a device: a device corresponds to a spatial organization of elements such that this configuration determines a temporal unfolding (Bachimont 2010).

A digital technical device is one whose general operation is based on information, memory and calculation. In this respect, we agree with Jean-Michel Salanskis in his booklet on the computational world (Salanskis 2011), who shows that the digital nature of a technical device introduces a radical break in technical evolution. The notion of artificial intelligence was formalized as an object of research at the Dartmouth College Conference in 1956[2]. Journalists are now talking about *artificial intelligences,* and we realize that certain digital technical devices are designed to regulate cognitive functions, which, up until recently, were deemed outside the scope of automation. These digital technical devices are taking over the cognition market, taking the form of behavioral recommendations, decision guidance, deciding what is "true" or not, judging cognitive abilities during learning, tirelessly classifying cognitive profiles for the benefit of market or security strategies and de facto replacing individual human interpretation for a growing number of tasks.

In this chapter, we propose to call such devices digital technical devices based on artificial intelligence (DTD-AI). It is in this shifting context, where marketing often prevails over rigor, that we propose to study what would be an *ethically-oriented design* of DTD-AI. By ethically oriented approach, we simply mean that the DTD-AI is designed to put the user in a position to *know what to do in order to do it right, when the question obviously arises.*

A DTD-AI cannot itself be ethical or unethical: it does not "think", as a philosopher might say. In any case, it cannot think *like a human*, because even though we extrapolate to an *autonomous consciousness*, it would then think like a particular DTD-AI and not like a human. Does this mean that a DTD-AI is neutral? Clearly not, as its use without appropriation of its

2 See: http://www-formal.stanford.edu/jmc/history/dartmouth/dartmouth.html [Accessed 16 September 2023].

functioning raises new ethical questions, pointed out by many institutions, as did the recent *Comité national pilote d'éthique du numérique*[3] (French National Digital Ethics Committee). Without waiting for the creation of this committee specialized in ethical issues, the *Conseil national du numérique* (CNnum)[4] (French National Digital Council) published a "Digital Ambition" report in June 2015, the long title of which clearly indicates the ethical issues associated with digital development: "Digital revolution: Delivering on the promise of *empowering* society and transforming the economy"[5].

Other groups, intellectuals and citizens' movements, particularly those involved in the "commons" movement[6], argue that users need to be *empowered* (Genard 2013) in their activities mediated by a digital technical device.

The digital technical device is often presented as a *pharmakon* – poison and remedy – for society. This chapter examines the technical and social conditions required for its use to *reveal itself explicitly* as a poison or a remedy in the user's context, enabling them to reflect on how to do the *right* thing with full knowledge of the facts.

The terms transparency, loyalty, traceability, fairness and explicability are often used in the recommendations made by institutions such as the CNnum, the CIGREF[7], the *Commission Nationale de l'Informatique et des Libertés* (CNIL) (French Data Protection Authority) and its report "How to enable Man to keep control"[8], as well as by associations such as the *Quadrature du Net*[9].

Academic research on the explicability of DTD-AIs is abundant but focuses mainly on the early stages of model learning, and not on their use in the actual user context (Chaput et al. 2021).

3 See: https://www.ccne-ethique.fr/fr/publications/comite-national-pilote-dethique-du-numerique-bulletin-de-veille-ndeg1 [Accessed 16 September 2023].
4 See: https://cnnumerique.fr/ [Accessed 16 September 2023].
5 See: https://www.ladocumentationfrancaise.fr/var/storage/rapports-publics/154000400.pdf [Accessed 16 September 2023].
6 See: https://en.wikipedia.org/wiki/Elinor_Ostrom [Accessed 18 September 2023].
7 See: https://www.cigref.fr/ [Accessed 16 September 2023].
8 See: https://www.cnil.fr/fr/comment-permettre-lhomme-de-garder-la-main-rapport-sur-les-enjeux-ethiques-des-algorithmes-et-de [Accessed 16, September 2023].
9 See: https://www.laquadrature.net/ [Accessed 16 September 2023].

In this chapter, we explore how to give substance to the recommendations for "more ethics" by proposing to facilitate an "ethics-oriented" approach to the design of the devices concerned.

These recommendations contribute to the specification of the *right properties* to be exhibited by DTD-AIs to facilitate this approach.

3.2. Expected properties of an ethics-oriented DTD-AI

Society, as philosophers see it, should function in an ethically oriented way: whatever the context or temporality, they make ethics the major subject of their reflections, and many consider it to be the very object of philosophy.

Viewpoints, stances and proposals evolve from one era and context to the next. This demonstrates, in the truest sense of the word, that it is not possible to build or design ethical technical systems on their own, outside the context of applications, regulations, time, culture, etc.

On the contrary, we believe that designing, building and knowing how to use ethically oriented DTD-AIs is necessary, though probably not sufficient, to enable the emergence of a society that knows what to do, to do it right in the era of the web and artificial intelligence.

What we are seeking, then, are generic properties that can be used to ethically orient a device, rather than specifying ethics for a precise device, which would mean nothing for a DTD-AI, artificial by nature.

Based on the arguments we think the philosophers and personalities interviewed would put forward (see Table 3.1) for ethical behavior in the use of technical devices, can we identify invariants to be integrated into the concrete capabilities that ethically oriented DTD-AIs should provide?

The arguments put forward by philosophers suggest the capabilities that a DTD-AI should offer the user in order to be considered ethically oriented. The aim is to provide the tools needed to develop ethical thinking when the ethical question arises in the context of using the DTD-AI itself.

To provide the starting point for our proposal, we have surveyed the writings of a number of philosophers on the subject of ethics and technology.

Table 3.1 shows the propositions we have attributed to them. From this list of propositions, we will synthesize them into two generically expected *good properties* for designing an ethics-oriented DTD-AI.

	Selected capabilities
Early sages and philosophers	
Lao Tseu (*Tao Te King*) (Lao 2008)	A digital technical system must be *observable* by the wise man if he is to remain in harmony with the world *as it is*. The *process*, the movement *is the main thing* to grasp.
From Aristotle to Democritus (Aristotle (translation Tricot and Sweller 2014; Tavoillot 2006; Plato 2018)	The technical device must facilitate access to the identification of the *target* to be aimed at in order to achieve the *sovereign good*. Identifying the target requires *studying its nature*, which the technical device must facilitate. Once the target has been identified, the technical device must facilitate the development of the *right* behavior.
Medieval/Renaissance - Modern era	
Michel de Montaigne (Nadeau 2010)	Ability to explore the contingency of the situation that *raises* an ethical question. This ties in with the notion of the *context* of a situation.
Descartes (Lallemand 2012)	*Calculation* is neutral and has no particular purpose in the world. Humans must, in all circumstances, be able to control it, to think it. The calculation integrated into the machine is human knowledge, which must therefore be verifiable. The induced property would therefore be accessible documentation of the reasoning carried out and the ability to *validate* it in the world in which it is carried out.
Spinoza[10] (Lord 2010)	The ability to support the processes of reasoning, deliberation, experimentation, capitalization and use of *experience* as inseparable capacities, from Spinoza's point of view, as constitutive of a *rational* being.
Philosophers of the Enlightenment (Dupuy et al. 2004; Stiegler 2015)	The ability to make knowledge available to anyone wishing to *enlighten themselves and enlighten others in return*.

10 Spinoza's Ethics is available in several languages. See: http://www.ethicadb.org/ [Accessed 17 September 2023].

	Selected capabilities
Modern times	
Immanuel Kant (Kant 1797; Sandel 2009)	Ability to assist *reasoning*, but not *replace it.* Ability to increase the ability to inform yourself so as to make *informed* choices.
Utilitarianism (Thiaw-Po-Une 2006)	Is it the notion of *indicators* that should be installed in the devices? These *danger indicators* would be continuously assessed on the basis of interactions and the state of the world as perceived by the digital technical device. The *indicators* would be constituted by public processes that could benefit from *deliberation* support mechanisms.
Husserl (Melle 2001; Trotignon 2006; Ferrarello 2007)	Ability to support the intersubjective construction of shared knowledge. Ability to keep individual experience and the intersubjective process of knowledge-building *articulated.*
Heidegger (and phenomenology) (Winograd 1993; Moreau 2004; Dreyfus 2007; Frère 2007; Seron 2016)	Heidegger implicitly sees technology as a possible site of solution, for "[...] without available technology, there are no more possible ethics, in the sense of a plurality of ways of dealing with oneself as the subject-object of moral consciousness". The *call* imposes itself and already possesses within it the elements of its understanding. Behavior can be *not to act*[11], as resistance, but it can also be to pursue activity (*doing*) as concrete thought, through investigations, trials, explorations, attempts, etc., as the construction of our *being.* As a result, it is the ability to allow *doing* after the *call,* enriched by *new* interactions on the activity, not so much on an *introspection* condemned in advance, but for personal construction in the *social co-being*[12] necessarily requiring *external inscriptions*.

11 Not acting is a form of *negative* action, not passivity.

12 Heidegger refuted the term intersubjectivity (Husserl), which implied the autonomy of each subject in the relationship, preferring instead "being-in-the-world-with".

	Selected capabilities
Positions on ethics and technology in contemporary philosophy	
Gilbert Simondon (Ellul 1977; Simondon 1989, 2005, 2014; Akrich 1993; Sebbah 2010 Guchet 2011; Barthélémy 2014; Saurin 2017)	The ability to put the user in the position of a *technician*; in other words, aware of their role in the regulations put in place by the digital technical system. By relying on its symbolic programmatic genesis, the digital technical device must be capable of restituting the *logic* that inhabits it.
Hans Jonas (Jonas 1998)	Ability to facilitate *thought* about the digital technical device by showing how it works, by being a support for *learning on demand*, by being a support for understanding the regulations in play.
Jürgen Habermas (Habermas 1999; Cusset 2001)	Ability to support discussion processes by providing, in a form accessible to all, the knowledge entries needed to understand, discuss and decide what to do. Ability to *reveal* the functions and regulations at work in *informed* discussion. Ability to integrate the explanatory elements of the ethical decisions made into the digital technical devices themselves, so that they can be appropriated and, if necessary, revived for discussion.
Emmanuel Levinas (Levinas 2000; Fontaine 2007)	Ability to withstand *face-to-face* contact in intersubjective relationships.
Paul Ricœur (Ricœur 1990, 2003; Barreau 2006)	Supporting memory, making it possible to tell the story of human activity and combating oblivion by exploiting the traces of activity as a source for constructing meaning. Modifying the relationship with work so that workers can exercise their responsibilities. Supporting the understanding of activity, so that the worker/user can appropriate and direct in some way the regulations at work in digital technical devices.
Francisco Varela (Varela 2004)	Ability to support *thought* processes when it is necessary *to understand a situation* in all its technical and social complexity. Ability to facilitate the process of transforming *experience* into *registered knowledge*.

Positions on ethics and technology in contemporary philosophy	Selected capabilities
Bernard Stiegler (Stiegler 1996, 2008)	Ability to provide users with all of the means to appropriate technical devices: user experience (UX) leading to self-learning of device operation, reflexivity of activity in the digital environment to support understanding of the regulations at work, ability to write-read knowledge inscriptions in the various tertiary retention devices, ability to provide the conditions for authentic and free *attention* by the user.
Antonio Damasio (Damasio 2017)	Ability to support the processes of understanding what provokes a *feeling* that an ethical question has arisen. Facilitate processes of *wonder* and *questioning* during the activity.

Table 3.1. *Table summarizing the implicit and explicit positions of various philosophers on "ethics and technology"*

In order to summarize the proposals in terms of *good* properties, it should be remembered that the aim is to ensure that a DTD-AI is designed to assist the user in investigating the ethical issues arising from their own use. Assistance is important when the ethical question emerges from use, but the design must also ensure that users have sufficient reflexivity about their activity to enable them to ask themselves the *ethical questions* that may be raised by their activity using a DTD-AI.

Here, the focus is on two good properties that characterize an ethically oriented DTD-AI design. Property I is the necessary but not sufficient condition for property II.

Property I of construction and memorization of knowledge of situated action for the technician (Simondon) as tertiary retentions (Stiegler):

– sub-property for observing and regulating activities;

– sub-property of familiarization/appropriation of activity traces;

– sub-property of user experience (UX) of current processes and regulations.

Property II to support the process of discussing activity and its regulation:

– sub-property to help the user find meaningful activity patterns;

– sub-property to assist in the deliberation of the ethical question.

Let us examine to what extent the satisfaction of these properties would already be more or less verified for a few historical or current DTD-AI classes.

3.2.1. *Property I: construction and memorization of knowledge of situated action for the technician (Simondon) as tertiary retentions (Stiegler)*

In this section, we look at the extent to which DTD-AIs using different classes of AI techniques already have, or do not have, a certain construction and memorization of situated action as tertiary retention, i.e. accessible as documentation of the activity mediated by the DTD-AI. It is the capacity of a DTD-AI to document its operation, which is questioned here for a few types of AI techniques that it can exploit:

1) *Expert systems*: expert systems are built from the knowledge of human experts and are able to propose an effective solution for a class of problems. An expert system uses an inference engine, i.e. an automaton based on logical inference, a list of facts – axioms or theorems – and a list of rules enabling facts to be logically deduced from other facts already known. The code of the inference engine is not accessible, but the corresponding algorithms are simple and well-documented. Most expert systems produce a trace of the *logical path* of reasoning. Reasoning can be documented[13], with facts used and produced, and rules selected. Expert systems thus satisfy the requirement for documentation, but experience shows that this trace can only be used by experts who can discuss it. To be a user-technician, the user must be trained in logical inference as well as in the field concerned. Some expert systems are designed to facilitate the user's appropriation of the expert knowledge mobilized in the device, but most encapsulate it without revealing it.

13 Documenting: the process of creating a narrative, of formalizing documentation by interpreting the traces of an activity. In this case, we are referring to the traces of reasoning that consist of linking inferences by applying rules from initial facts or facts to be demonstrated.

2) *Knowledge-based systems*: it was Alan Newel who proposed differentiating the *knowledge* level from the *reasoning* level (Newell 1982). *What is known about a domain* is described in a graph of terminological concepts and semantic relations. Relationships carry semantics that enable inference. The realization of a knowledge-based system is then a matter of separate engineering (Schreiber et al. 1994) for tasks such as diagnosis, prognosis, classification, decision support, etc. It is possible to establish *encyclopedias or knowledge repositories*, which can be used to characterize the information available on the *Semantic Web* (Lee et al. 2011). The natural user-technician is the one who participates in the construction of the ontology. Discovering the semantics encapsulated in these ontologies remains difficult for non-technical users[14].

3) *Bio-inspired:*[15] *types* are very numerous, but we will only mention here the neural inspiration, which today constitutes the main contemporary branch of AI encapsulated in the most popular DTD-AIs. Bio-inspired approaches abandon the idea of symbolically capturing *expert* knowledge to build knowledge models and instead build purely numerical models from an initial model that is gradually modified by learning from input data. This is essentially the neural network as conceived by learning specialists, the *data scientists* who master the learning implementation chain. Artificial neural networks were reinvented in 1982, and the reader can discover them in the highly educational introduction to Touzet (2016). Today, this reference forms the basis of the LLMs exploited by what is known as generative artificial intelligence. Learning from these models is highly sensitive to the quality and quantity of the input data and to the parameterization of the learning process. The apparent quality of the results of generative AI is impressive but raises new questions.

In this case, documenting the process is virtually impossible at the network learning level, and non-existent when implemented in a DTD-AI like ChatGPT, to name one of the best-known devices[16]. The learning phase remains *inexplicable* for the moment, even in the mathematical sense of the term, as Stéphane Mallat clearly demonstrates[17]. The complexity of the

14 See: https://en.wikipedia.org/wiki/Ontology_learninghttps://en.wikipedia.org/wiki/Ontology_learning [Accessed 17 September 2023].

15 See: http://choicereviews.org/review/10.5860/CHOICE.46-4490 [Accessed 17 September 2023].

16 For a quick review of generative AI, see: https://en.wikipedia.org/wiki/Generative_artificial_intelligence [Accessed 17 September 2023].

17 See: https://www.college-de-france.fr/site/stephane-mallat/inaugural-lecture-2018-01-11-18h00.htm [Accessed 17 September 2023].

learning process is abyssal and requires enormous computing resources and energy. The use of learned models[18] for generative AI is based on a Markovian *gamble*: billions of data described by billions of variables are needed to generate something corresponding to the end-user's expectations, with *no possibility of guaranteeing its correctness.* Generative AI-type DTD-AIs combine other tools to try to *control* the result and avoid displaying results that are problematic from a regulatory, moral or other point of view. In addition, a wealth of *training courses* on how to *properly use ChatGPT* is appearing on the networks, but none of these courses really explain how the answers are produced from the questions. They just explain tricks for *orienting* the queries so that it works "well". How then can the user become a user-technician of such a technology?

3.2.2. *Property II: supporting the process of discussing and regulating activity*

General digital technical devices have been devised to facilitate participative discussion processes between different people[19]. Digital technical devices designed for collaboration also facilitate discussion, some of which will be mentioned below. However, although the range is quite extensive, none of them, as far as we know, makes it easy to discuss the interaction with the DTD itself, whether AI or not. Moreover, the DTD as a collaborative discussion medium is difficult to use for new user-members unless, for example, they are trained and have community animators.

When discussing the functioning of a DTD, the processes at work must be described, both the actions linked to the user's activity and the actions linked to the processes at work on the DTD's side.

Realizing what activity is taking place is necessary for representing it and understanding its regulations. In this second part, we will look at the qualities of reflexivity and affordance that digital technical devices should possess if this explicit consideration of activity is to be built into their use. Secondly, we will look at the possibilities then open for assisting processes of appropriation of the mechanisms at work during the actual use of digital technical devices, particularly for activities that may raise ethical questions.

18 See: https://en.wikipedia.org/wiki/Language_model [Accessed 17 September 2023].

19 See, for example, the range of participatory tools available from: https://cap-collectif.com/ [Accessed 17 September 2023].

This section would benefit from a review of the theories of adaptation to new modes of activity organization, particularly studied in the field of management science (Millerand 2002; Dourish 2003; De Vaujany 2006; Hussenot 2009). These studies demonstrate the importance of the appropriation process in engaging users in their activities. The big difference is that the DTD's actions cannot be discussed by users. Users serve processes for which they are not the user-technicians. These works on adaptation specifically study workflows[20]. These works often start from the question of how users adapt to new ways of organizing work; they demonstrate that the issue is not adaptation, but the very difficult appropriation of these processes. Paul Dourish's work (Lindtner et al. 2012) is particularly noteworthy, demonstrating that cultural issues need to find their place in appropriation processes, rather than being represented as variables in a user profile.

3.2.2.1. *The importance of reflexivity and affordance in digital technical devices*

Every DTD has a minimum level of reflexivity, so that the user realizes which interaction they are engaged in. The simplest illustration is the character that appears on the screen when a key is pressed on a keyboard. The user takes the echo of their keystroke as confirmation that the elementary typing interaction has been successful. If the terminal is slow to display the echo, the user becomes anxious. Research into human–computer interaction is very active[21], and it is within this framework that Winograd, quoted in the first part, places most of his message on the design of computer systems. In the same conference, Gray et al. (2018) study the different classes of interaction *dark patterns*[22] implemented with the aim of favoring the *shareholder* over the user. Fortunately, there are also collections of *user friendly patterns*[23].

During our literature search, we did not identify any works specifically devoted to interaction design with the aim of accompanying moments of reflection and deliberation on a question, ethical, for example, at the initiative of the user, and even less so when this question was raised by the very use of the DTD. However, users show an interest in doing so by seeking

20 See: https://datascientest.com/workflow-tout-savoir [Accessed 17 September 2023].

21 See: https://sigchi.org/conferences/conference-history/ [Accessed 17 September 2023].

22 See: https://www.deceptive.design/ [Accessed 17 September 2023].

23 See: https://www.interaction-design.org/literature/article/10-great-sites-for-ui-design-patterns [Accessed 17 September 2023].

explanations on the forums, where discussions are held that are sources of knowledge for many others. Spontaneously, to illustrate their situation, users take screenshots, produce extracts from event logs, provide contextual information following the advice of other, more technical users than themselves, and thus go behind the scenes of the DTD concerned.

This approach shows that reflexivity about activity cannot be reduced to reflexivity about immediate interaction but concerns activity over time, mobilizing technical functions and situated in a social context, in relation to other users. Dourish (1995) was one of the first to point out the importance of this kind of reflexivity for the development of Computer Supported Cooperative Work systems. He proposed a way of designing an environment that could adapt to the reality of collaborative work as it was actually taking place. To achieve this, he proposed the use of a meta-object approach, enabling the model of a behavior to be modified dynamically at runtime, according to the user's needs. The language used, MOP CLOS (Meta Object Protocol Common Lisp Object System[24]), is a language developed within the framework of artificial intelligence techniques for the dynamic representation of knowledge.

To illustrate our point, and without claiming to be exhaustive, we will distinguish a few broad categories of situations to be taken into account:

1) *Digitally mediated individual activity*: by individual, we simply mean that the activity does not involve direct contact with other people. It takes place, for the most part, in interaction with a digital technical device. For example, writing this chapter using LibreOffice and Zotero is a digitally mediated individual activity. In addition to the writing itself, it is possible to go on the web, read texts on screen, enrich the bibliography, follow a scientific lecture, etc.

2) *Digitally mediated collective activity*: the activity mobilizes several people who use different digital tools for their collective activity: web, shared spaces, email, smartphone, etc. This is the setting most often encountered today. Digital technical devices interact via digital terminals: computer, microcomputer, tablet, telephone, connected object, etc. UX is built on the basis of interactions *experienced* with these terminals. This requires reflexivity and affordance: immediate reflexivity in the activity of document production is sometimes less obvious than in category 1, but collaborative document production devices are trying to get closer to

24 See: https://www.cliki.net/MOP.

Wysiwyg, where the user drags documents, texts, images, sounds, from one place to another in a symbolized form. De facto norms are gradually being put in place to represent others (labels, photos, video, images, etc.) with affordances, evidence of use. *Activity traces* emerge, as the contributions of others are *revealed.* Activity traces are rich in types of interaction considered interesting, and include temporally situated information, involving collaborators represented by their identifiers.

3) *Digitally assisted group activity*: the digital technical device is designed to assist with tasks corresponding to a predefined model. There are countless devices of this type, particularly in the context of the "collaborative" economy. These devices are designed according to activity models either:

– *Not chosen* by the "collaborators"[25], including by checking that they behave in accordance with the expectations of the collaboration platform on the basis of indicators to be met. Users *serve* the platform without becoming user-technicians.

– *Chosen* by the "collaborators" themselves by configuring a generic platform[26] that brings together all of the functions useful for collective activity. In this scenario, it is indeed as user-technicians that collaborators organize the use of the platform, specializing it to their needs.

In reality, if we distinguish these activities, their microworlds are interconnected: for example, the document I write on my own (category 1), will be made available on a Google sharing platform (category 2) and referenced in a Framateam (category 3) as part of a more general editorial preparation activity. This means that any activity could fall into category 3. When Google becomes involved in assisting the user in their activity, its platform moves from category 2 to category 3 in the *unchosen* version: Eric Schmidt, its Chairman, is quoted as saying: "I think most people don't want Google to answer their questions. They want Google to tell them what to do next"[27]. When a collective decides to organize the use of its shared spaces with a tool like Framateam[28], it also becomes a category 3 activity, but this time in

25 These are the models used in the business world: from Business Process Management (BPM) to Business Activity Monitoring (BAM) but also models from the "collaborative" economy such as Mechanical Turk. See: https://www.mturk.com/ or UBER https://www.uber.com/fr/fr/ [Accessed 17 September 2023].

26 See: https://yeswiki.net pour un exemple dans le libre [Accessed 17 September 2023].

27 See: https://www.journaldunet.com/ebusiness/le-net/1142653-15-declarations-insolites-d-eric-schmidt-president-de-google/ [Accessed 25 September 2018].

28 See: https://framateam.org is based on the open-source software https://mattermost.com/.

the *chosen* version. This category 3 should include an environment for discussing ethical issues, whether they arise individually or collectively.

3.3. Illustrations of DTDs integrating activity reflexivity for individual and collective documentation purposes

To make it easier to read the illustrations that follow, a summary is given below:

– A digital technical device is not ethical or unethical by nature. It must enable users to take ownership of how it works, so that they learn to know what to do when their attention is drawn to an ethical issue that concerns them. The digital technical device must be ethically oriented if it is to succeed.

– The necessary (but not sufficient) conditions are: documentarization, i.e. the transformation into a document of digital traces observed during a digitally mediated activity. The digital functions mobilized are articulated with the activity process, enabling reflexivity on the activity and revealing the adapted affordance (or otherwise) of the devices designed.

We have chosen illustrations from our team's research work. The illustrations implement the *M-Trace* (modeled trace) mechanisms proposed by the team and presented in detail in Champin et al. (2013).

The principle behind these applications is to provide the user with a device for *voluntarily* tracing their activity on a DTD-AI or non-AI according to a *trace model* defined by them. A trace model consists of a description of *obsels* (observed elements) that the user wishes to integrate into the reflexive observation of their activity. The user is assisted in building this model from observable elements in their environment: operating system elements (events traced by default), web browser elements (possible user interactions on the browser, interactions with servers) and personal elements (added manually by the user).

Each traced element is characterized by intrinsic properties (text, numerical value, symbol, image, video, sound, etc.) and a time stamp. The trace collected is visualized in real time and can be *transformed* to interpret it in different ways, for example, by associating meaningful *sequences* within the activity. This modeling task is not trivial but can be carried out progressively, starting with an *initial* trace that can be directly understood, as it is marked out by the actions consciously carried out by the user. Real-time visualization enables the user to grasp this basic level. Transformations can be carried out a posteriori, to search for patterns in the trace and benefit from the experience of other users' transformation operations. The illustrations below show how the modeled trace can be implemented and interacted with in different contexts.

A study of the potential use of traces was carried out by Magali Beldame (Ollagnier-Beldame 2011b), who identified four types of use of activity traces to facilitate adaptation of the IT environment. In Ollagnier-Beldame (2011a), the way in which the reflexive trace participates in the construction of meaning is demonstrated during a joint activity. Our review of the literature and the state of the art of platforms did not identify any digital technical devices explicitly interested in providing, in a generic way, a user reflexivity augmented by interaction traces. We will therefore present illustrations from our own work.

The devices presented here are not direct solutions to the question addressed in this chapter but illustrations of the technical and organizational feasibility of a reflexive approach involving the user as user-technician.

We will add a thought experiment to illustrate the use of this approach to participate in an explanatory process in the context of an ethical question posed when using a ChatGPT-type DTD-AI.

3.3.1. *Support from M-Traces for a corporate community of practice*

The project chosen for this scenario, led by a company, was financed by ANR[29] funds. Community users in a large company were provided with a reflexive interface to their activity, based on modeled traces, to enrich a collaborative work environment, supporting content management: validation circuits, document production progress, etc. A zoom of the visualized and interactive trace is shown in Figure 3.1.

Users have access to the following "business ownership" functions:

– temporal navigation in the trace, with different levels of activity grouping (patterns);

29 ANR: *Agence Nationale de la Recherche* (French National Research Agency).

– cross-functional navigation via document objects exchanged (documents, emails, etc.) with other users;

– documenting and formatting activity traces to enable integration into document production;

– assistance in viewing the activity in terms of business models. This is the standardized way of performing the activity. The models are named, and visible in concrete terms of the activity actually implemented;

– assistance in discovering patterns of activity that emerge in actual practice. This is particularly useful when a group is setting up and needs to find its best practices quickly.

Users have shown their interest in such an approach for two main reasons: to help them cross-learn how to use the device and to help them cooperate in deciding which business routines to implement.

The trace-based model discovery system has been validated for its knowledge discovery capabilities but has not yet been studied in its UX dimension.

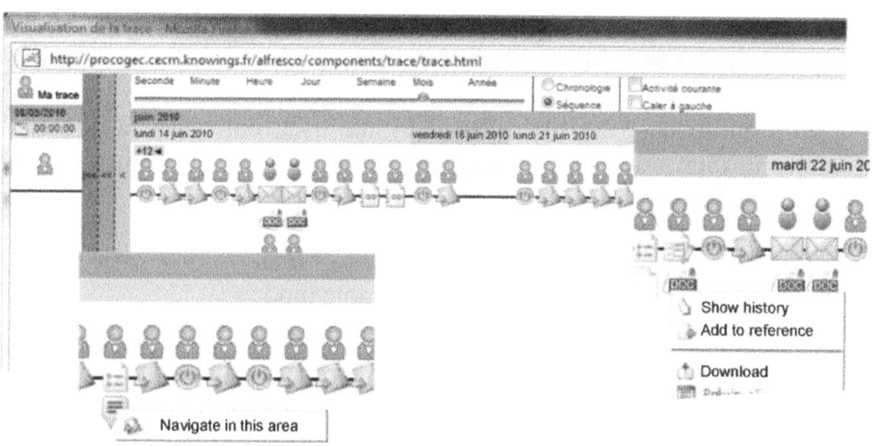

Figure 3.1. *Procogec trace management interface. For a color version of this figure, see: www.iste.co.uk/abel/ethics.zip*

3.3.2. *Support for human learning activity*

During a CNRS[30] mission on the phenomenon of MOOCs (2014)[31], our team carried out the instrumentation of an MOOC-type digital technical device, providing all users with the possibility of regulating the tracking of their activity and discussing the semantics of the indicators used[32].

This experiment enabled us to observe the two "good properties" that would be very useful for a digital technical device and that we defend here as necessary to guide its ethical use:

– user ownership of the tracing process:

- starting, suspending, resuming and stopping tracing under the user's control,

- choice of what to track on the terminal for a given activity: learners often chose to track access to resources other than those offered by the MOOC platform,

- storage in a private environment,

- real-time interactive visualization, with a reflexive effect on the activity in time and space;

– the user's action-perception experience of their interactions;

– platform actions, not experienced by the user, but revealed in visual proximity to their own interactions, providing keys to internal functioning (configurable layout: symbols, colors, text fields, etc.);

– tools for exploring, interrogating and exploiting traces:

- a trace analysis tool based on configurable models,

- a tool for managing shared indicators in a "store", providing access to indicator models, and for uploading your own, developed with the design tool (back office). Indicators are displayed in the learning environment (front office). The learner has access to both the back office and the front office.

---

30 CNRS: *Centre National de Recherche Scientifique* (French National Scientific Research Center).

31 See: https://projet.liris.cnrs.fr/coatcnrs/wiki/doku.php.

32 This work was invited for presentation at MIT (2014). See: https://prezi.com/zyuf8wzkonwe/observing-a-learning-activity/ [Accessed 17 September 2023].

This system has been tested in MOOC training courses and during a CNRS summer school. In reality, MOOC platforms are rarely used as cooperative workspaces. Instead, learners use the generic web tools they are familiar with to work together, outside the platform. The articulation between platform and other tools is not generally assured, and the instrumentation we have proposed fills this gap with a private activity management extension, based on modeled traces. Those interested in other scenarios are invited to consult the publications of the LIRIS TWEAK team[33].

3.3.3. *Example of an activity involving a ChatGPT-type DTD-AI*

Let us engage in a thought experiment here, imagining what a documenting assistant for an activity that has integrated the use of ChatGPT might look like.

The hypothesis involves someone who has recently been hired by a structure that helps people set up their own business. The initial prompt is: "I need to advise someone who wants to set up a glass recycling business. What are the first questions I should ask?" Readers are invited to test this prompt on OpenAI[34].

For this person, an ethical question quickly arises: "Can I use ChatGPT's answers directly, or do I really need to check all its answers and how?". ChatGPT recommends verifying everything and provides no references to support its claims.

We assume that this person wants to check the answers.

ChatGPT cannot be trained on all of the questions it will be asked, but this person can continue to use the DTD to:

– query the Internet using a search engine;

– read documentation suggested by answers to queries;

– summarize what interests this person in a notebook;

– contact colleagues or people found on the Internet to discuss a particular question with them;

33 See: https://liris.cnrs.fr/.

34 See: https://chat.openai.com/.

– look for situations similar to those of the person seeking to set up the activity;

– look for contact details of more specialized people who can be contacted.

This is a lot of work, and there is no guarantee that even the list of questions proposed by ChatGPT, like the ones that will be asked, is exhaustive or relevant. However, our character is fortunate enough to have installed a reflexive tracking plugin on their browser.

Therefore, this person starts by simply by Googling "creating a glass recycling business in France", and the first suggestion is "https://www.creerentreprise.fr/creer-une-entreprise-de-recyclage/[35]. Most of the generalities indicated by ChatGPT are there, while other recommendations do not seem necessary, and, above all, this time many links identify specific information while other questions, not cited by ChatGPT, are listed.

Our character will be able to navigate to these links, retrieve information, find references, identify resource persons, make contacts, etc. As we have seen, this was a glass recycling company, and they will specialize their queries in this area of recycling.

This person therefore has the history of all their queries and interactions in the form of a modeled trace. By transforming the trace, they will be able to organize their search for information into typical patterns. They document their work at low cost and, at the same time, realize that ChatGPT has only served to kick-start their activity by providing them with a few "prompts" to feed their own research.

A new ethical question arises, however, concerning the way in which the character should handle the personal information given to them by the person they are going to advise: financial capabilities, level of technical skill, network of partners, ability to manage a business, etc.

They ask ChatGPT, who draws up a long list of general recommendations, ending with a recommendation to talk to a specialist.

35 At the time of writing, ChatGPT filters the generation of bibliographic references, often revealing hallucination phenomena. This was the case at the time of writing in May 2023.

This time, intimidated by the fact that they were not doing things properly, the character wrote an email to their line manager who suggested that they let the person present themselves freely and that they organize themselves to help them when they asked, rather than estimating their abilities *a priori*.

Several meetings are organized with the client, some remote and others face-to-face. Our character and the client use the services of their DTD to take things further. The client's documents, sent by email or made available on a file-sharing system, and any information they have found on the web, are integrated into the trace, either automatically if they are accessible via our character's DTD or by annotation. Our character recommends that the person they are advising also install the reflexive tracing plugin, and both can now narrate their interactions, comparing them more easily.

They now have a replayable method for dealing with similar situations. They have measured what a text generator can and cannot do, however powerful and impressive it may be, and the importance of keeping control of recommendations and estimating the value of a recommendation in an explicit way.

Above all, our character has a basis for recounting the counseling activity with this person, facilitating the follow-up report and guaranteeing the possibility of returning to the activity itself on the basis of this account. This account highlights the ethical approach of our character throughout their activity.

Finally, troubled by their experience with ChatGPT, they sought to join think tanks on how it worked, but... found none. In fact, although ChatGPT is offered by an OpenAI structure, there is no accessible documentation on how ChatGPT actually works, and we have not found any organized collective to help its users better understand how it works and how to verify claims, in the image of, for example, fake checking organizations.

3.4. Conclusion

This chapter looks at how a digital technical device based on artificial intelligence techniques (DTD-AI) can be instrumented so that the end-user can be supported in their activity, particularly when ethical questions arise. This article focuses on the digital web and artificial intelligence, as they are invading cognitive activities, a sector hitherto considered difficult to automate. Society is taking up the ethical question raised by such an orientation. In the media, on think tanks and in the regulatory arena, opinions, projections and protections are provoking partisan debate. The question is now widely raised at national (Villani 2018), European[36] and international levels (IEEE 2019).

First, let us question the philosophy to remind ourselves of two things:

1) Ethics is one of the main issues dealt with by philosophers.

2) Ethics only makes sense to humans who reflexively question and organize themselves individually and collectively to answer the ethical questions that arise.

Among all the contributions we have heard, we have highlighted those of Gilbert Simondon in the context of contemporary philosophy marked by phenomenology. Following Bernard Stiegler in his intuitions, and Bruno Bachimont in what concerns more specifically the notion of knowledge inscriptions, we chose to study how it would be possible for digital technical devices to provide the remedy for the poison it can itself spread. Two other choices were possible:

1) Consider that digital technical devices are neutral, which was until now the doxa of modernity, but which the cognitive orientation of current digital applications has undermined. The proponents of transhumanism are even announcing a singularity in human evolution based on devices that increase human cognitive capacities, promising – without saying how – to study the ethical issues involved[37].

2) Digital technical devices are toxic by construction. This stance extends to technical devices in general. Bernard Stiegler reminds us that Socrates considered writing to be a technique that alienates man from the truth. Technology is human by construction, so technology cannot be intrinsically alienating for a user-technician, but it can easily be so if it is not possible for any user to become a user-technician. In a totalitarian society, total control could thus be imposed, but even in a democratic society, the alienation of humans by machines is a major risk but not an inevitability. The position we are taking seems a reasonable one for a society that recognizes the human in

36 See: https://www.europarl.europa.eu/news/fr/headlines/society/20230601STO93804/loi-sur-l-ia-de-l-ue-premiere-reglementation-de-l-intelligence-artificielle.

37 This Wikipedia article seems like a good way to raise the question of transhumanism: https://en.wikipedia.org/wiki/Transhumanism.

technology and knows how to live accordingly. Living with technology may seem like a contradiction in terms, but this is how we live, coupled with nature via human technology. A well-understood coupling would be a demonstration of the wisdom acquired through real-world experience, built up by our interactions, which today are often mediated by digital technical devices. We therefore conclude that we have a meta-ethical responsibility to think of digital technical devices as *ethically oriented*.

This analysis of philosophical postures then led us to study the right properties that digital technical devices providing cognitive functions should have in order to support the management of situations of disruption of activity, when the user is called upon to reflect on the direct or indirect ethics of activity as mediated by the digital technical device. More specifically, we want to study the conditions that enable a user to become a user-technician.

What makes a user-technician? This is the person who demonstrates an implicit understanding, illustrated by their interactions with the digital technical device: they feel they are doing the right thing without having to think about it. They demonstrate a form of wisdom, and their behavior is spontaneously "good-natured", not asking any ethical questions until a surprise in the process causes them to think again, alerting them to the fact that they *need* to reconsider before continuing.

Is it possible for a user to develop this form of wisdom at the current level and complexity of digital technical devices, just by using them, through experience alone, without assistance? Obviously, given the very dynamics of digital technical devices, natural appropriation cannot be guaranteed, and the answer to this question is undoubtedly *no*.

Given that we cannot be content with such a conclusion, which would lead us to renounce technology, as seems to be the conclusion of figures such as Ellul, it seems reasonable to strive to ensure that activities mediated by digital technical devices facilitate the identification and reflection on an ethical question that they would pose, through good properties designed to facilitate humanity's own ethical process.

To get out of this apparent deadlock, we propose to rephrase things in a different way: although the user alone cannot achieve the status of a wise person in a world integrating digital technology, the user must (1) be able to alert themselves to behavior they sense as unethical; (2) be able to reflect on the reality of the behavior they sense; and (3) be able to collectively co-construct ethical behavior. The aim is no longer to understand everything, but to be able to question everything when it comes to developing a new knowledge of *what to do*.

The good properties selected are formulated as follows:

– construction and memorization of situated action knowledge for the technician (Simondon) as tertiary retentions (Stiegler);

– support for the process of discussing and regulating activity.

We have detailed the first property, which goes far beyond digital technology. It involves knowing how to read and write the knowledge inscriptions encapsulated as tertiary retentions in digital technical devices. This literacy does not guarantee illiteracy, however, if the tertiary retentions are not accessible to just anyone. The tertiary retentions containing the necessary knowledge inscriptions are mainly the computer code (the functions) and the traces kept during interactions of the activity in all its possible complexity. We have studied a number of conditions for documenting these tertiary retentions, to bring them back into the human register of writing–reading, via reformulation in text or in standardized forms that can be discovered through learning and appropriated through experience.

The second property, supporting discussion of activity and regulation, has received very little attention in the computer science literature. We had intended to imagine how Habermas's ideas might apply at this level, but the study is not sufficiently advanced to risk doing so. We have dealt with this part by pointing out the qualities required of the digital technical device for the right property to develop, but we have not yet found any specific work on this question. However, to give a more concrete idea of what a device supporting discussion of activity and its regulation might look like, we have chosen two scenarios from our research team's work: in the field of corporate knowledge management and, more recently, in the field of appropriating a human learning activity when using MOOCs. The sole aim of these scenarios is to render visible what is usually hidden in devices and to show what types of interaction could be developed by designers to imagine the ethically oriented digital technical devices we feel are indispensable.

We have also devised a scenario integrating a DTD-AI, with ChatGPT providing reflexive trace-type assistance to enable users to put their DTD-mediated activity into a narrative for themselves and for others interacting with this activity. This scenario emphasizes reflection and the ability to argue about the value of the activity.

The implementation of a modeled trace computer object introduces a new complexity into the description of digital technical devices and the possible interactions with this object to support ethical deliberation are not immediately clear. We believe that this object is a potential mediator of ethical discussion for several reasons, arising from our observations of interactive uses of the modeled trace:

1) Understanding what this trace represents is *obvious* if the trace is immediate during interaction. An object that cannot be observed one way or another in its creation, development and transformations may have good technical properties, but it cannot be appropriated by the user, let alone serve as an appropriation tool available for deliberation to identify the regulations at work.

2) In scenarios, the trace is always a support for debriefing and reformulation between the actors in the interaction, facilitating understanding of the DTD's role for the individual or collective user.

These observations are not demonstrations, nor do they replace a research program, but they are certainly worth mentioning in this discussion. They provide hypotheses to be investigated in order to study what could be functions to assist ethical deliberation: revisiting experience, replaying situations with new ways of proceeding, identifying signature patterns of known ethical issues and facilitating their resolution, etc. Web and AI technologies could be specifically studied to provide the technical functions needed for these deliberative processes. However, we would again only be pushing the problem back a little: if there is no clear organization of spaces and times for physical deliberation with others, then assistance would not make much sense.

We would therefore like to end this chapter with a call for the development of specific research programs, inclusive of society, to think about, design and experiment together with thoughtful, ethically oriented digital technical devices. For example, it would be interesting to exploit the possibilities of collaborative work available in open source and/or free software as grounds for investigating and experimenting with processes and tools enabling ethical deliberation to be set up under clear conditions of documentation, recounting of the deliberative process and support schemes to be put in place to facilitate its integration into digital technical devices.

It is not easy for designers and developers alone to come up with these devices. We need to bring together researchers, designers and, above all, users who are motivated to become user-technicians. Today, marketing managers prescribe devices. They must now integrate this movement, by changing their approach and thinking about devices so that they become interesting for life. By interesting for life, we mean that human beings must be able to develop ethics that guarantee the conditions for living well. What is outlined in this chapter may seem impossible to achieve, but we maintain that it is not possible for it to be impossible.

3.5. References

Akrich, M. (1993). Les formes de la médiation technique. *Réseaux*, 11(60), 87–98.

Aristotle (2014). *Éthique à nicomaque*. Les échos du Maquis, Paris [Online]. Available at: https://philosophie.cegeptr.qc.ca/wp-content/documents/éthique-à-Nicomaque.pdf [Accessed 12 August 2018].

Bachimont, B. (2010). *Le sens de la technique : le numérique et le calcul*. Les Belles Lettres, Paris.

Barreau, H. (2006). L'éthique de Paul Ricœur à partir de "Soi-même comme un autre" (1990) [Online]. Available at: https://halshs.archives-ouvertes.fr/halshs-00108135 [Accessed 18 September 2018].

Barthélémy, J.-H. (2014). *Simondon*. Les Belles Lettres, Paris.

Champin, P.-A., Mille, A., Prié, Y. (2013). Vers des traces numériques comme objets informatiques de premier niveau. *Intellectica*, 59, 171–204.

Chaput, R., Cordier, A., Mille, A. (2021). Explanation for humans, for machines, for human-machine interactions? In *Explainable Agency in Artificial Intelligence WS. AAAI-2021*.

Cusset, Y. (2001). *Habermas l'espoir de la discussion*. Michalon, Paris.

Damasio, A. (2017). *L'ordre étrange des choses*. Odile Jacob, Paris.

De Vaujany, F.-X. (2006). Pour une théorie de l'appropriation des outils de gestion : vers un dépassement de l'opposition conception-usage. *Management & Avenir*, 9(3), 109. doi: 10.3917/mav.009.0109.

Dourish, P. (1995). Developing a reflective model of collaborative systems. *ACM Transactions on Computer-Human Interaction (TOCHI)*, 2(1), 40–63.

Dourish, P. (2003). The appropriation of interactive technologies: Some lessons from placeless documents. *Computer Supported Cooperative Work (CSCW)*, 12(4), 465–490.

Dreyfus, H.L. (2007). Why Heideggerian AI failed and how fixing it would require making it more Heideggerian. *Philosophical Psychology*, 20(2), 247–268.

Dupuy, J.P., Hountondji, P.J., Rouanet, S.P., Scarantino, L.M. (2004). Philosophie, science et éthique. Report, UNESCO, Première journée internationale de la philosophie, 77.

Ellul, J. (1977). *Le système technicien*. Liberté de l'Esprit, Paris.

Ferrarello, S. (2007). L'idée de science éthique et ses implications dans le cadre de la science phénoménologique. *Etudes Phénoménologiques*, 8, 23.

Fontaine, P. (2007). Emmanuel Levinas (1906-1995). Présentation générale de sa philosophie. Table ronde consacrée à 'La découverte de Levinas', Project, Europe Éducation École [Online]. Available at: http://melies.ac-versailles.fr/projet-europe/telecharge-levinas.wmv.

Frère, B. (2007). Max Scheler et la phénoménologie française. *Revue philosophique de la France et de l'étranger*, 132(2), 177. doi: 10.3917/rphi.072.0177.

Genard, J.L. (2013). De la capacité, de la compétence, de l'empowerment, repenser l'anthropologie de la participation. *Politique et sociétés*, 32(1), 43–62.

Gray, C.M., Kou, Y., Battles, B., Hoggatt, J., Toombs, A.L. (2018). The dark (patterns) side of UX design. In *Proceedings of the 2018 CHI Conference on Human Factors in Computing Systems*. ACM Press, Montreal, 1–14. doi: 10.1145/3173574.3174108.

Guchet, X. (2011). Les technosciences : essai de définition. *Philonsorbonne*, 5, 83–95. doi: 10.4000/philonsorbonne.348.

Habermas, J. (1999). *De l'éthique de la discussion*. Flammarion, Paris.

Hussenot, A. (2009). Manager l'appropriation des solutions TIC : des controverses aux modes d'appropriation. *Systèmes d'information & management*, 14(2), 65. doi: 10.3917/sim.092.0065.

IEEE (2019). ETHICALLY ALIGNED DESIGN: A vision for priotizing human well-being with autonomous and intelligent systems. Standard [Online]. Available at: https://standards.ieee.org/content/dam/ieee-standards/standards/web/documents/other/ead_v2.pdf [Accessed 13 April 2019].

Jonas, H. (1998). *Le principe responsabilité : une éthique pour la civilisation technologique*. Flammarion, Paris.

Kant, E. (1797). *Anthropologie du point de vue pragmatique*, Foucault, M. (trans). Vrin, Paris.

Lallemand, J.-D. (2012). L'éthique cartésienne de la pensée. PhD Thesis, Université de Bourgogne, Dijon.

Lao, T. (2008). *Tao Te King (traduction Stephen Mitchell), un voyage illustré.* Synchronique, Paris.

Lee, T.B., Hendler, J., Lassila, O. (2011). The Semantic Web. *Scientific American*, 284(5), 34–43.

Levinas, E. (2000). *Totalité et infini essai sur l'extériorité.* Le Livre de Poche, Paris.

Lindtner, S., Anderson, K., Dourish, P. (2012). Cultural appropriation: Information technologies as sites of transnational imagination. In *Proceedings of the ACM 2012 Conference on Computer Supported Cooperative Work.* ACM Press, Seattle, 77. doi: 10.1145/2145204.2145220.

Lord, B. (2010). *Spinoza's Ethics: An Edinburgh Philosophical Guide.* Edinburgh University Press, Edinburgh.

Melle, U. (2001). La théorie husserlienne du jugement. *Revue Philosophique de Louvain*, 99(4), 683–714.

Mille, A. (2019). Vers des dispositifs techniques numériques orientés éthiques ? *Intellectica. Revue de l'Association pour la Recherche la Cognition (ARCo)*, 1. doi: hal.archives-ouvertes.fr/hal-02142666.

Millerand, F. (2002). *La dimension cognitive de l'appropriation des artefacts communicationnels. Internet : nouvel espace citoyen.* L'Harmattan Paris.

Moreau, D. (2004). Heidegger et la question de l'éthique : la construction d'un interdit. *Horizons philosophiques*, 14(2), 1. doi: 10.7202/801261ar.

Nadeau, C. (2010). *Montaigne contre l'éthique de la vertu.* Classiques Garnier, Paris. doi: 10.15122.

Newell, A. (1982). The knowledge level. *Artificial Intelligence*, 18, 87–127.

Ollagnier-Beldame, M. (2011a). Les traces numériques dans les activités conjointes : leviers de la construction du sens. *Journal of Human Mediated Interactions (RIHM)*, 11(2), 1–23.

Ollagnier-Beldame, M. (2011b). The use of digital traces: A promising basis for the design of adapted information systems? *International Journal on Computer Science and Information Systems, Special Issue 'Users and Informations Systems'*, 6(2), 24–45. doi: hal-00669019.

Plato (2018). La République, Livre VII (traduction Chambry). *Wikisource* [Online]. Available at: https://fr.wikisource.org/wiki/La_République_(trad_Chambry)/Livre_VII [Accessed 12 August 2018].

Ricœur, P. (1990). *Soi-même comme un autre.* Le Seuil, Paris.

Ricœur, P. (2003). L'aventure technique et son horizon planétaire. *Autres Temps. Les cahiers du christianisme social*, 76(1), 67–78. doi: 10.3406/chris.2003.2410.

Salanskis, J.-M. (2011). *Le monde du computationnel.* Les Belles Lettres, Paris.

Sandel, M.J. (2009). C'est l'intention qui compte, Emmanuel Kant. In *Justice*. Flammarion, Paris, 153–206.

Saurin, I. (2017). Comprendre la technique, repenser l'éthique avec Simondon. *Esprit*, 3, 157. doi: 10.3917/espri.1703.0157.

Schreiber, G., Wielinga, B., de Hoog, R., Akkermans, H., Van de Velde, W. (1994). CommonKADS: A comprehensive methodology for KBS development. *IEEE Expert*, 9(6), 28–37. doi: 10.1109/64.363263.

Sebbah, F.-D. (2010). *Qu'est-ce que la 'technoscience' ? Une thèse épistémologique ou la fille du diable ?* Les Belles Lettres, Paris.

Seron, D. (2016). Introduction historique à la philosophie phénoménologique. Master's Thesis, Université de Liège, Liège [Online]. Available at: https://orbi.uliege.be/bitstream/2268/186476/1/seron-introd-hist-phil-phenomenolog.pdf [Accessed 19 August 2018].

Simondon, G. (1989). *Du mode d'existence des objets techniques*. Aubier, Paris.

Simondon, G. (2005). *L'individuation à la lumière des notions de forme et d'information*. Jérôme Million, Paris.

Simondon, G. (2014). *Sur la technique*. Presses Universitaires de France, Paris.

Stiegler, B. (1996). *La technique et le temps*. Galilée, Paris.

Stiegler, B. (2008). Industrie relationnelle et économie de la contribution. In *Le design de nos existences à l'époque de l'innovation ascendante*. Mille et une nuits, Paris.

Stiegler, B. (2015). L'esprit des lumières à l'époque du philosophical engineering. In *De la trace à la connaissance à l'ère du Web*, Mille, A. (ed.). Intellectica, Paris, 29–40.

Tavoillot, P.-H. (2006). L'épicurisme et l'idée de la sagesse. In *Questions d'éthique contemporaine*, Thiaw-Po-Une, L. (ed.). Stock, Paris, 84–94.

Thiaw-Po-Une, L. (2006) (ed.). L'utilitarisme. In *Questions d'éthique contemporaine*. Stock, Paris, 409–423.

Touzet, C. (2016) Les réseaux de neurones artificiels, introduction au connexionisme [Online]. Available at: https://hal-amu.archives-ouvertes.fr/hal-01338010.

Tricot, A. and Sweller, J. (2014). Domain-specific knowledge and why teaching generic skills does not work. *Educational Psychology Review*, 26, 265–283.

Trotignon, P. (2006). La phénoménologie de Husserl et la Science [Online]. Available at: http://societe-sciences-agriculture-arts-lille.fr/wp-content/uploads/2014/08/Sol_2006_p4-7_Trotignon.pdf.

Varela, F. (2004). *Quel savoir pour l'éthique ?* La Découverte/Poche, Paris.

Villani, C. (2018). Donner un sens à l'intelligence artificielle. Report, Mission parlementaire [Online]. Available at: https://www.aiforhumanity.fr/pdfs/9782111457089_Rapport_Villani_accessible.pdf [Accessed 9 November 2019].

Winograd, T. (1993). Heidegger et la conception des systèmes informatiques. *Intellectica*, 2 [Online]. Available at: https://www.intellectica.org.

4

Ethical Autonomous Agents: Literature Review and Illustration for Markov Decision Processes

4.1. Introduction

The emergence of questions about the responsibility and governance of algorithms has raised a number of ethical issues, particularly with regard to the development of autonomous artificial agents interacting with human beings. Beyond the ethical issues relating to the use of these systems, the absence of an ethical component in the decision-making mechanisms of these agents can cause problems. For example, in the field of autonomous vehicles, the automatic choice of a driving speed may be considered more or less ethical, depending on the circumstances. It may be preferable to drive at a reduced speed in front of a school at the end of the school day, rather than simply obeying the speed limit. In this case, ethics is not a strict constraint, but rather a recommendation to which the agent should adhere if possible. Still by way of example, in the field of healthcare, and projecting ourselves into a hypothetical future where nursing robots have to take care of patients, interactions with human beings should intuitively respect patients' dignity, regardless of the therapeutic efficacy of the agent's decisions (or even in contradiction with them). Here, ethics calls on notions, in this case human dignity, that are difficult to implement, subjective, plural and whose definition may have to be adapted to the current situation. More generally, as Weizenbaum pointed out as long

Chapter written by Grégory BONNET, Nadjet BOURDACHE, Abdel-Illah MOUADDIB and Mihail STOJANOVSKI.

ago as 1976, any automated decision-making that influences human destinies can be problematic, as these same decisions made by human beings rely, among other things, on compassionate, empathetic, cultural and ethical factors, from which autonomous artificial agents are exempt (Weizenbaum 1976).

From these issues, it follows that providing tools for modeling, programming and integrating ethics into the decision-making mechanisms of autonomous agents, in other words proposing models of *ethical autonomous agents*, is a matter of interest. This does not, of course, remove the more general issues of use and regulation of artificial intelligence systems, but it can provide tools for implementing such regulation. Thus, these agent models must enable them to represent and reason about ethical notions, to judge their decisions and those of others in moral and ethical terms, and to take account of the plural dimension of ethics in their decisions. To this end, numerous approaches are proposed in the literature. Some are qualitative, based, for example, on valued argumentation frameworks (Bench-Capon 2003), modal logic (Lorini 2012), non-monotonic logic (Berreby et al. 2017) or BDI architectures (Cointe et al. 2016). Other approaches are quantitative, relying mainly on decision theory (Svegliato et al. 2021) or machine learning methods (Chaput et al. 2021). Whichever approach is chosen, work in the field of ethical autonomous agents generally seeks to produce models that are generic and that allow for a rich expression of the range of concepts involved in ethical decision-making.

This chapter is divided into two parts.

The first part aims to present a review of the state of the art in terms of ethical autonomous agents. Section 4.2 introduces the problem by presenting a high-level view of the different components involved in ethical decision-making. We then identify the main questions an ethical autonomous agent designer needs to answer, in order to implement adequate decision-making mechanisms. Section 4.3 presents a state-of-the-art review of architectures and models used to integrate the ethics of autonomous artificial agents.

The second part focuses on fleshing out the issues involved in designing ethical autonomous agents, and to this end, we propose to describe in detail the original model of *ethical Markov decision processes* (E-MDP), a quantitative and explicit approach based on decision theory. Section 4.4 presents this model and an algorithm for solving it. Finally, as an example, we instantiate the model with three distinct ethical principles in section 4.5.

4.2. Issues specific to the integration of ethics

Before reviewing different models and architectures of ethical autonomous agents, we need to define what ethics is, identify its key components and the specificities this notion implies in terms of models. Our aim is not to provide a complete and exhaustive review of moral and ethical philosophical issues, but to present a synthetic view that is practical for autonomous agents. Section 4.2.1 therefore aims to identify the main components to be integrated into an autonomous agent architecture. Section 4.2.2 then presents the computational issues specific to the introduction of ethics in autonomous agents, and highlights the fundamental questions that any model must answer.

4.2.1. *A high-level approach to ethics*

First, we need to distinguish between what is moral and what is ethical. As Deleuze sums up:

> Morality presents itself as a set of binding rules of a special kind, which consists in judging actions and intentions by relating them to transcendent values (this is right, this is wrong, etc.); ethics is a set of optional rules that assess what we do and say according to the mode of existence it implies (Deleuze 1990).

Here, in the context of decision-making, options are first evaluated in moral terms, meaning associating them with causing good or harm in relation to their conformity to the mores, values and customs of a group or person (Timmons 2012). Morality is in fact based on moral values, which are abstract notions – positive (e.g. courage, a sense of justice) or negative (e.g. greed or cruelty) – characterizing a wide range of objects: states, actions or even norms. Making a decision that promotes a positive moral value causes good, while demoting one generally corresponds to causing harm. When two options are supported by different moral values, each bringing a certain amount of regret given that the execution of both is impossible, this is a moral dilemma. The social sciences have shown that these values vary in importance and form hierarchical organizations called value systems (Wiener 1988).

Secondly comes ethics, which plays a triple role. First of all, ethical reasoning is the way in which moral values are elicited, meaning that, depending on the context, the values that are important to the decision-maker are chosen, with arguments to support these choices (Haidt 2001). Secondly, ethical reasoning is the process of attributing to decisions the underlying moral values; in other words, those that are demoted or promoted according to the context and the different types of responsibility of the decision-maker in the effects of these decisions. Lastly, ethical reasoning is, in the case of a moral dilemma, the process of aggregating – or more generally compromising – between different moral evaluations in order to make a just decision (Hirose 2014).

Early thinking on ethics distinguished between obligations, prohibitions and recommendations (positive or negative): not fulfilling an obligation or violating a prohibition should be sanctioned by a significant penalty, while doing a non-recommended action or not doing a recommended action should be sanctioned more lightly (Averroes 1178). Other ideas – for example, the doctrine of double effect (Foot 1967) – refute the duality between causing good and causing evil: we cannot easily justify causing evil by causing good, since one is not the negation of the other. Moreover, the doctrine of doing and allowing (Rickless 1997) highlights the difference between doing evil and allowing evil to occur. Indeed, causing harm is more blameworthy than allowing harm to occur in the future.

Although we are aware that these notions of morality and ethics can be criticized or refined, they help to highlight a number of constituent components of ethical decision-making, illustrated by the model of Cointe (2017) in Figure 4.1.

Therefore, ethical decision-making involves deciding on the right actions or behaviors to adopt, based first and foremost on a contextual evaluation of these actions or behaviors in terms of morality. The latter is based on values, which can be organized into value systems, and moral rules. It should be noted that research in psychology indicates that some moral choices are underpinned by decision-makers' ability to experience emotions. The rightness of actions then depends not only on their morality, but on other factors such as the desires they enable to be realized, the concrete ability of an agent to carry them out (i.e. an agent cannot be blamed for not having done what it could not in practice do) and the ethical principles that aggregate these different factors. Integrating ethics into autonomous agents therefore requires modeling the various components.

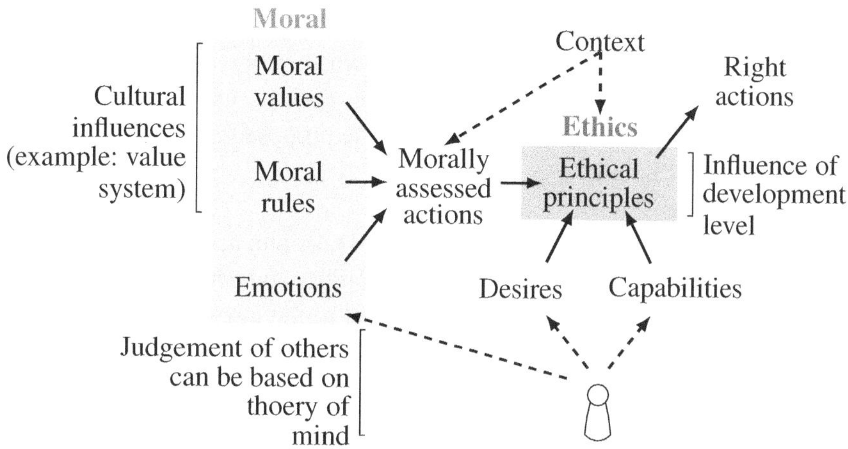

Figure 4.1. *Components of ethical decision-making, adapted from Cointe (2017). For a color version of this figure, see www.iste.co.uk/abel/ethics.zip*

4.2.2. *Programming ethical autonomous agents*

First of all, it should be remembered that programming an ethical autonomous agent does not mean that this agent is ethical in itself, but that its decisions can be judged as ethical by an external human observer: it is therefore a simulation of ethics (just as an emotional agent simulates emotions, or a decision-making agent simulates decision-making).

This raises the question: can ethical decision-making be reduced to a calculation, an optimization problem or a constraint satisfaction problem?

A radical position would be to say yes, and consider that existing artificial intelligence tools (planning methods, deontic logics, social choice theory, etc.) are sufficient to represent and deal with ethical problems. However, as Powers (2006) points out, reducing ethics to problem solving is in itself problematic. Ethics is also a question of choice: choice in representations, in the values considered, and in the way exceptions and other agents are taken into account.

A less radical position would be to consider that the problem of computational ethics is to provide a multitude of tools for identifying or dealing with specific aspects of ethical questioning, and to leave it up to the designer to choose the tools best suited to their problem. Thus, the aim would be to provide autonomous agent models, which can explicitly represent multiple value systems, shared or not between more agents, and always explicitly represent elicitation and evaluation criteria, as well as notions of responsibility and causality. In this context, the proposed models must address three fundamental issues.

1) What definition of ethics does the model take into account? For example, some models may not distinguish between morality and ethics, and consider all ethical reasoning as a constraint to be applied to the agent's decisions. Other models may assume the prior existence of elicited values, then use them to reason in terms of constraints. Finally, others may consider the respect of ethical principles as an end in itself, and thus as an explicit objective of the agent. Whatever definition of ethics is chosen, it will necessarily be a reduction of what ethics is in general, which has implicit meanings that system designers need to be aware of.

2) Which modeling approach should be chosen? Irrespective of the choice of objects to be modeled (morals, ethics, value systems, etc.), it is necessary to decide how to model them. Some models may be qualitative, while others may be quantitative, and will involve questions of aggregation. Finally, how should the modeling be carried out in concrete terms: should the objects considered be specified, or can they be learned, and from which dataset? These are just some of the questions whose answers will produce distinct models.

3) How can we evaluate an ethical autonomous agent model? Many fields of artificial intelligence rely on well-known *benchmarks* to evaluate themselves, as these are based on ground truth and enable performance measures to be calculated. However, what is performance in ethical terms? Intuitively, evaluation can only be based on a broad category of notions, such as concepts used in social choice theory (fairness, non-discrimination, envy-freeness), and, on the other hand, on concepts used in contingent planning (risk, safety). Other notions such as expressiveness or complexity of description (for reasons of readability) may also be relevant.

4.3. Ethical autonomous agents: state of the art

We can distinguish three main types of ethical agent models: qualitative implicit architectures (section 4.3.1), which do not separate the ethics model from the agent's operational model, qualitative cognitive architectures (section 4.3.2) and quantitative cognitive architectures (section 4.3.3), which separate ethical reasoning from the operational model by explicitly representing the different components of ethics. These three types of architectures require specification of the ethical concepts being modeled. We can then consider a fourth type of architecture: those based on learning mechanisms (section 4.3.4). This study excludes formal verification approaches – such as Mermet and Simon (2016) – which do not so much propose agent architectures as methodologies for proving ethical behavior a posteriori.

4.3.1. *Qualitative implicit architectures*

The first type of ethical agent architectures is what we call qualitative implicit architectures. A typical example of this type of architecture is *Ethical Governor* proposed by Arkin et al. (2009) for military missions where an artificial agent must apply the "laws of war" to decide whether or not to engage in actions. This architecture is illustrated in Figure 4.2 and is a hybrid reactive/deliberative architecture. This means that the agents have no mental states, and they execute a given policy a priori. To this end, each perceived situation (possibly weighted by a degree of certainty) is reactively associated with a commitment action. The agent then deliberates on the set of activated actions and decides on their permissibility according to the ethical constraints associated with each.

Here, every action has its own ethical constraints defined according to the situation and which must be verified, as well as its own exception procedures.

Thus, the agent's decision-making process is not described in terms of morals and ethics distinct from the concrete situation, but in terms of situation-specific constraints that only make sense from a global point of view. What is moral and ethical is thus already arbitrated – without distinguishing between the different concepts involved – at the level of constraints for each situation. In this sense, the architecture is not very generic, and does not distinguish between operational procedures (what the agent must do independently of any ethical question) and moral and ethical reasoning itself. This is what we find in other architectures such as that of Winfield et al. (2014) for mobile robotics. We can see this type of architecture as an instantiation in the field of autonomous agent architectures of an approach based on *value-sensitive design* (Cummings 2006). For this reason, an important line of work has been devoted in parallel to defining more generic, higher-level architectures, separating ethical reasoning itself from the decision-making model.

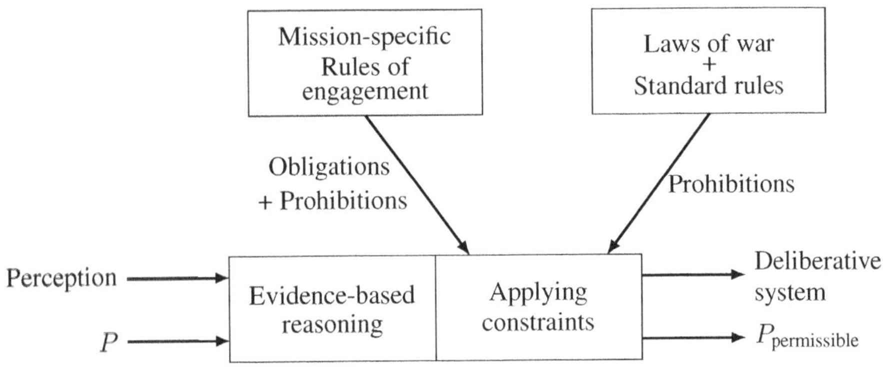

Figure 4.2. *Ethical governor architecture from Arkin et al. (2009)*

4.3.2. *Qualitative cognitive architectures*

As seen earlier, not explicitly separating morality and ethics from operational procedures can be reductive, and cognitive approaches, i.e. considering agents with mental states, may be relevant to overcome this problem (Robbins and Wallace 2007). We can identify two main types of cognitive architectures. On the one hand, some approaches focus on moral issues, meaning reasoning to plan the satisfaction of a maximum number of moral values, and rely mainly on modal logic. On the other hand, other approaches focus on ethical issues, meaning reasoning to take account of preemptions, exceptions and contextual preferences, and rely on non-monotonic reasoning, formal argumentation or inference with negation by failure.

A first natural way to model ethical reasoning is to draw on work in deontic modal logic, and more specifically, the work of Horty (1996), implemented in the Athena prover by Arkoudas et al. (2005), which axiomatizes an STIT logic (expressing that an agent wants a formula to be true) with a universal deontic operator and agentive deontic operators. Here, these operators are used to express formulas such as "it is obligatory to ensure that ϕ" (universal) and "the agent should ensure that ϕ" (agentic), which in the latter case relies on the agent's preferences for traces. These preferences capture the agent's internal value system. Other operators, multi-agents this time, interesting for ethics, have also been proposed to express, for example, epistemic blame (Naumov and Tao 2020) ("a group of agents is responsible for π if it ensures that ϕ and knew that it had a strategy ensuring $\neg\phi$") or multi-agent dilemmas (Naumov and Yew 2021) ("a group of agents necessarily ensures a formula within an option set by incurring a (fixed) penalty"). However, in these frameworks, actions are abstracted by the choice operator, and the concepts of morality and ethics also remain abstracted by the deontic operators. So, as in implicit architectures, there is no distinction between these two concepts. This approach is extended by Lorini (2012) with the DL-MA[1]. This model then explicitly expresses the agent's actions, abilities, knowledge, operational goals (desire) and moral ideals. Ethics is then modeled by the agent's preference between their operational objectives and their moral ideals according to the trace.

Recently, several approaches have built on this line of work to propose moral planning models. For example, Lindner et al. (2020) propose a framework restricted to the SAS+ language. Still by way of example, Grandi et al. (2022) restrict themselves to LTL logic to propose a moral planning model that unifies ways of resolving inconsistencies between goals, desires via a notion of priority or lexicographic order. In general, all of these approaches have difficulty representing context-dependent notions of exceptions, which are central to ethical reasoning. This is why other work has focused on non-monotonic reasoning, starting with models based on formal argumentation.

Formal argumentation has always been naturally linked to issues of legal decision-making, and expressing arguments about norms is a guiding thread in this field (Oren 2013; Prakken and Sartor 2013). Naturally, arguing about norms with varying degrees of force, and depending on the preferences of the reasoning agents, can be used to model ethical reasoning. This has led Atkinson and Bench-Capon to develop *valued argumentation frameworks*

1 Dynamic logic of mental attitudes and joint actions.

(VAFs). In a VAF, arguments are associated with a moral value or are objective facts. For example, Figure 4.3 represents reasoning around the question "is it right to steal medicine from one sick person for another sick person with no money?". A first argument, here C, can say "it is forbidden to steal" and can therefore promote a *property* value. A second, here D, can say "a person without money has the right to steal medicine" and can promote a *life* value (argument D). Arguments attack each other, and ethical reasoning consists of finding, for preferences over values, a subset of arguments with desirable properties (e.g. conflict-free, which defend each other and attack all other arguments) to support a decision.

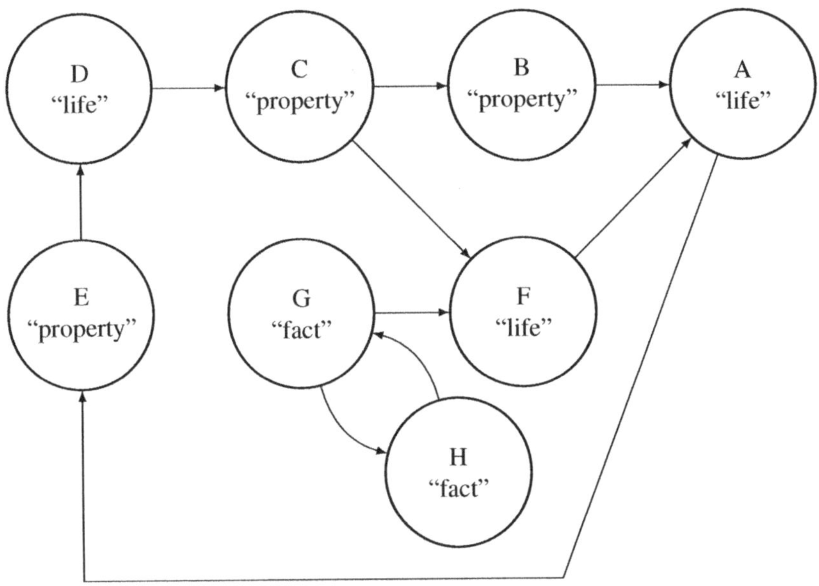

Figure 4.3. *An example of a value-based argumentation framework from Bench-Capon (2003)*

There are several extensions of this framework, in particular multi-valued frameworks where arguments can be supported by several values (Kaci and van der Torre 2008) or where the values associated with arguments depend on a context (Wu 2020). However, in a VAF, the associations between argument structure and values remain abstract, characterized only by their association. Moreover, by default, VAFs model immediate reasoning, not sequential decision problems.

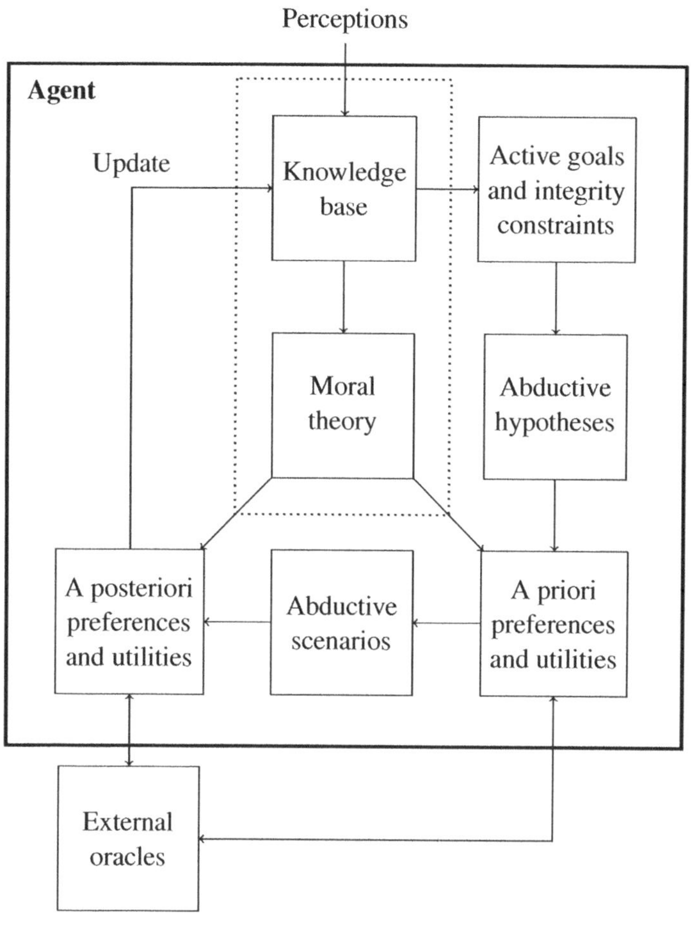

Figure 4.4. *Prospectic logic architecture from Saptawijaya and Pereira (2015)*

Another line of work on non-monotonic reasoning relies on logics that take advantage of negation by failure, to express exceptional cases. This line of work is illustrated in particular by those of Pereira and Saptawijaya (2007a, 2007b); Saptawijaya and Pereira (2014, 2015), which fit into the general architecture illustrated in Figure 4.4. Here, however, ethical evaluation is specified by action-specific statements. This effectively captures deontological statements, but does not capture consequentialist aspects. Indeed, ethics is not extracted here by any form of understanding of the environment and the ethical rules in place. There is no representation of causality, so action and its consequences are not dynamically linked; their relationship is therefore stated rather than inferred. Consequentialist aspects were then initially dealt with by Ganascia (2007), where the direct consequences of actions are represented. Ethics can then be expressed in terms of these consequences, rather than the actions themselves. This model was then extended to sequential aspects, namely the consequences of consequences, as well as events in nature by Berreby et al. (2017).

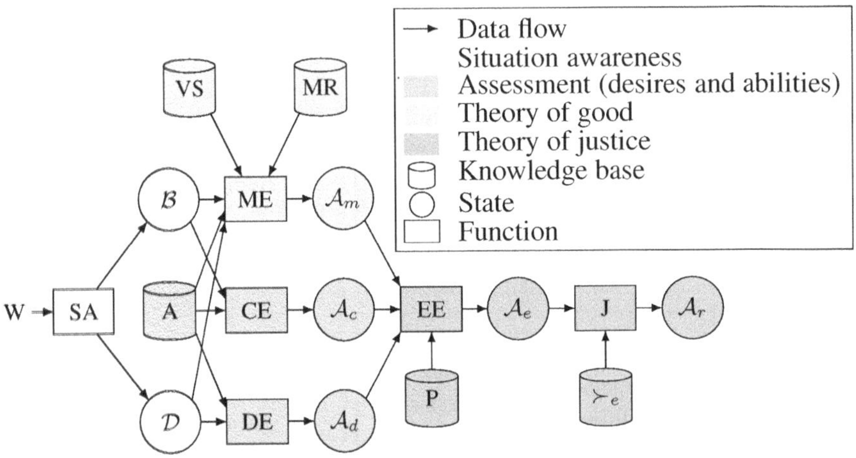

Figure 4.5. *EJP architecture from Cointe et al. (2016). For a color version of this figure, see www.iste.co.uk/abel/ethics.zip*

The preceding architectural approaches are basically reasoning models for representing moral or ethical reasoning. The operational aspect, very present in qualitative implicit architectures, is treated secondarily. This is why BDI architectures, such as those proposed by Dennis et al. (2015), Cointe et al. (2016) and Bremner et al. (2019), bridge the gap between reasoning models and the reactive aspect of implicit architectures. As an example, the EJP architecture, for *ethical judgment process*, proposed by Cointe et al. (2016), is illustrated in Figure 4.5. Here, the architecture is based on non-monotonic reasoning implemented in AgentSpeak, which triggers reactive judgment procedures based on the agent's perceptions. As with Pereira and Saptawijaya, actions associated with direct consequences are evaluated in terms of desires (agent goals) and moral values. Preferences on different criteria aggregating these evaluations then model the ethical reasoning itself. The specificity of this approach is that, based on the theory of mind, it enables us to judge another agent according to different moral or ethical criteria.

However, the previous BDI architectures do not explicitly represent causal aspects related to ethics. Only the direct consequences of an action, or the action itself, are evaluated. This is why other architectures, such as the one proposed by Mao and Gratch (2012) and Bourgne et al. (2021), integrate a causal inference between the agent's perceptions and the ethical judgment process. This is also the case for the ACE architecture Bourgne et al. (2021) and Sarmiento et al. (2023) illustrated in Figure 4.6. This architecture is structured in three layers: (i) a factual layer describing the situation and its evolution as a function of decisions via a STRIPS fragment of PDDL; (ii) a relationship analysis layer, centered on causality, which establishes positive causal relationships (causing an event) and negative causal relationships (preventing an event); and finally, (iii) an ethical layer which evaluates the ethical permissibility of the options under consideration by distinguishing between the theory of the good (moral) and the theory of the just (ethical).

4.3.3. *Quantitative cognitive architectures*

In the previous architectures, the qualitative aspect implies that values are promoted or demoted, decisions are deemed ethical or not, and situations are not subject to quantified uncertainty. This is why quantitative approaches seek to explicitly model this. In the literature, the vast majority of quantitative sequential decision-making methods under uncertainty are based on the Markov decision process model or MDP[2]. A number of approaches have been proposed for integrating ethics into MDPs, which can be divided into three categories.

A first way of integrating ethics into MDPs is to use a *reward function shaping* technique, meaning to modify the reward function that evaluates the quality of the agent's decisions. To do this, rewards and penalties based on the morality of the actions chosen are added to this function. For example, in the case of an autonomous vehicle, De Moura et al. (2020) use a reward function based on proximity to other road users, respect for the law and distance to the goal. In the event of unavoidable collisions, the reward function is modified according to ethical preferences to decide on the most acceptable collision. As with quantitative implicit architectures, there is no explicit separation between ethics and the agent's operational goal.

2 The reader can find a formal presentation of MDPs in section 4.4.1.

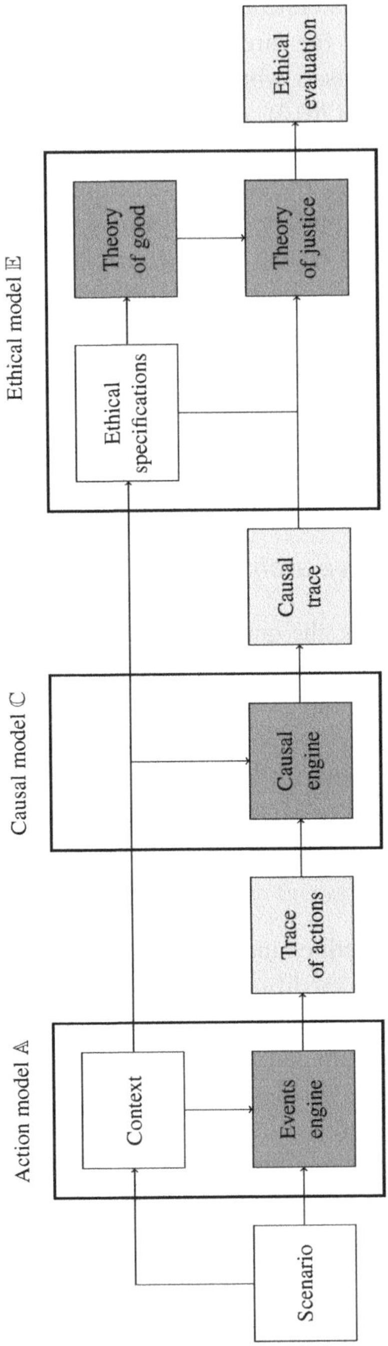

Figure 4.6. *ACE architecture, adapted from Sarmiento et al. (2023)*

Another approach is to add an ethical component to MDPs. For example, Svegliato et al. (2021) define *ethically compliant autonomous systems* (ECAS) that incorporate a particular moral principle. To achieve this, a constraint not directly expressed in the MDP is added to the model. The approach is then based on constrained optimization, meaning the search for a policy that satisfies this constraint. Consequently, if the constraints are inconsistent, an ethical policy may not exist. A multi-agent extension of ECAS is proposed by Nashed et al. (2021). Here, each agent has a particular state space and a value function on it. The moral principle is defined to take account of the moral communities to which the agent belongs. In these approaches, each new moral principle requires a specific constraint.

Another approach proposed by Loreggia et al. (2022) consists of calculating two policies on two distinct reward functions, an amoral one and a multicriteria function representing moral values. Morality is thus a constitutive element of the model, and ethics consists of deciding on the most moral action among a set of options. Depending on an aggregation criterion, an orchestrator chooses in each state whether to follow the amoral or the moral policy. In the same vein, Rodriguez-Soto et al. (2020) combine several reward functions directly in the value function: an evaluative function that rewards the agent for following obligations and a normative function that penalizes the agent who violates a norm (acts in a forbidden way or neglects an obligation). An ethical policy is one that does not violate any norm and is praiseworthy at the same time. Such a policy may not always exist. However, in both approaches, these models cannot differentiate between policies with many violated norms or values and many praiseworthy actions, and those with a few violated norms or values and a few praiseworthy actions.

4.3.4. *Learning an ethical model*

Focusing on autonomous agent architectures, we will not consider learning-based approaches that focus primarily on classification tasks. These include works that train a neural network (Wiedeman et al. 2020) or a Bayesian classifier (Kim et al. 2018) to predict the results of the *MIT Moral Machine Experiment*, or those that seek to learn the values associated with words in a corpus (Araque et al. 2020).

In the case of qualitative cognitive architectures, research into learning for ethical decision-making is essentially based on inductive logic programming

(ILP) (Muggleton 1991). Given a knowledge base and positive and negative examples, ILP enables hypotheses to be learned in the form of complete (covering all positive cases) and consistent (covering no negative cases) rules. Anderson et al. (2006) and then Anderson and Anderson (2014) proposed the *case-supported principle-based behavior* (CPB) paradigm. Here, the agent's actions are associated with sets of duties that are more or less fulfilled, and the examples consist of saying whether an action is acceptable. The system then learns a preference relationship between actions by explicitly deducing the duty constraints that lead to preferring one action to another. This approach produces large rules that are disjunctions of all duty fulfillment conjunctions. This is why Dyoub et al. (2020) have proposed a method still based on ILP on an ASP model, making it possible to take advantage of negation by failure to learn more readable rules.

In the case of quantitative cognitive architectures, learning an ethical decision-making model is generally based on reinforcement learning.

For example, Balakrishnan et al. (2018, 2019) propose to teach ethical "constraints" on one-armed bandits, a model called *behavior constrained Thompson sampling* (BCTS). Ethics is represented here as a generalized contextual multi-armed bandit problem. In this model, each agent's decision is represented by an arm whose reward function, originally unknown, is stochastic and depends on a context defined as a vector of features. Each time the agent makes a decision, it receives a context-dependent reward, as well as Boolean feedback on whether or not the decision was ethical in that context. The idea is that the agent first learns a policy that satisfies the ethical constraint, before subsequently learning a policy that is a linear combination of the reward and the ethical reward (which is no longer observed). Here, the model mixes a qualitative and contextual approach to ethics (a decision is ethical or not) with a quantitative approach where the violation of the ethical constraint is weighed against the value of the reward. Note also that there is no explicit distinction between morality and ethics.

In the field of MDPs, a first series of works relies on human intervention to judge the morality of the agent's actions. For example, Abel et al. (2016) rely on the expertise of a human to judge a priori the morality of each action, while Wu and Lin (2018) use a database that aggregates numerous human responses for a POMDP (partially observable MDP). In both cases, this is a tabular reinforcement learning method (the transition function is learned explicitly) and the reward obtained by the agent is a regret that depends on the difference between the morality of the best decision and the morality of the one actually taken by the agent. Here again, the distinction between morality and ethics is not explicit. This is why Rossini et al. (2020) propose a deep neural network that explicitly separates the latent space of amoral evaluation from that of ethical evaluation according to a set of values. Chaput et al. (2021) generalizes this type of neural approach to the multi-agent framework and the continuous domain via the encoding of MDP states by a Kohonen map. In this approach, illustrated in Figure 4.7, an unknown reward function subject to ethical judgment is to be learned. There are three main differences from the previous model: (1) the exploration algorithm for learning is noisy to explore continuous states; (2) judgments are given by external ethical autonomous agents which can be based on a qualitative cognitive architecture (e.g. an argumentation model or a BDI architecture) or a simple quantitative architecture (e.g. classical reward functions); (3) the learning algorithm generates a policy for each independently judging agent (thus modeling a moral aspect where each judge promotes a particular value) and then identifies dilemma situations which are sets of similar states where the judges' evaluations differ.

4.3.5. *Intermediate conclusion*

We have reviewed the main types of ethical agent models and architectures. The main finding is that each approach is based on necessarily reductive modeling choices regarding the representation of ethics. The fundamental problem is not so much the resolution mechanisms proposed by each approach, but rather their ability to be as generic and expressive as possible in order to explicitly represent the various concepts underlying ethical decision-making: notions of values, value systems, moral evaluation, ethical principles, contextual preferences, exception cases, causality and responsibility (ontic, linked to the agent's actions per se, or epistemic, linked to what the agent knew or did not know) for the consequences of decisions. We can note that the explicit representation (and resolution) of multi-agent ethical issues is less represented, namely theory-of-mind-based mechanisms for judging others, value alignment, fair and non-discriminatory decision-making, although these are topics traditionally addressed in the field of social choice theory (Baum 2020; Fioravanti et al. 2022).

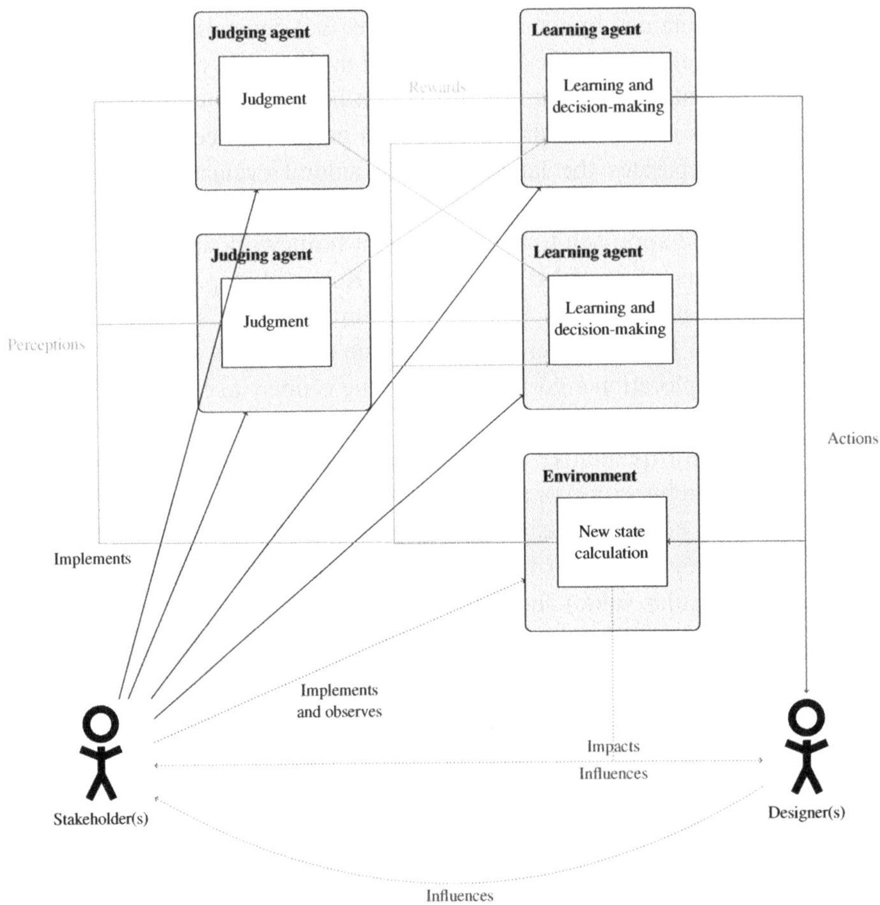

Figure 4.7. *General architecture for ethical learning from Chaput et al. (2021). For a color version of this figure, see www.iste.co.uk/abel/ethics.zip*

4.4. Ethical Markov decision processes

In the remainder of this chapter, we will illustrate the concepts discussed above with an example of quantitative cognitive architecture, based on *Markov decision processes* (MDPs). We have seen that models in this category either deal with a single rule from a set of ethical rules, called *ethical principles* – indicating exogenously to the model which moral values are important and which decisions are permissible – or do not explicitly distinguish between what is moral and what is ethical. We propose here the *ethical Markov decision process* (E-MDP) model, which extends MDPs with explicit moral values and uses a multi-criteria reward function that represents the different cases in which these values are satisfied (promoted) or violated (demoted). The aim of this model is to:

1) Have an explicit representation of the moral values that can be elicited as positive or negative by the decision-maker.

2) Explicitly consider harm and good as distinct, i.e. causing harm (respectively preventing harm) does not necessarily mean that the good has been prevented (respectively, the good has been caused).

3) Distinguish between causing harm (respectively good) and allowing harm (respectively good).

4) Be able to express obligations, prohibitions and recommended actions.

The rest of this chapter is structured as follows. Section 4.4 introduces what Markovian decision processes are and how we can extend them to model morality and ethics. Section 4.5 then presents three model instances to capture different ethical principles we can find in the literature, namely divine command theory, duties prima facie and virtue ethics.

4.4.1. *Markov processes and ethical contexts*

A *Markov decision process* (Puterman 1994) is a decision-making model in a fully observable stochastic environment. An MDP is a quadruplet $\langle S, A, \mathcal{T}, R\rangle$ where S is a finite set of states, A is a finite set of actions, $\mathcal{T} : S \times A \times S \rightarrow [0, 1]$ is a function such that $\mathcal{T}(s, a, s')$ is the probability that choosing the action $a \in A$ in the state $s \in S$ produces the resulting state $s' \in S$, $R : S \times A \times S \rightarrow \mathbb{R}$ is a function such that $R(s, a, s')$ is the immediate reward the agent will receive for arriving at state $s' \in S$ after choosing action $a \in A$ in state $s \in S$.

A solution to MDPs is a function, called *policy*, which associates an action (or a set of actions) with each state of the MDP. There are several types of policy, such as deterministic or stochastic policies (Puterman 1994) or non-deterministic policies (Fard and Pineau 2011). Deterministic policies $\pi : S \rightarrow A$ describe what action the agent should take in each state s, while stochastic policies $\pi : S \times A \rightarrow [0, 1]$ describe for each state s the probability of choosing the action a. A non-deterministic policy $\pi : S \rightarrow 2^{|A|}$

describes the set of action choices the agent can make in each state. In this chapter, we focus on deterministic policies. An optimal solution to an MDP is an *optimal policy* π^*, which maximizes the expected cumulative reward in each state $s \in S$ by solving Bellman's equation. For maximization, Bellman's equation takes the form $\forall s \in S$:

$$V^*(s) = \max_a \sum_{s' \in S} \mathcal{T}(s, a, s')[\mathcal{R}(s, a, s') + \gamma V^*(s')]$$

The main algorithms for solving an MDP and obtaining optimal policies are *value iteration* (VI) (Bellman 1957) and *policy iteration* (PI) (Howard 1960). For our purposes, we use a variant of VI that uses Q-values (Watkins 1989).

Deciding from an ethical point of view requires an *ethical context* that is specific to the decision-maker. This context represents the agent's moral values, which can be divided into positive, negative and neutral values. The polarity of values can differ from one agent to another. For example, *obedience* is a value that can be positive or negative, depending on the agent's philosophical position.

DEFINITION 4.1.– *Let* $\mathcal{V} = \{v_1, \ldots, v_k\}$ *be a set of moral values. An* ethical context $\mathcal{C}$ *is a tuple* $\{mathcal{C}_1, \ldots, \mathcal{C}_k\}$, *where* $\mathcal{C}_i \in \{1, -1, 0\}$. *An evaluation of* 1 *(respectively* -1 *and* 0*) means that the value is considered positive (respectively negative and neutral) for the agent. Let* $\mathcal{G}_\mathcal{C}$ *(respectively* $\mathcal{B}_\mathcal{C}$ *and* $\mathcal{N}_\mathcal{C}$*) be the set of positive (respectively negative and neutral) values in the context* $\mathcal{C}$*:* $\mathcal{G}_\mathcal{C} = \{v_i \in \mathcal{V} : \mathcal{C}_i = 1\}$ *(respectively* $\mathcal{B}_\mathcal{C} = \{v_i \in \mathcal{V} : \mathcal{C}_i = -1\}$ *and* $\mathcal{N}_\mathcal{C} = \{v_i \in \mathcal{V} : \mathcal{C}_i = 0\}$*).*

Note that values do not differ in importance: a positive value cannot be considered better than another (respectively negative, worse). We leave it to future studies to take into account a hierarchy of values. At this point, the question arises: how should an agent make a decision in an ethical context? From a general point of view, a value can be promoted or demoted by a decision. Promoting a value means that the agent's behavior is consistent with it, while demoting a value means that it is violated by the agent's behavior (whether the value is positive or negative). It therefore seems natural that an interesting ethical decision-making maximizes the positive moral values promoted and minimizes the negative values promoted. Furthermore, it should maximize the negative values demoted and minimize the positive values demoted. As the positive or negative values promoted and demoted are not dual, such a decision process is a multi-criteria decision process. Ideally, it should satisfy the following property.

PROPERTY 4.1.– *An ethical decision-making process maximizes the promotion of positive values and the demotion of negative ones, while minimizing the demotion of positive values and the promotion of negative ones.*

However, it is not always possible to satisfy Property 4.1. Therefore, we propose the compromise expressed by Property 4.2.

PROPERTY 4.2.– *An ethical decision-making process first minimizes evil by minimizing the negative values promoted and maximizing those demoted (the first criterion being more important than the second), then maximizes good by maximizing the positive values promoted and minimizing those demoted (the first criterion being more important than the second).*

From this, we can define E-MDPs, which are extended MDPs with a moral, represented by promoted or demoted values associated with transitions, and an ethic, which dictates how the agent optimizes a decision with respect to the moral.

DEFINITION 4.2 (ETHICAL MDPS).– *E-MDPs consist of a sextuplet* $\langle S, A, \mathcal{T}, \mathcal{C}, \mathcal{E}, \mathcal{R}\rangle$*, where* S, A *and* $\mathcal{T}$ *are the classical sets of states, actions and the transition function respectively,* $\mathcal{C}$ *is an ethical context (see Definition 4.1),* $\mathcal{E}$ *is a moral evaluation function (see Definition 4.3) and* $\mathcal{R}$ *is an ethical reward function (see Definition 4.4).*

To express ethical principles, we need to describe the alignment of agent behavior with moral values. We therefore introduce the moral evaluation of transitions, which measures whether a transition promotes, demotes or does not consider a given value of the context.

DEFINITION 4.3 (MORAL EVALUATION OF TRANSITIONS).– *Each transition* $(s, a, s') \in S \times A \times S$*, where* $\mathcal{T}(s, a, s') > 0$*, is associated with a tuple* $\mathcal{E}(s, a, s') = \langle \mathcal{E}(s, a, s')_1, \ldots, \mathcal{E}(s, a, s')_k\rangle$ *representing its moral evaluation. The i-th element* $\mathcal{E}(s, a, s')_i$ *of* $\mathcal{E}(s, a, s')$ *takes a value in* $\{1, -1, 0\}$*, which means that the moral value* $v_i \in \mathcal{V}$ *is respectively promoted, demoted or not considered.*

4.4.2. *Modeling ethics*

E-MDPs' reward function describes how the moral values of the agent's ethical context are aligned with their behavior. The agent can promote or demote a value, resulting in four distinct behaviors: the promotion of a positive or negative value – i.e. *causing good or harm* – and behaviors promoting a positive or negative value – i.e. *preventing good or harm.*

DEFINITION 4.4 (ETHICAL REWARD FUNCTIONS).– *The reward function $\mathcal{R}$ produces a quadruplet where Δ counts the good caused, ∇ the harm caused, $\overline{\Delta}$ the good prevented, $\overline{\nabla}$ the harm prevented. Thus, $\mathcal{R}(s, a, s') = \langle \Delta, \nabla, \overline{\Delta}, \overline{\nabla} \rangle$ with $\Delta, \nabla, \overline{\Delta}, \overline{\nabla}$ such that:*

$$\Delta = \sum_{v_i \in \mathcal{G}_C} x_i \text{ and } \nabla = \sum_{v_i \in \mathcal{B}_C} x_i \text{ where } x_i = \begin{cases} 1 & \text{if } \mathcal{E}(s, a, s')_i = 1 \\ 0 & \text{or} \end{cases}$$

$$\overline{\Delta} = \sum_{v_i \in \mathcal{G}_C} x_i \text{ and } \overline{\nabla} = \sum_{v_i \in \mathcal{B}_C} x_i \text{ where } x_i = \begin{cases} 1 & \text{if } \mathcal{E}(s, a, s')_i = -1 \\ 0 & \text{or} \end{cases}$$

We denote $\mathcal{R}_\star(s, a, s')$ by $\star \in \{\Delta, \nabla, \overline{\Delta}, \overline{\nabla}\}$ the $\star$ component of the reward function for a given transition. Following the Definition 4.4, an E-MDP policy can be evaluated according to several ethical value functions that give the value of a policy in a given state according to a $\star$ component of $\mathcal{R}$.

DEFINITION 4.5 (ETHICAL VALUE FUNCTIONS).– *An ethical value function $V_\star^\pi(s)$ for $\star \in \{\Delta, \nabla, \overline{\Delta}, \overline{\nabla}\}$ is defined as:*

$$V_\star^\pi(s) = \max_{a \in \pi(s)} \sum_{s' \in S} \mathcal{T}(s, a, s') \left[\mathcal{R}_\star(s, a, s') + \gamma V_\star^\pi(s')\right]$$

Since causing and preventing harm and good are distinct and potentially conflicting, the notion of optimality becomes subjective. As a result, we want to be able to express them explicitly, and we refrain from aggregating the four aspects, as we risk losing information necessary for decision-making. With regard to the Properties 4.1 and 4.2, a question arises: "does the end justify the means? In other words, do we seek to produce the greatest good, which may result from harm, or do we focus on doing as little harm as possible, which may in some circumstances preclude doing much good?". As there is no hierarchy between values, we consider it more important for the agent to avoid causing harm as much as possible, and then focus on doing as much good as possible in the remaining decision space. To this end, we use a lexicographic ordering that consists of favoring policies that cause the least harm, and then, from the set of these policies with the least harm, we choose those that do the most good, as shown in the following definitions.

DEFINITION 4.6.– *The optimal π_B^* policies with respect to negative values are given by:*

$$\pi_B^* \in \underset{\pi}{\operatorname{argmin}}\ V_{\nabla}^{\pi}(s) - V_{\overline{\nabla}}^{\pi}(s) + \epsilon V_{\overline{\nabla}}^{\pi}(s) \text{ where } \epsilon > 0$$

The third term, which is the weighted value of the harm prevented, measures the importance of harm prevention, which avoid the agents from being absolved from causing harm by preventing it (totally or partially). This encourages the agent to avoid harm altogether, rather than intentionally causing it in order to repair it later. Furthermore, if only a subtraction between harm caused and harm prevented were taken into account, policies in which harm was caused and fully prevented would be indistinguishable from those in which no harm was caused. This also applies to policies that are optimal in terms of positive context values.

DEFINITION 4.7.– *The optimal π_G^* policies with respect to positive values, taken from the optimal policies with respect to negative values, are given by:*

$$\pi_G^* \in \underset{\pi \in \pi_B^*}{\operatorname{argmax}}\ V_{\Delta}^{\pi}(s) - V_{\overline{\Delta}}^{\pi}(s) - \epsilon' V_{\overline{\Delta}}^{\pi}(s) \text{ where } \epsilon' > 0$$

Note that the optimal policy with respect to good is chosen from among the policies that are already optimal with respect to harm. This choice constrains the notion of a good-optimal policy, but ensures that the agent will not consider it optimal to do harm in order to obtain a greater good.

PROPERTY 4.3.– *Solving E-MDPs using the Definitions 4.6 and 4.7 allows us to compute a policy that satisfies the Property 4.1 when such a policy exists, or that satisfies the Property 4.2 otherwise.*

DEMONSTRATION (SKETCH) 4.1.– *If a policy satisfying the Property 4.1 exists, then calculating a policy using Definition 4.6 and then Definition 4.7 returns that policy. Indeed, if such a policy exists, let us denote it π^*, then it is such that for any other policy π, and for any $s \in \mathcal{S}, V_{\bigstar}^{\pi^*}(s) \geq V_{\bigstar}^{\pi}(s)$*

(respectively $V_{\bigstar}^{\pi^*}(s) \leq V_{\bigstar}^{\pi}(s)$) for $\bigstar \in \{\Delta, \overline{\nabla}\}$ (respectively $\bigstar \in \{\overline{\Delta}, \nabla\}$). Consequently, π^* is optimal for the criteria given by Definitions 4.6 and 4.7 and will therefore be returned by any algorithm optimizing these. If there is no policy satisfying Property 4.1, then any algorithm optimizing the criteria given by Definitions 4.6 and 4.7 will return a policy satisfying Property 4.2 by definition. □

Once these two criteria have been satisfied, we obtain a set of policies where the agent does as much good as possible while causing as little harm as possible. To illustrate these optimal policies, we present a comparative example in Figure 4.8.

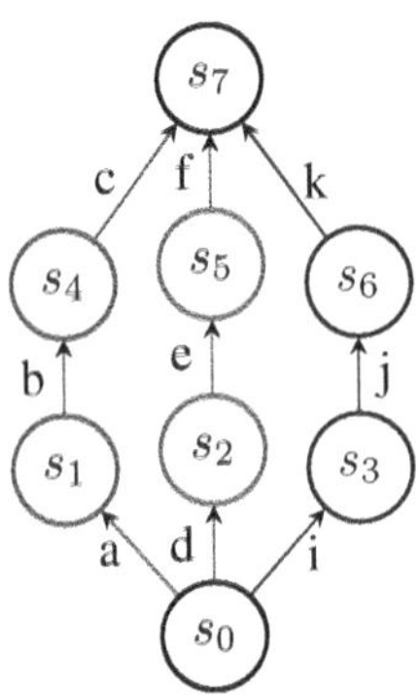

τ	$\mathcal{E}(\tau)_n$	$\mathcal{E}(\tau)_p$
(s_0, a, s_1)	1	1
(s_1, b, s_4)	1	1
(s_4, c, s_7)	0	1
(s_0, d, s_2)	1	1
(s_2, e, s_5)	1	1
(s_5, f, s_7)	−1	0
(s_0, i, s_3)	1	1
(s_3, j, s_6)	0	1
(s_6, k, s_7)	0	0

Figure 4.8. *The figure shows three policies: red, green and blue. For a color version of this figure, see www.iste.co.uk/abel/ethics.zip*

COMMENTS ON FIGURE 4.8.– *The table shows the positive ($\mathcal{E}(\tau)_p$) and negative ($\mathcal{E}(\tau)_n$) moral evaluations for each transition of these policies. As we mentioned, a policy that satisfies Property 4.1 does not always exist. In this example, we can easily see that no policy optimizes all criteria at the same time. Indeed, the red policy maximizes the good caused (Δ =3 vs. Δ =2 for the blue and green policies), the green policy maximizes the amount of harm prevented ($\overline{\nabla} = 1$ vs. $\overline{\nabla} = 0$ for the red and blue policies), while the blue policy minimizes the amount of harm caused ($\nabla = 1$ vs. ∇ =2 for the red and green policies). Using Definitions 4.6 and 4.7, we can deduce the following order of preference: the blue policy is the best policy (it causes the least harm), the green policy is the second best (it causes as much harm as the red, but* *prevents some of it) and the red policy is the least good (even though it does the most good).*

Note that since the ethical reward function only takes morality into account, processing an amoral task requires special treatment. A first approach might be to consider that performing this task promotes a specific positive value. Thus, this particular value will serve as an incentive (in an ethical sense) for the agent to also strive to achieve their goal while behaving ethically. However, as there is no hierarchy between values, if the model contains other positive moral values, the amoral task could be neglected in favor of other positive values. For this reason, we explicitly add another optimization criterion. We then assume that we have a classical reward function $\mathcal{R}_C$ and, given an optimal policy with respect to positive values, we use this reward function to select the best policy with respect to the task.

4.4.3. *Solving E-MDPs*

To solve E-MDPs, we adapt Algorithm 4.1 to take into account the specificities of the ethical reward function and our definitions of optimal policies with respect to negative and positive values. Note that it is not possible to simultaneously calculate Q-values according to each criterion. It is possible for actions that are non-optimal with respect to the harm to be optimal with respect to the good. Thus, Q-values propagated from state to state will not be based on the same actions according to criterion. For this reason, the Q-values and the policy must be calculated in succession and refined: a policy with respect to a criterion must be calculated by considering only the actions that are optimal for the preceding criterion. This is why our algorithm provides sets of policies, i.e. several optimal actions are associated with each state. Our approach therefore follows the steps below:

1) Calculate the Q-values with respect to the harm and extract an optimal policy, starting from a policy with all possible actions for each state.

2) Calculate the Q-values with respect to the good and extract an optimal policy, considering only the actions of the optimal policy with respect to the bad in each state.

3) If an amoral task is to be performed, calculate the Q-values with respect to $\mathcal{R}_C$ and extract an optimal policy, considering, in each state, only the actions of the optimal policy with respect to the good.

Algorithm 4.1 Iteration of lexicographical value

Input: the π policy and the $\bigstar$ criterion
Output: the optimal $\pi^*_\bigstar$ policy

for all $s \in S$ **do**
    for all $a \in \pi(s)$ **do**
        $Q_\bigstar(s, a) \leftarrow 0$
    end for
end for
$\Delta \leftarrow 0$
while $\Delta \geq \Delta_o$ **do**
    $\Delta \leftarrow 0$
    for all $s \in S$ **do**
        for all $a \in \pi(s)$ **do**
            $\texttt{temp} \leftarrow Q_\bigstar(s, a)$
            $Q_\bigstar(s, a) \leftarrow f(Q_\bigstar(s, a))$
            $\Delta \leftarrow \max(\Delta, |\texttt{temp} - Q_\bigstar(s, a)|)$
        end for
    end for
end while
$\pi^*_\bigstar(s) \leftarrow Opt_\bigstar(Q^*_\bigstar, \pi, s) \quad \forall s \in S$
return π^*

This procedure ensures that the final optimal policy is the one that first adheres to the ethical criteria and then, if there is an amoral task, completes the task if possible.

For each step, we use a variant of Algorithm 4.1, the generic form of which is presented in Algorithm 4.1:

– The $\bigstar$ parameter indicates the criterion for which policies are calculated: $\nabla\overline{\nabla}$ is the criterion for harm, and $\Delta\overline{\Delta}$ is the criterion for good.

– For the $\nabla\overline{\nabla}$ criterion, the input policy is a generic policy that considers all possible actions for each state. For the $\Delta\overline{\Delta}$ criterion, the input policy is the optimal policy with respect to harm, which only considers actions that are optimal for harm. In the case of a task, the input policy considers only the optimal actions extracted from the $\Delta\overline{\Delta}$ criterion.

– The f function calculates Q-values either with respect to harm, or with respect to good, or classically with respect to $\mathcal{R}_C$. In the case of harm or good, the following formulas are those presented in Definitions 4.6 and 4.7. Formally:

$$f(Q_{\nabla\overline{\nabla}}(s,a)) = \sum_{s'} \mathcal{T}(\tau)\Big[\big[R_{\nabla}(\tau) - R_{\overline{\nabla}}(\tau) + \epsilon R_{\overline{\nabla}}(\tau)\big] + \gamma \min_{a'} Q_{\nabla\overline{\nabla}}(s',a')\Big]$$

$$f(Q_{\Delta\overline{\Delta}}(s,a)) = \sum_{s'} \mathcal{T}(\tau)\Big[\big[R_{\Delta}(\tau) - R_{\overline{\Delta}}(\tau) - \epsilon' R_{\overline{\Delta}}(\tau)\big] + \gamma \max_{a'} Q_{\Delta\overline{\Delta}}(s',a')\Big]$$

where $\tau = (s, a, s'), \epsilon > 0, \epsilon' > 0$.

– Similarly, the Opt function focuses on the minimum or maximum value given by Q for an action $a \in A$ as a function of $\bigstar$. For harm, we want policies in which the least harm has been done. For good, we want the policies in which the most good has been done. Formally:

$$Opt_{\nabla\overline{\nabla}}(Q_{\nabla\overline{\nabla}}, \pi, s) = \big\{a \in \pi(s) : Q_{\nabla\overline{\nabla}}(s,a) = \operatorname*{argmin}_{\pi(s)} Q_{\nabla\overline{\nabla}}(s, \pi(s))\big\}$$

$$Opt_{\Delta\overline{\Delta}}(Q_{\Delta\overline{\Delta}}, \pi, s) = \big\{a \in \pi(s) : Q_{\Delta\overline{\Delta}}(s,a) = \operatorname*{argmax}_{\pi(s)} Q_{\Delta\overline{\Delta}}(s, \pi(s))\big\}$$

4.5. Establishing ethical principles in E-MDPs

In order to apply the concepts presented in section 4.4, we model the ethical frameworks considered by Svegliato et al. (2021): *divine command theory* (DCT), prima facie duties (PFD) and *virtue ethics* (VE). These ethical frameworks are interesting because they focus respectively on states, state-action pairs and transitions. For each, we define the ethical context and the constraints it implies on the moral evaluation function. In the following, we denote by T the set of transitions with non-zero probability:

$$T = \{(s, a, s') \in S \times A \times S \mid \mathcal{T}(s, a, s') > 0\}$$

4.5.1. *Theory of divine command*

DCT assumes that certain states are forbidden, and that the agent causes harm by entering them. We define these states below, and the constraints they impose on the moral value function.

DEFINITION 4.8 (FORBIDDEN STATES).– *Let* $\mathcal{F} = \{\mathcal{F}_1, \dots, \mathcal{F}_k\}$ *be a set of forbidden state sets* $\mathcal{F}_i \subseteq S$. *Each* $\mathcal{F}_i$ *is associated with a negative value* $v_i \in \mathcal{B}_\mathcal{C}$ *of the context.*

Having several subsets of forbidden states allows us to associate them with different moral values. For example, one state might be forbidden to avoid endangering people, while another might be forbidden to protect people's privacy.

As these are different values, each state will belong to a different subset of forbidden states.

Transiting to a state belonging to a forbidden subset promotes the associated negative value, as the agent causes harm by doing so.

DEFINITION 4.9 (ENTERING A FORBIDDEN STATE).– *Transitions that end in a forbidden state promote the associated value:*

$$\forall (s, a, s') \in T, \forall \mathcal{F}_i \in \mathcal{F} : s' \in \mathcal{F}_i \implies \mathcal{E}(s, a, s')_i = 1$$

When the agent finds itself in a forbidden state, it must leave it as quickly as possible. To encourage the agent to leave these states, transiting from a forbidden state to one that is not is a way of preventing harm.

DEFINITION 4.10 (EXITING A FORBIDDEN STATE).– *Transitions that start in a forbidden state and end in a state that is not forbidden demote the associated value:*

$$\forall (s, a, s') \in T, \forall \mathcal{F}_i \in \mathcal{F} : (s \in \mathcal{F}_i \wedge s' \notin \mathcal{F}_i) \implies \mathcal{E}(s, a, s')_i = -1$$

Transitions in which neither the start state nor the resultant state is forbidden have a moral evaluation that considers no value.

DEFINITION 4.11 (OTHER TRANSITIONS).–

$$\forall (s, a, s') \in T, \forall \mathcal{F}_i \in \mathcal{F} : (s \notin \mathcal{F}_i \wedge s' \notin \mathcal{F}_i) \implies \mathcal{E}(s, a, s')_i = 0$$

Figure 4.9 illustrates the previous definitions.

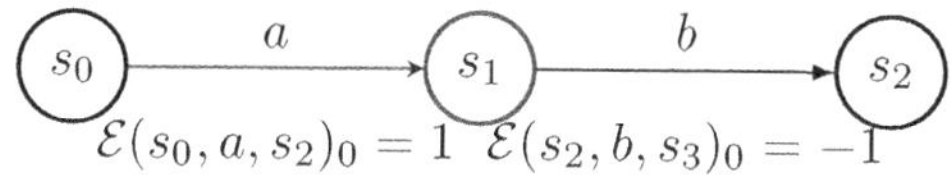

Figure 4.9. *An example of a DCT framework. Consider the ethical context $C = \langle -1 \rangle$ and the forbidden states $\mathcal{F}_0 = \{s_1\}$. The s_1 state is forbidden, and the transition that enters it promotes harm. The transition that leaves it and arrives in s_2 (which is not forbidden) demotes the negative value, and thus prevents harm. For a color version of this figure, see www.iste.co.uk/abel/ethics.zip*

4.5.2. *Prima facie duties*

PFDs presuppose the existence of fundamental duties that the agent must fulfill. Below, we define these duties and the constraints they impose on the moral evaluation function.

DEFINITION 4.12 (DUTY).– *Let $\mathcal{D} = \{delta_1, \ldots, \delta_k\}$ be a set of duties. A duty δ_i is a set of state-action pairs: $\delta_i = \{(s_0, a_0), \ldots, (s_n, a_n)\}$. Each duty is associated with a negative value v_i in $\mathcal{C}$.*

The agent *fulfills the duty* by choosing the duty action in the associated state, and *neglects the duty* if a different action is chosen.

Fulfilling or neglecting a duty can be interpreted in two ways: *positively*, where the agent causes good whenever a duty is fulfilled, and *negatively*, where the agent causes evil whenever a duty is neglected. In this particular case, the notions of *causing good* and *causing harm* become dual, so we can either focus on fulfilled duties (on maximizing good), or focus on neglected duties (on minimizing evil). Here, we choose to focus on the negative interpretation. Since duties are considered fundamental, meaning that the agent is obliged to perform them, returning to a state where a duty was previously neglected and fulfilling it will not be considered to prevent harm. Consequently, only a new harm can be prevented and, due to the nature of duties, the harm caused cannot be prevented at all within this framework.

DEFINITION 4.13 (NEGLECTING A DUTY).– *Neglecting a δ_i duty consists of going through (s, a, s') transitions where there exists $(s, a') \in \delta_i$ and where $(s, a) \notin \delta_i$. In this case, (s, a, s') promotes the negative value v_i:*

$$\forall (s, a, s') \in T : \exists\, \delta_i \in \mathcal{D}, (s, a') \in \delta_i \wedge (s, a) \notin \delta_i \implies \mathcal{E}(s, a, s')_i = 1$$

Other transitions do not take any value into account in their evaluation.

DEFINITION 4.14 (OTHER TRANSITIONS).– *All transitions* (s, a, s') *where the pair (start state, action) is not part of a duty* δ_i *have a moral evaluation not applicable for the associated negative value* $v_i \in \mathcal{B}_C$*:*

$$\forall (s, a, s') \in T, \forall\, \delta_i \in \mathcal{D} : (s, a) \notin \delta_i \implies \mathcal{E}(s, a, s')_i = 0$$

Figure 4.10 illustrates the previous definitions.

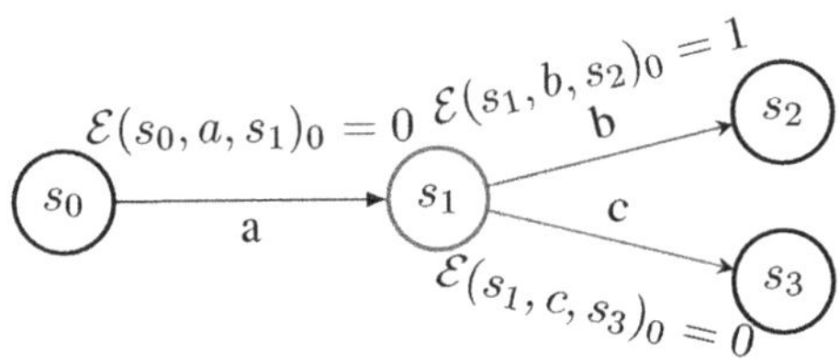

Figure 4.10. *An example of a PFD framework. Consider a context* $C = \langle -1 \rangle$ *and the duty* $\delta = (s_1, c)$*. Choosing action* c *in* s_1 *fulfills the duty and causes no harm. Choosing* b *promotes the negative value and therefore causes harm. For a color version of this figure, see www.iste.co.uk/abel/ethics.zip*

4.5.3. *Virtue ethics*

The VE framework assumes that there is a moral exemplar that behaves as we want our agent to behave. The agent must then conform to this behavior, represented by *moral trajectories* (MTs).

DEFINITION 4.15 (MORAL TRAJECTORY).– *A moral trajectory of a moral exemplar is a set* $MT = \{(s_0, a_0, s'_0), \ldots, (s_m, a_m, s'_m)\}$ *of transitions. A moral trajectory is associated with two moral values* v_n *and* v_p *such that* $C_n = -1$ *and* $C_p = 1$*:* v_n *is a negative value and* v_p *is a positive value.*

Since the results of actions are not deterministic, there may be unintended path departures: the agent tries to follow the path but fails to do so due to stochastic effects. In other ethical frameworks, this is irrelevant, as they are based on prohibitions, such as not attaining a state or neglecting a duty. In virtue ethics, on the other hand, these accidental outcomes do matter, because it is not so much the result of the action that counts as the intention behind it. Two values are then needed to take this into account, one to reward intentional follow-through or penalize unintentional outputs, and the other to penalize intentional outputs. In the following, we distinguish between *morally good trajectories* (MGT) and *morally bad trajectories* (MBT); respectively, the moral trajectories we want the agent to follow and the trajectories we want the agent to avoid. The constraints on the moral evaluation function then depend on the type of MT.

4.5.3.1. *Morally good trajectories*

Following a trajectory defined by a moral exemplar is considered morally good. Thus, transitions that are part of an MGT promote the associated positive value and cause good.

DEFINITION 4.16 (MAINTAINING AN MGT).– *Transitions belonging to an MGT promote the associated positive value:*

$$\forall(s, a, s') \in MGT : \mathcal{E}(s, a, s')_p = 1$$

When the agent chooses an action that follows an MGT, but the successor state is not the one expected, it accidentally exits the MGT. Since the agent had no intention of leaving the path, it only prevents good, without causing harm.

DEFINITION 4.17 (ACCIDENTAL EXIT FROM AN MGT).– *Transitions that have the same start state and action as a transition in an MGT, but whose successor state is different, demote its positive value:*

$$\forall(s, a, s') \in T : \exists(s_g, a_g, s_g') \in MGT,$$
$$s = s_g \wedge a = a_g \wedge s' \neq s_g' \wedge (s, a, s') \not\in MGT \implies \mathcal{E}(s, a, s')_p = -1$$

On the other hand, if in an MGT the agent chooses an action that is not part of the trajectory, while still having the possibility of choosing a correct action, it intentionally leaves the trajectory. As a result, it not only prevents good, but also causes harm.

DEFINITION 4.18 (INTENTIONAL EXIT FROM AN MGT).– *Transitions with a start state that is a start state in an MGT, but whose action is different from that of the MGT, promotes its negative value and demotes its positive value:*

$$\forall(s, a, s') \in T : \exists(s_g, a_g, s_g') \in MGT, s = s_g \wedge a \neq a_g$$
$$\implies \mathcal{E}(s, a, s')_n = 1 \wedge \mathcal{E}(s, a, s')_p = -1$$

For all other transitions, the moral assessment considers neither positive nor negative values.

DEFINITION 4.19 (OTHER TRANSITIONS).– *Transitions that do not satisfy Definitions 4.16, 4.17 and 4.18 are evaluated as follows:*

$$\mathcal{E}(s, a, s')_n = 0 \wedge \mathcal{E}(s, a, s')_p = 0$$

Figure 4.11 illustrates the previous definitions.

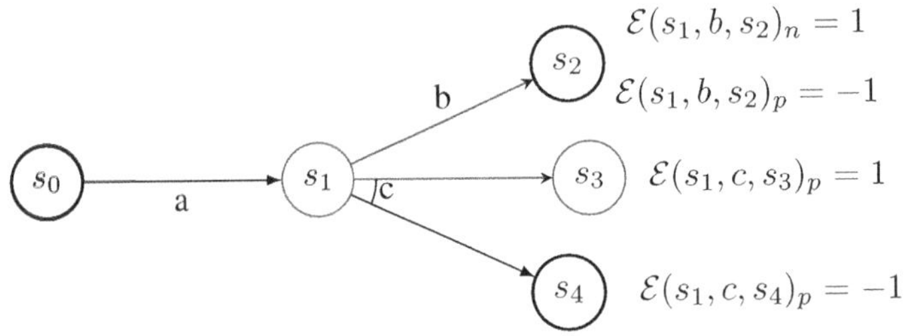

Figure 4.11. *An example of an MGT for a VE frame. Consider the context* $C = \langle -1, 1 \rangle$ *and an MGT containing* (s_1, c, s_3). *If the agent performs action* c, *it may end up in* s_3 *and causes good, or in* s_4 *and prevents good. If the agent chooses* b, *it intentionally leaves the trajectory, causing harm. For a color version of this figure, see www.iste.co.uk/abel/ethics.zip*

4.5.3.2. *Morally bad trajectories*

An agent in a state that is part of an MBT must not stay there. Therefore, transitions that start from this state and return to it cause harm, even if they do not belong to the MBT.

DEFINITION 4.20 (STAYING IN AN MBT).– *Transitions whose start state and successor state are the same, and which are also a start state of a transition in an MBT, promote the negative value:*

$$\forall(s, a, s') \in T : \exists(s_b, a_b, s'_b) \in MBT, s = s_b \wedge s = s' \implies \mathcal{E}(s, a, s')_n = 1$$

Following an MBT is also considered to cause harm.

DEFINITION 4.21 (FOLLOWING AN MBT).– *Transitions belonging to an MBT promote its negative value:*

$$\forall(s, a, s') \in MBT : \mathcal{E}(s, a, s')_n = 1$$

Due to stochasticity, accidental exits from MBTs are also possible. This means that the agent has chosen to remain in an MBT but has failed.

Such a transition causes good, because the agent has left the MBT, but it also causes harm, because the intention was to stay in the MBT.

DEFINITION 4.22 (ACCIDENTAL EXIT FROM AN MBT).– *Transitions with the same start state and action as a transition in an MBT, but whose successor state is different, promote both its negative and positive values:*

$$\forall(s, a, s') \in T : \exists(s_b, a_b, s_b') \in MBT, s = s_b \wedge a = a_b \wedge s' \neq s_b'$$
$$\implies \mathcal{E}(s, a, s')_n = 1 \wedge \mathcal{E}(s, a, s')_p = 1$$

In an MBT, if the agent chooses to leave the trajectory when it has the possibility of following it, it prevents harm and causes good.

DEFINITION 4.23 (INTENTIONAL EXIT FROM AN MBT).– *Transitions whose start state is a start state of an MBT transition, but whose action is not part of it, demote the negative value and promote the positive value:*

$$\forall(s, a, s') \in T : \exists(s_b, a_b, s_b') \in MBT, s = s_b \wedge a \neq a_b \wedge \exists a' = a_b$$
$$\implies \mathcal{E}(s, a, s')_n = -1 \wedge \mathcal{E}(s, a, s')_p = 1$$

For all other transitions, the moral assessment considers neither positive nor negative values.

DEFINITION 4.24 (OTHER TRANSITIONS).– *Transitions that do not satisfy Definitions 4.20, 4.21, 4.22 and 4.23 are evaluated as follows:*

$$\mathcal{E}(s, a, s')_n = 0 \wedge \mathcal{E}(s, a, s')_p = 0$$

Figure 4.12 illustrates the previous definitions.

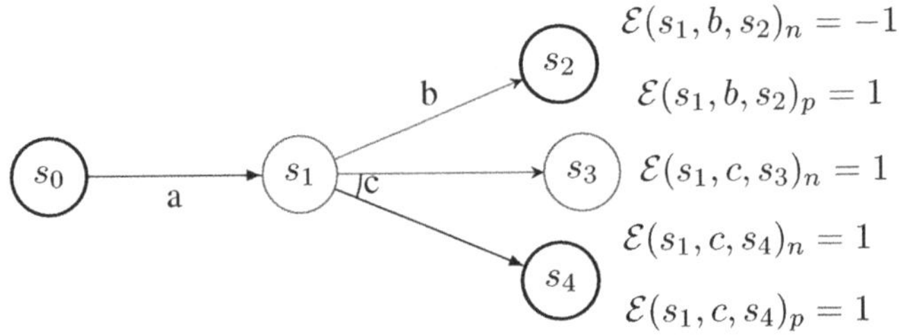

Figure 4.12. *An example of an MBT for a VE frame. For a color version of this figure, see www.iste.co.uk/abel/ethics.zip*

COMMENTS ON FIGURE 4.12.– *Consider the context* $\mathcal{C} = \langle -1, 1 \rangle$ *and the MBT containing* (s_1, c, s_3)*. If the agent performs action* c*, it may find itself in* s_3 *and causing only harm, or in* s_4 *and causing both harm and good, because the agent chooses to follow the wrong trajectory, but had an accidental exit. If the agent chooses* b*, it actively chooses to exit the trajectory, thus causing good and preventing harm.*

4.6. Conclusion

In conclusion, questions of responsibility and governance of algorithms are raising ethical issues in the development of autonomous artificial agents. Over and above questions of use, the aim of this chapter was to deal with the integration of an ethical component into the decision-making mechanisms of these agents. The problem is not so much to reduce ethical decision-making to a calculation, optimization or constraint satisfaction problem, but to provide tools and architectures that are sufficiently expressive to explicitly represent all the components of moral and/or ethical reasoning. So, from a general point of view, building ethical artificial agents requires confronting three questions:

1) What definition of ethics should we take into account?

2) Which modeling approach should be chosen?

3) How do we evaluate the models and architectures designed?

Our literature review has enabled us to distinguish three main types of ethical agent models: qualitative implicit architectures, which do not separate the ethical model from the operational model of the agents, qualitative and quantitative cognitive architectures, which separate ethical reasoning from the operational model by explicitly representing the different components of ethics. The difference between the latter two lies in the way morality or ethics are evaluated, either qualitatively (a behavior is ethical or not), or quantitatively (a behavior is more or less ethical to a certain degree). The main observation is that each approach is based on necessarily reductive modeling choices regarding the representation of morality and ethics, and that explicit approaches make it easier for the designer to highlight these choices.

To conclude this chapter, we have illustrated the concepts presented above through a quantitative cognitive architecture in particular: the E-MDP model. This E-MDP model explicitly integrates ethics into Markov decision processes as positive and negative moral values, promoted or demoted. It uses a quadruplet reward function to optimize first causing as little harm as possible, then causing as much good as possible. We have illustrated this model on three ethical frameworks – divine command theory, based on prohibitions; duties, based on obligations; and virtue ethics, based on exemplary trajectories – which can be combined. Naturally, this approach is necessarily reductive and, as a future perspective, it would be relevant to extend this model to hierarchical values (i.e. a given value is more important to the agent in a certain context) and to value systems (i.e. promoting a given value has an influence on the promotion or demotion of another value). In addition, multi-agent ethical issues, such as fairness and diversity, are not expressed. To extend this framework to a multi-agent setting, each agent would intuitively have its own ethical context, and it would be interesting if moral values would represent how agents take others into account. For example, an egalitarian value could be promoted when a decision promotes or demotes an equivalent or close number of values for all agents.

4.7. References

Abel, D., MacGlashan, J., Littman, M.L. (2016). Reinforcement learning as a framework for ethical decision making. *AAAI Workshop on AI, Ethics, and Society*, 54–61.

Anderson, M. and Anderson, S. (2014). Toward ensuring ethical behavior from autonomous systems: A case-supported principle-based paradigm. *Industrial Robot*, 42(4), 324–331.

Anderson, M., Anderson, S., Armen, C. (2006). An approach to computing ethics. *IEEE Intelligent Systems*, 21(4), 56–63.

Araque, O., Gatti, L., Kalimeri, K. (2020). MoralStrength: Exploiting a moral lexicon and embedding similarity for moral foundations prediction. *Knowledge-Based Systems*, 191(105184), 11.

Arkin, R.C., Ulam, P., Duncan, B. (2009). An ethical governor for constraining lethal action in an autonomous system. Technical Report, University of Nebraska, Lincoln.

Arkoudas, K., Bringsjord, S., Bello, P. (2005). Toward ethical robots via mechanized deontic logic. *AAAI Fall Symposium on Machine Ethics*, 17–23.

Atkinson, K. and Bench-Capon, T. (2008). Addressing moral problems through practical reasoning. *Journal of Applied Logic*, 6(2), 135–151.

Averroes (1178). The decisive treatise. Treatise.

Balakrishnan, A., Bouneffouf, D., Mattei, N., Rossi, F. (2018). Using contextual bandits with behavioral constraints for constrained online movie recommendation. In *27th International Joint Conference on Artificial Intelligence*, New York, 5802–5804.

Balakrishnan, A., Bouneffouf, D., Mattei, N., Rossi, F. (2019). Using multi-armed bandits to learn ethical priorities for online AI systems. *IBM Journal of Research and Development*, 63(4–5), 1–13.

Baum, S. (2020). Social choice ethics in artificial intelligence. *AI & Society*, 35(1), 165–176.

Bellman, R. (1957). A Markovian decision process. *Indiana University Mathematics Journal*, 6, 679–684.

Bench-Capon, T. (2003). Persuasion in practical argumentation using value-based argumentation frameworks. *Journal of Logic and Computation*, 13(3), 429–448.

Berreby, F., Bourgne, G., Ganascia, J.-G. (2017). A declarative modular framework for representing and applying ethical principles. In *16th International Conference on Autonomous Agents and Multiagent Systems*, São Paulo, 96–104.

Bourgne, G., Sarmiento, C., Ganascia, J.-G. (2021). ACE modular framework for computational ethics: Dealing with multiple actions, concurrency and omission. In *1st International Workshop on Computational Machine Ethics*.

Bremner, P., Dennis, L.A., Fisher, M., Winfield, A.F. (2019). On proactive, transparent, and verifiable ethical reasoning for robots. *Journal of the IEEE*, 107(3), 541–561.

Chaput, R., Boissier, O., Guillermin, M., Hassas, S. (2021). A multi-agent approach to combine reasoning and learning for an ethical behavior. In *4th AAAI/ACM Conference on AI, Ethics, and Society*, 13–23.

Cointe, N. (2017). Jugement éthique pour la décision et la coopération dans les systèmes multi-agents. Doctoral Thesis, Université de Lyon, Lyon.

Cointe, N., Bonnet, G., Boissier, O. (2016). Ethical judgment of agents' behaviors in multi-agent systems. In *15th International Conference on Autonomous Agents and Multiagent Systems*, Singapore, 1106–1114.

Cummings, M. (2006). Integrating ethics in design through the value-sensitive design approach. *Science and Engineering Ethics*, 12(4), 701–715.

De Moura, N., Chatila, R., Evans, K., Chauvier, S., Dogan, E. (2020). Ethical decision making for autonomous vehicles. *Science and Engineering Ethics*, 26(7729).

Deleuze, G. (1990). *Pourparlers (1972 – 1990)*. Éditions de Minuit, Paris.

Dennis, L., Fisher, M., Winfield, A. (2015). Towards verifiably ethical robot behaviour. *1st International Workshop on AI and Ethics*, Austin.

Dyoub, A., Costantini, S., Lisi, F.A. (2020). Towards an ilp application in machine ethics. In *29th International Conference on Inductive Logic Programming*, 26–35.

Fard, M.M. and Pineau, J. (2011). Non-deterministic policies in Markovian decision processes. *Journal of Artificial Intelligence Research*, 40, 1–24.

Fioravanti, F., Rahwan, I., Tohmé, F. (2022). Properties of aggregation operators relevant for ethical decision making in artificial intelligence. Technical Report, Red Nacional de Investigadores en Economía Buenos Aires.

Foot, P. (1967). The problem of abortion and the doctrine of the double effect. *Oxford Review*, 5, 5–15.

Ganascia, J.-G. (2007). Ethical system formalization using non-monotonic logics. *Proceedings of the Annual Meeting of the Cognitive Science Society*, 1013–1018.

Grandi, U., Lorini, E., Parker, T., Alami, R. (2022). Logic-based ethical planning. In *21st International Conference of the Italian Association for Artificial Intelligence*, Udine, 198–211.

Haidt, J. (2001). The emotional dog and its rational tail: A social intuitionist approach to moral judgment. *Psychological Review*, 108(4), 814–834.

Hirose, I. (2014). *Moral Aggregation*. Oxford University Press, Oxford.

Horty, J.F. (1996). Agency and obligations. *Synthese*, 108, 269–307.

Howard, R.A. (1960). *Dynamic Programming and Markov Processes*. MIT Press, Cambridge.

Kaci, S. and van der Torre, L. (2008). Preference-based argumentation: Arguments supporting multiple values. *International Journal of Approximate Reasoning*, 48(3), 730–751.

Kim, R., Kleiman-Weiner, M., Abeliuk, A., Awad, E., Dsouza, S., Tenenbaum, J.B., Rahwan, I. (2018). A computational model of commonsense moral decision makin. In *1st AAAI/ACM Conference on AI, Ethics, and Society*, Cambridge, 197–203.

Lindner, F., Mattmüller, R., Nebel, B. (2020). Evaluation of the moral permissibility of action plans. *Artificial Intelligence*, 287, 103350.

Loreggia, A., Mattei, N., Rahgooy, T., Rossi, F., Srivastava, B., Venable, K.B. (2022). Making human-like moral decisions. In *5th AAAI/ACM Conference on AI, Ethics, and Society*, Oxford, 447–454.

Lorini, E. (2012). On the logical foundations of moral agency. In *11th International Conference on Deontic Logic in Computer Science*. Springer-Verlag, Berlin, 108–122.

Mao, W. and Gratch, J. (2012). Modeling social causality and responsibility judgment in multi-agent interactions. *Journal of Artificial Intelligence Research*, 44, 223–273.

McConnell, T. (2018). Moral dilemmas. In *The Stanford Encyclopedia of Philosophy*, Zalta, E.N. (ed.). The Metaphysics Research Lab, Stanford.

Mermet, B. and Simon, G. (2016). Formal verification of ethical properties in multiagent systems. *Workshop on Ethics in the Design of Intelligent Agents*, 26–31.

Muggleton, S.H. (1991). Inductive logic programming. *New Generation Computing*, 8, 295–318.

Nashed, S., Svegliato, J., Zilberstein, S. (2021). Ethically compliant planning within moral communities. In *4th AAAI/ACM Conference on AI, Ethics, and Society*, 188–198.

Naumov, P. and Tao, J. (2020). An epistemic logic of blameworthiness. *Artificial Intelligence*, 283, 103269.

Naumov, P. and Yew, R.-J. (2021). Ethical dilemmas in strategic games. In *35th AAAI Conference on Artificial Intelligence*, 11613–11621.

Oren, N. (2013). Argument schemes for normative practical reasoning. In *2nd International Workshop on Theory and Applications of Formal Argumentation*, Beijing, 63–78.

Pereira, L. and Saptawijaya, A. (2007a). Modelling morality with prospective logic. *Lecture Notes in Artificial Intelligence*, 4874, 99–111.

Pereira, L. and Saptawijaya, A. (2007b). Moral decision making with ACORDA. In *14th International Conference on Logic for Programming, Artificial Intelligence, and Reasoning*.

Powers, T. (2006). Prospects for a Kantian machine. *IEEE Intelligent Systems*, 21(4), 46–51.

Prakken, H. and Sartor, G. (2013). Formalising arguments about norms. In *26th Annual Conference on Legal Knowledge and Information Systems*, Amsterdam, 121–130.

Puterman, M. (1994). *Markov Decision Processes: Discrete Stochastic Dynamic Programming*. Wiley, New York.

Rickless, S.C. (1997). The doctrine of doing and allowing. *The Philosophical Review*, 106(4), 555–575.

Robbins, R.-W. and Wallace, W.-A. (2007). Decision support for ethical problem solving: A multi-agent approach. *Decision Support Systems*, 43(4), 1571–1587.

Rodriguez-Soto, M., Lopez-Sanchez, M., Rodriguez-Aguilar, J.A. (2020). A structural solution to sequential moral dilemmas. In *19th International Conference on Autonomous Agents and Multiagent Systems*, Auckland, 1152–1160.

Rossini, D., Croce, D., Mancini, S., Pellegrino, M., Basili, R. (2020). Actionable ethics through neural learning. *34th AAAI Conference on Artificial Intelligence*, 5537–5544.

Saptawijaya, A. and Pereira, L.M. (2014). Towards modeling morality computationally with logic programming. In *16th International Symposium on Practical Aspects of Declarative Languages*, San Diego, 104–119.

Saptawijaya, A. and Pereira, L.M. (2015). The potential of logic programming as a computational tool to model morality. In *A Construction Manual for Robots' Ethical Systems: Requirements, Methods, Implementations*, Trappl, R. (ed.). Springer, New York, 169–210.

Sarmiento, C., Bourgne, G., Inoue, K., Cavalli, D., Ganascia, J.-G. (2023). Action languages based actual causality for computational ethics: A sound and complete implementation in ASP. Technical Report, Sorbonne Université, Paris.

Svegliato, J., Nashed, S., Zilberstein, S. (2021). Ethically compliant sequential decision making. In *35th AAAI Conference on Artificial Intelligence*, 11657–11665.

Timmons, M. (2012). *Moral Theory: An Introduction*. Rowman & Littlefield Publishers, Lanham.

Watkins, C. (1989). Learning from delayed rewards. Doctoral Thesis, Cambridge University, Cambridge.

Weizenbaum, J. (1976). *Computer Power and Human Reason: From Judgment to Calculation*. W.H. Freeman and Company, London.

Wiedeman, C., Wang, G., Kruger, U. (2020). Modeling of moral decisions with deep learning. *Journal of Visual Computing for Industry, Biomedicine, and Art*, 3(27), 27–36.

Wiener, Y. (1988). Forms of value systems: A focus on organisational effectiveness and cultural change and maintenance. *Academy of Management Review*, 13(4), 534–545.

Winfield, A., Blum, C., Liu, W. (2014). Towards and ethical robot: Internal models, consequences and ethical action selection. In *Advances in Autonomous Robotics Systems*, Mistry, M., Leonardis, A., Witkowski, M., Melhuish, C. (eds). Springer, Berlin, 85–96.

Wu, Z. (2020). A context-based argumentation framework with values. *20th Workshop on Computational Models of Natural Argument*, Perugia, 1–10.

Wu, Y.-H. and Lin, S.-D. (2018). A low-cost ethics shaping approach for designing reinforcement learning agents. In *32th AAAI Conference on Artificial Intelligence*, New Orleans, 1687–1694.

5

Ethics and Ecology in Production Systems

5.1. Introduction

The ecological transition, the sustainable transformation of our society or the Anthropocene are all names that designate the necessary change in our lifestyles to move towards the construction of a society consistent with the physical limits of the Earth system. These transformations are necessary today if we are to face up to the fact that planetary limits are gradually being exceeded, rendering the earth uninhabitable for the human species (Richardson et al. 2023). Industry is considered to be the third largest source of CO_2 emissions (after electricity generation and transport) and the main contributor to heavy metal pollution (Calvin et al. 2023). In 2002, ICSU had already defined production and consumption patterns as one of the three major topics of study in sustainability science (ICSU 2002). For this reason, this chapter focuses on the production systems of the future.

An interesting concept for thinking about this change is that of the industry of the future. In the literature, whether French or international, the concept of industry of the future is seen in a perspective of "reindustrialization" or "industrial sovereignty" to increase the share of industry in Europe. From our point of view, the industry of the future goes beyond the mere concept of "Industry 4.0". Indeed, the general approach of Industry 4.0 consists of adding digital tools (sensors on production lines, massive data harvesting, cloud-oriented infrastructures) to develop the automation of production lines, with a view to making industries more

---

Chapter written by Emmanuel CAILLAUD and Lou GRIMAL.

competitive (lowering production costs) (Lasi et al. 2014). This approach does not take into account planetary limits and the potential decrease in production levels. This is why more recent approaches, entitled 5.0 or 6.0, attempt to take environmental impact into account, as in the European policy of 2021[1]. Unfortunately, this approach is still based on marginally reducing the impact of production systems on the environment and is a long way from considering respect for the physical limits of the Earth system as a whole.

We propose a different vision of the industry of the future that takes into account the current ecological context. In an industry where the aim is to produce without destroying natural capital, and therefore potentially to produce less, what is the role of digital tools? Our aim is to understand the role of digital tools in this new proposal. IT tools are seen here as a tool in the service of production, not as an end in themselves.

The ecological situation calls for a major change in production methods and potentially a shift in industry priorities. In this context, it is important to address the ethical dilemmas posed by this major change. For example, arbitration on the distribution of resource use will be difficult both for territories and for preservation choices for future generations. Should we use "green hydrogen" resources to remove sulfur from oil in refineries, as Total is planning to do, or use the electricity generated by renewable energies directly for other purposes, or even question the need for energy?

We believe that the industry of the future, digitalization, sustainability and ethics are intimately linked. This is why this chapter will be structured as follows: explanation of the ecological context and the link with issues of industrialization and (de)digitization (section 5.2), analysis of the place of ethics in the industry of the future (section 5.3) and a proposal for an ethical approach to the industry of the future, understood as a mode of production consistent with the physical limits of the Earth system (section 5.4).

5.2. Ecological context

Every week brings its share of disasters: every region of the world is affected by fires, floods and rising temperatures. In the summer of 2023 alone, we can mention fires in Canada and South America, floods in Libya

1 European Commission. See: https://research-and-innovation.ec.europa.eu/knowledge-publications-tools-and-data/publications/all-publications/industry-50-towards-sustainable-human-centric-and-resilient-european-industry_en [Accessed July 2024].

and record-breaking temperatures around the Mediterranean. The consequences for the environment, and therefore for living conditions, are far-reaching. Everyone can see from the news that the extreme climatic events predicted in the various IPCC reports (Calvin et al. 2023) did not wait until 2050. These events are taking place in a France below +2°C (Ribes et al. 2022), but could reach almost +4°C by the end of the century with the climate policies currently implemented around the world.

This dramatic ecological context can be synthesized by the planetary limits model. This model shows the nine limits that must not be exceeded if we are to remain in a safe operating space, meaning a climate similar to that experienced during the Holocene, which enabled the development of human societies. The planetary limits are: biosphere integrity, climate change, new entities, stratospheric ozone depletion, land-use change, freshwater change, biogeochemical fluxes, ocean acidification and atmospheric aerosol load.

Knowledge of planetary limits is progressing, and in the summer of 2023, researchers at the Stockholm Resilience Center were able to confirm that six of the nine planetary limits had been exceeded (Richardson et al. 2023), as shown in Figure 5.1.

The ecological problem for production and consumption systems cannot therefore be limited to a calculation of CO_2. The integrity of the biosphere, the use of fresh water, the use of land, the production and diffusion of new entities in our environments, the impact of production chains on biogeochemical flows and the release of aerosols are also crucial issues to be taken into account to ensure the habitability of planet Earth. It should be remembered that although planetary limits are assessed separately, they are, of course, interconnected. For example, climate change is accelerating the decline in biodiversity. While it has been possible in the past to remedy the depletion of the ozone layer, exceeding certain thresholds is irreversible.

Integrating this context into the development strategies of companies and industries has become a survival issue for the human species. It will be necessary to adapt mankind, and therefore production systems, to respond to ecological transformations. This raises a number of questions.

On a national scale, what types of production will governments prioritize? Is it possible to transform a polluting company into a nonpolluting one, or does this require too much time in view of the ecological emergency? At the company level, other questions arise: how can we limit or stop production? How to choose the intensity of production? How can we rethink our business model with a view to respecting planetary limits?

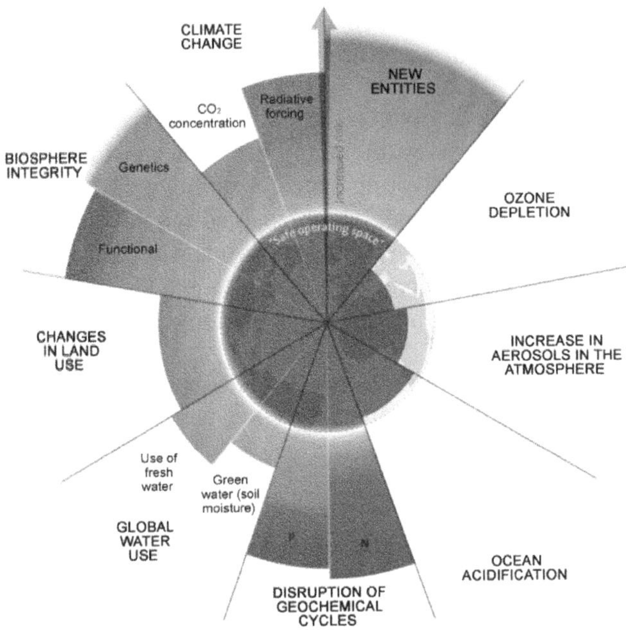

Figure 5.1. *Planetary limits (Richardson et al. 2023). For a color version of this figure, see www.iste.co.uk/abel/ethics.zip*

By way of illustration, we can refer to the changes proposed by Décathlon (2023) to develop equipment rental, the purchase of reconditioned products and their repair. The Décathlon brand aims to make sport accessible to all. However, in a world at +4°C, the practice of sport becomes limited, as practicing sport at over 35°C can be fatal for the human body. We can see here the extent to which the ecological situation is calling certain human activities into question and how companies need to evolve.

These elements are difficult for companies to take into account, which is why a model by production sector unit has been proposed by the "absolute center for sustainability" (Hjalsted et al. 2021). The proposed approach reduces planetary limits to an individual and then allows for a breakdown by sector, or by company, as shown in Figure 5.2.

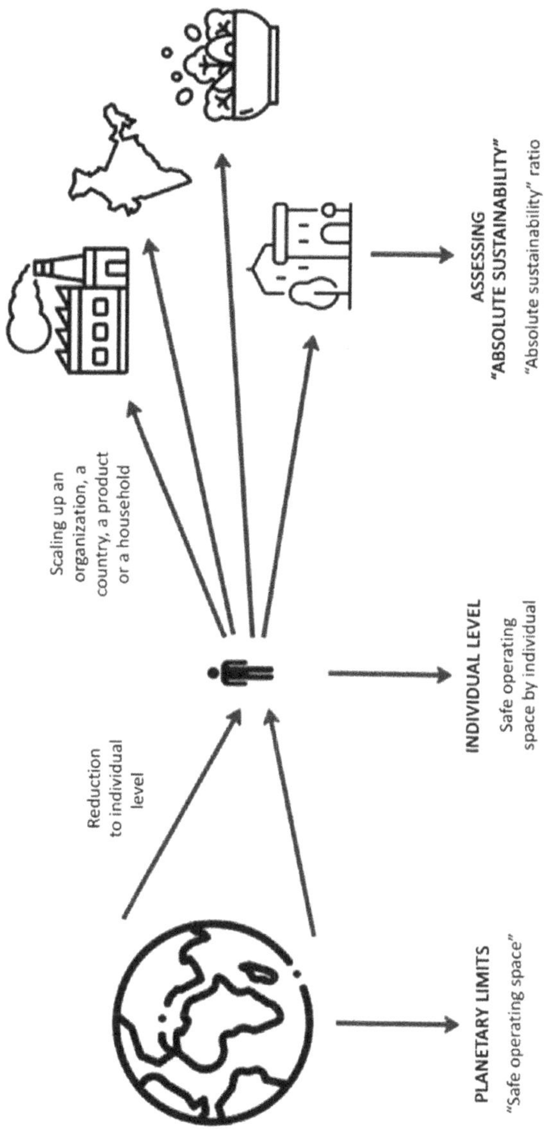

Figure 5.2. *Sharing safe space for humanity taken from (Hjalsted et al. 2021)*

Planetary limits were designed at a macroscopic level. This model proposes to allocate planetary limits for each individual (definition of a safe operating space per individual), in order to reduce calculations to the level of an individual. How can we do this? A first option is to divide by the number of individuals on the planet (perfect equality between individuals). But is this fair? Does everyone need the same thing, regardless of geographic location or metabolic rate? This simple proposition raises ethical questions. A second option is to take the emissions currently emitted by countries (or companies) and reduce them to a defined level. However, to what extent can this option allow other sectors to grow? A third option is to take into account the past responsibilities of countries/companies. Some countries or regions have built their wealth on the exploitation of ecosystems. As a result, countries or regions with a high GDP today need to cut back more than countries or regions with a lower GDP.

This description of the different options for allocating environmental impacts makes ethical issues obvious. For instance:

– Not all companies pollute in the same way: how can we identify these differences?

– Some companies have grown by exploiting ecosystems: do they now have to pay for this?

– Which human societies in the world should contribute more to the ecological effort?

Although different distribution options are considered and reduced to equations, these methods raise ethical questions of resource allocation and consideration of social foundation criteria. For this reason, we have chosen to focus on the ethical aspects of transforming production methods in line with a sustainable ecological footprint.

5.3. Integrating ethical issues into an industry in ecological transition

Today, ethics is often seen as the implementation of moral rules (Comte-Sponville 2002). Three ethical approaches are usually considered, as in Deslandes (2012):

– Deontology, as proposed by Kant. In this approach, rules must be strictly observed (e.g. not to lie, regardless of the consequences).

– Consequentialist and utilitarian, as proposed by Mill and Bentham. For each situation, benefits and risks are assessed. An action is taken if the benefits outweigh the negatives, or the action with the fewest negative effects is chosen. This ethical approach is illustrated by the famous streetcar dilemma defined in Foot (1967), where the streetcar driver must choose between injuring one person or five.

– By virtue, as proposed by Aristotle. This approach asks which virtues are mobilized by actions. To act courageously, the decision-maker needs to be neither heroic nor cowardly.

Value ethics is an extension of the individual virtues approach, associating others with oneself (Ricoeur 1984). To illustrate, Paul Ricoeur details justice as a value in the same text: "justice means: let your freedom be worth as much as mine. Value is the mark of excellence of actions that satisfy this requirement".

This approach, which links the individual and the collective, seems a promising way for ethics to manage the transition to greater sustainability, since we are all linked on a planetary scale.

There are different levers for transforming human societies (Meadows 1972). Drawing on a systemic approach, the author stresses that the most effective approach is that of modifying the mindset, which we consider in this chapter as a set of shared values, and going beyond paradigms.

On this basis, Abson et al. (2017) propose leverage points for the sustainable transformation of society: with a society's values and way of thinking (paradigm) as the most effective leverage points, and also the most profound and therefore the most complex to implement. The authors emphasize three axes: the role of institutions, the connection of people to nature, and the production and use of knowledge in transformation processes.

For this reason, this section focuses on the values embedded in product design and production systems. Along with Meadows and Abson, we believe that a change in values is a promising way to meet the essential challenges of future transitions (Van Der Weij et al. 2023) and move towards a sustainable industry of the future.

What products, processes, raw materials, energy and skills are needed to meet what needs in what environment? In the following sections, we take a closer look at value ethics and then focus on ecological ethics.

5.3.1. *Attempts to meet standards*

In response to the need for companies to demonstrate their social responsibility, an IEEE 7000[2] standard was published in 2021. It includes:

> The objective of this standard is to enable organizations to design systems by explicitly taking into account individual and societal ethical values, such as transparency, sustainability, privacy, fairness and responsibility, as well as values generally considered in systems engineering, such as efficiency and effectiveness.

A value is defined as "a conception that influences the selection of available modes, means and ends of action". Examples of values are given below:

– Positive values: love, friendship, privacy, security, transparency, responsibility, generosity, dignity, courage, fairness, beauty, equity, freedom, dignity and sustainability.

– Negative values: bias, lack of transparency, lack of privacy, selfishness and greed.

An ethical value is defined as "a value that, in the context of human culture, supports a judgment about what is right or wrong (a virtue is an example of an ethical value)". Appendix G of the standard provides an informative list of ethical values to be taken into account in systems engineering, such as autonomy, equity and sustainability.

This standard is therefore based on ethical values. It is complementary to the IEEE Code of Ethics, which is very general. The purpose of this standard is to help take into account the ethical dimension in systems engineering, notably:

– to understand the ethical values at stake in the system to be designed;

2 "IEEE Standard Model Process for Addressing Ethical Concerns during System Design", 2021.

– to integrate ethical values into specifications;

– to assist in the decision-making process between design alternatives, taking into account ethical values;

– to take ethical values into account throughout the design process.

It is based on a two-stage design process: (1) exploration of system solution concepts (Figure 5.3a) and (2) system development or detailed design (Figure 5.3b). These two stages are a limited version of the system life cycle as defined in ISO/IEC/IEEE 24748-1. Values are elicited and prioritized in step (1) by identifying stakeholders and their values. In step (2), the selected values are integrated into the system specifications, as well as into the design risk management process. A transparency management process supports these two stages.

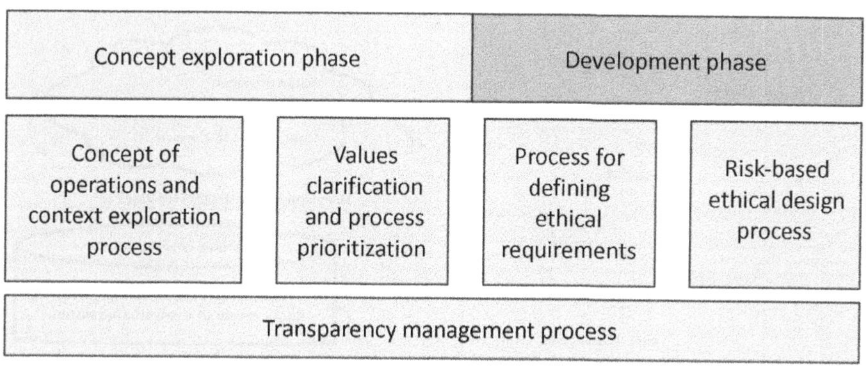

a) b)

Figure 5.3. *Processes and stages in the standard (adapted from IEEE 7000-2021). For a color version of this figure, see www.iste.co.uk/abel/ethics.zip*

Sociotechnical systems are the bearers of values and ethical principles. The aim of this standard is to help designers consciously implement the values identified as fundamental (core values) in the system under consideration.

Values can be derived from different ethical approaches and different parties involved (see the left-hand side of Figure 5.4). A core value groups together several values, which can be illustrated in different ways (value demonstrator).

The standard gives the example of the fundamental value "privacy", which can cover several values such as "confidentiality", itself illustrated by "the right to be alone" (value demonstrator). These illustrations of value implementation help to express the needs of the parties involved and contribute to the definition of specifications in terms of ethical values (EVR in the right-hand side of Figure 5.4). An EVR enables the expression of one or more value-based system requirements.

To summarize, values are first translated into specifications and then into risks if they are not met, meaning if the system is not aligned with the value-based specifications.

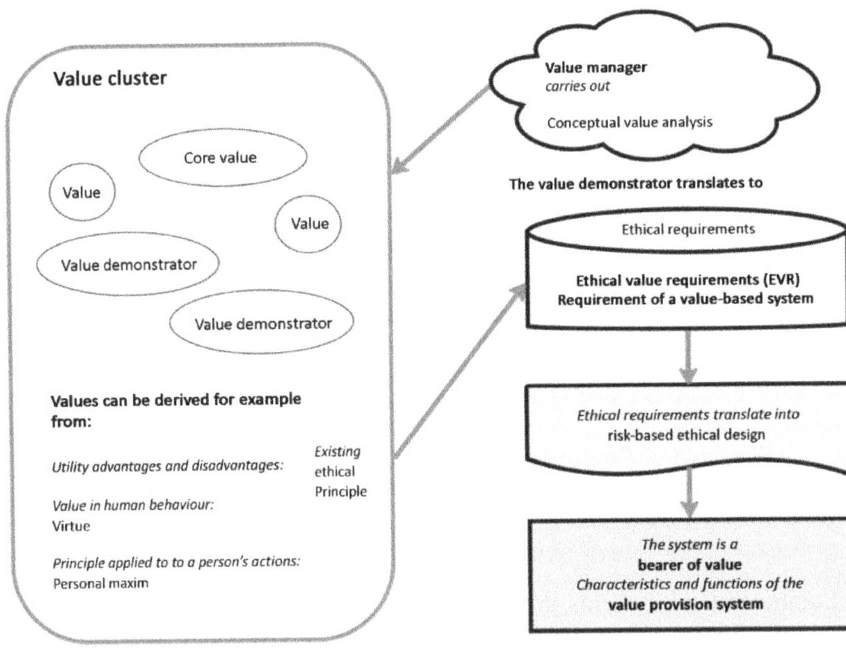

Figure 5.4. *Value concepts (IEEE 7000-2021). For a color version of this figure, see www.iste.co.uk/abel/ethics.zip*

It seems important to us to raise several criticisms of this normative approach.

The standard states (page 13): "the processes described in this standard do not prescribe what is ethical and what is unethical". Given the IPCC's knowledge of the current trajectory towards a +4°C world, can we remain non-prescriptive?

The standard also states (page 13): "the use of IEEE Std 7000 does not imply that an organization following its processes is ethical in all other aspects of its mission, product or service development, or discharge of its social responsibility". Although a few pages later (page 25), the standard specifies that the product's context of use must be taken into account, the standard does not provide for the mission of the producing company to be taken into account. From an ethical point of view, this position seems problematic. Is it possible to analyze the ethics of a technical system without considering the context in which the product/service is developed? On page 26, we can read: "the ethical decisions made in one organization can affect its suppliers and customers, the entire economy, and public well-being". This clearly shows that ethics cannot be confined to a limited perimeter, but must be perceived in a systemic way.

Finally, this standard is interesting in that it encourages those involved in production systems (in connection with IT) to spell out the values of their products/services and to make their design choices legible in relation to these values. The standard also stresses the importance of ethical choices throughout the product life cycle (page 36): "stakeholders involved with the envisaged system throughout its life cycle are identified and their representatives are chosen".

There is one final problem to raise, and it has to do with ecological issues. In the IEEE 7000-2021 standard, sustainability is considered to be a value among others. But is this really the case? Isn't sustainability more a goal to be achieved? In a strong sustainability approach, natural capital cannot be weighed against other forms of capital, such as human capital (human strength) or physical capital (the machines we build, for example). If the standard's developers see sustainability as a "*value*" among others, then it becomes a value to be respected among a list of values. This does not necessarily correspond to an approach in which respect for planetary limits is paramount when developing a new production system. However, we know that standards can gradually help to change paradigms, and in this respect, the IEEE 7000-2021 standard is interesting. The hierarchy of values is a question of ethics, and the place of sustainability in this hierarchy raises the question of environmental and ecological ethics. This is why section 5.3.2 focuses on this topic.

5.3.2. *From environmental ethics to ecological ethics*

In the standard presented in section 5.3.1, ecology (sustainability) was seen as just one of several values to be respected. Designers have a list of constraints to respect, and environmental protection is just one of them. Is this perspective really relevant if we want to produce within planetary limits?

Another option considered in environmental ethics is to give value (monetary or symbolic) to ecosystems or to what is considered "nature". From this point of view, it is worthwhile to "protect the environment" or set up "conservation" processes, as the degradation of ecosystems would be detrimental to human societies (health risks, reduced yields, etc.). Berque (2004) illustrates the ambiguity of such a stance with the example of the *huyang* forest in China: the preservation policy is first and foremost put forward to protect nature for the purposes of economic development for human activities. By wanting to "protect" nature – not for what it is in itself, but for what it brings us – does the creation of areas free of human activity not distance humans from this nature?

In short, from the perspective of environmental ethics, ecosystems (or anything nonhuman) have no intrinsic value. They have value only in the light of their usefulness to humans. From this perspective, although nature does have a value and it is important to preserve it, we can question its utilitarian and anthropocentric aspect. Indeed, this utilitarian approach focuses on benefits and risks and distances us from the necessary paradigm shift. The environmental ethics explained above confer on humans a mission to protect nature by separating themselves from it, by ensuring that humans do not interfere with ecosystems (constitution of conservation zones, for example). Another vision involves linking communities of humans and nonhumans to relearn how to interact together (the family of relational ethics, such as that explained by Metz and Miller (2016)).

In this way, human beings are no longer distanced from so-called natural ecosystems, but brought back into relationship with them. These ethics are referred to in this chapter as "ecological ethics" and thus focus on relationships.

Like Bruno Latour, we can consider that the ecological crisis is the manifestation of the loss of the link between culture and nature. Today's human activities were conceived in the context of modernity, with the idea that human activities could be freed from the state of the Earth system. The ecological crisis reminds us that this idea of a human being detached from his living environment is no more than a belief. So how do we land on Earth (Latour 2017)? How do we reintegrate the link between human systems, engineered technical systems and ecosystems?

5.3.3. *Ecological ethics and technology*

This section is dedicated to clarifying the relationships between ecology and technical systems. It highlights how computer scientists and production systems specialists relate to nonhumans.

First, let us point out that very few articles on ecological ethics and computer tools were found in the IEEE database. We have therefore extended our search with these two keywords to other communities.

A study by Jenkins and McCauley (2006) shows how IT tools can have a real impact on ecosystem management. The example chosen by the authors concerns geographic information systems (GIS) and, in particular, their algorithms. These systems deal directly with nonhuman entities (forests, fields, watercourses, etc., i.e. elements containing a diversity of species). The users of these computer systems are specialists in ecology, and their practices reflect strong ecological ethics. Their decisions are based on GIS results. Thus, the way in which these GIS tools work (algorithmic logic, underlying assumptions) is of the utmost importance to them. As computer tools need categories, some isolated wetlands may find themselves outside a "wetland" category and therefore be left out of the results (bad taking into account). The authors of the article show that the computer scientists developing the GIS tools, although not a priori important players in GIS, actually have a key role, as they define the implicit assumptions embedded in the systems. As such, they hold a form of power. The power shift from users to the technical designers of information systems has also been documented in one community (Ghoshal 2020).

According to Jenkins and McCauley (2006), following Jonas and Churchill, greater power brings greater responsibility. Are computer software developers aware of their increased power over the world, and therefore of their responsibility? This example illustrates how ecological ethics challenge the skills of professionals (Minteer et al. 2008).

5.4. Proposed areas of work

In this section, we first look at the skills required to create and maintain a production system (section 5.4.1), then consider what needs to be produced, and therefore the very existence of certain production systems (section 5.4.2), and finally look at the production system's material and technological resources (section 5.4.3).

5.4.1. *Competence of production system players*

In the introduction to our chapter, we stated that our aim was to understand what role digital tools would play in an industry grappling with ecological issues. Of course, this chapter does not cover the whole of this question, but it does raise a number of issues, notably the link between ethics, ecology and the industry of the future. We have seen that IT tools can condition or orient the results of a process of experts dealing with an issue (see section 5.3.2). Thus, it seems undesirable to separate IT expertise from the expertise linked to the purpose of the IT tool. However, it seems difficult to ask IT specialists to be experts on different themes, as this takes time and is sometimes incompatible with the person's skills.

We agree with Berardy et al. (2011) that computer scientists should develop their interaction skills. This skill "describes the kind of knowledge needed to communicate effectively with experts in technical disciplines, even without practicing the discipline in question" (Seager et al. 2011). This interactional competence has also been identified by Seager et al. (2011) as a crucial expertise to develop for engineers leading projects involving sustainable transformations of society.

Interestingly, Wiek, one of the co-authors of the paper on interactional expertise, is also one of the leading authors in the literature on competencies for sustainability. Back in 2011, Wiek synthesized five key competencies for sustainability: systems thinking, normative competence, visioning and anticipation, strategic competence and interpersonal competence.

Ten years later, this model has been validated and completed with three key competencies (intrapersonal competence, integration competence, implementation competence) (Brundiers 2021).

These profiles are ideal for implementing company transformation and need to be placed in transformative contexts to exploit their full potential. What are these contexts?

5.4.2. *Purpose of the production system*

Throughout this chapter, we have discussed various ethical frameworks in which certain production systems are anchored or could become anchored in the near future.

The perspective of relational ethics seems promising to us, as it relates the biosphere to human needs, meaning that it establishes the relationship between nature and culture. Our development has left little room for human needs.

However, the production system only makes sense if it serves human needs. The production system should therefore meet essential human needs while respecting planetary limits and the men and women who are mobilized as human resources.

The needs to be considered are those of the people who receive the products and services produced, as well as those of the people involved in the production system.

The framework proposed by Manfred Max-Neef in Clair (2017) is used for the needs to be satisfied. We find the capabilities defined by Nussbaum and Chavel (2012), but here the fundamental needs are specified, and the way of satisfying them sheds light on the products to be produced within the limits of planetary resources.

Max-Neef proposes a matrix cross-referencing fundamental needs and the means of satisfying them: being, having, doing and interacting. By way of illustration, we present this matrix for the "sustenance" need and the means of satisfying in Figure 5.5.

Needs	Means to satisfy needs Being	Having	Doing	Interacting
Sustenance (basic needs)	Physical health, mental health, balance, sense of humor, adaptability	Food, housing, work	Feeding, procreating, resting, working	Living and social environment
...	...	...	...	...

Figure 5.5. *Illustration of the basic needs matrix from Clair (2017). For a color version of this figure, see www.iste.co.uk/abel/ethics.zip*

We will focus on the *having* part of the Max-Neef matrix. However, for the human resources of the production system, all the means of satisfying needs must be considered.

The products to be realized would therefore be: food, shelter, the means to ensure health and safety, literature and the educational system, games and entertainment.

As far as human resources are concerned, the diversity of ways of satisfying needs is much broader, since they are not limited to possession, and also take into account who we are, what we do and how we interact.

If production systems do not meet these fundamental needs, is their existence necessary in a world where resources are becoming scarce and energy use is to be considered with caution in a logic of sobriety?

5.4.3. *Returning to planetary limits with available technical systems*

Planetary limits pose real tensions for production systems. How can we produce with limited quantities of raw materials? How can we ensure that this production does not emit excessive amounts of pollution? These are the same questions asked by the Club of Rome[3] when applied to production systems. We cannot consider that this world is limitless and seek infinite growth. Physical and raw material limits are imposed on everyone. We are already witnessing tensions over raw materials, against a backdrop of strong geopolitical tensions between major powers and states (Western Europe, the United States, China, Russia, etc.). Each wants to ensure its "sovereignty" and get its hands on the resources of the others. The European Union has defined a list of rare raw materials. The risks of supply disruptions for 25 raw materials are studied and linked to the technologies and sectors concerned.

The particular sensitivity of rare earths is highlighted, posing particular challenges to the technologies needed for wind power generation and electric motors, at a time when these technologies are considered essential by European policies to limit CO_2 emissions.

In this chaotic world, anticipating the technology that will be needed is difficult. It is therefore wise to consider a range of technologies that need to be mastered in order to face the coming years. The concept of technodiversity, in other words, the desire to consider a broad portfolio of technologies to master, is essential to resilience. We must continue to develop cutting-edge technologies to satisfy certain essential needs, but we must also know how to conserve and develop technologies adapted to limited resources (Bihouix 2014).

Production systems therefore need to consider both the fragility of their raw material supplies and their ability to master a diversity of technologies. It can be useful to consider the available resources of the environment in which a technology or production system as a whole is produced.

5.5. Conclusion

This chapter has shown that the current ecological emergency calls for a radical change in production systems. However, the transformation of these production systems raises ethical questions: which companies should reduce their production? How should this choice be made? Who should decide what to produce? Attempts to integrate ethics into production systems do not strike us as sufficient to achieve a return to sustainable production for the Earth system. This also calls into question the role of information technology

3 Meadows (1972). See: https://archive.org/details/limitstogrowthr00mead/mode/2up [Accessed July 2024].

in these systems. We have proposed three areas of focus: the skills of the players in the production system, a reflection on the purpose of the production system and the resources available for these systems.

This leads us to conclude that the role of IT in the transition of production systems towards respect for planetary limits cannot be left to computer scientists alone. In fact, interdisciplinary teams need to take charge of these issues, with skills in change management, industrial systems, alternative economic models to capitalism, models for assessing sustainable issues and the design of IT systems.

Finally, we would like to emphasize that the players in production systems are intermediaries between the environmental sciences and the humanities and social sciences. A production system will draw on the resources of the biosphere to create artifacts and support the development of products or services that will modify society and our world as a whole. Given the end of the habitability of the entire planet as we have known it up to now, the players in production systems must reflect deeply on their role as intermediaries between the biosphere and human societies, and therefore on the relationship they maintain between nature and culture.

5.6. Acknowledgments

The authors thank Maureen Prunier for her support and for making the completion of this chapter a reality.

5.7. References

Abson, D.J., Fischer, J., Leventon, J., Newig, J., Schomerus, T., Vilsmaier, U., Von Wehrden, H. (2017). Leverage points for sustainability transformation. *Ambio*, 46(1), 30–39. doi: 10.1007/s13280-016-0800-y.

Aurousseau, M., Ballot, E., Bernard, A., Brissaud, D., Caroly, S., Frein, Y., Grabot, B., Rocchi, V. (2013). FUTURPROD – Les systèmes de production du futur. Report, Agence Nationale de la Recherche, Paris.

Berardy, A., Seager, T.P., Selinger, E. (2011). Developing a pedagogy of interactional expertise for sustainability education. In *Proceedings of the 2011 IEEE International Symposium on Sustainable Systems and Technology*, Chicago, 1–4. doi: 10.1109/ISSST.2011.5936891.

Berque, A. (2004). Ce qui fonde l'éthique environnementale. *Diogène*, 207(3), 3–14.

Bihouix, P. (2014). *L'Âge des low tech : vers une civilisation techniquement soutenable*. Éditions du Seuil, Paris.

Brundiers, K., Barth, M., Cebrián, G., Cohen, M., Diaz, L., Doucette-Remington, S., Zint, M. (2021). Key competencies in sustainability in higher education – Toward an agreed-upon reference framework. *Sustainability Science*, 16, 13–29.

Calvin, K., Dasgupta, D., Krinner, G., Mukherji, A., Thorne, P.W., Trisos, C., Romero, J. (2023). Climate Change 2023: AR6 Synthesis Report. IPCC, Geneva. doi: 10.59327/IPCC/AR6-9789291691647.

Chavel, S. (2012). Martha Nussbaum et les usages de la littérature en philosophie morale. *Revue philosophique*, 137(1), 89–100.

Clarke, W.C. (2002). Science and technology for sustainable development. *ICSU Series on Science for Sustainable Development*, 9.

Comte-Sponville, A. (2002). *Présentations de la philosophie*. Librairie générale française, Paris.

Décathlon (2023). La relation durable [Online]. Available at: https://engagements.decathlon.fr/la-relation-durable.

Désaunay, C. and de Jouvenel, F. (2021). Scénarios de rupture à l'horizon 2040–2050. Report, Futuribles International, Paris.

Deslandes, G. (2012). *Le management éthique*. Dunod, Paris.

European Commission (2020). Critical raw materials for strategic technologies and sectors in the EU: A foresight study. Report, EU Publications Office, Luxembourg [Online]. Available at: https://data.europa.eu/doi/10.2873/865242.

European Commission (2021). Industry 5.0: Towards a sustainable, human centric and resilient European Industry. Report, EU Publications Office, Luxembourg [Online]. Available at: https://data.europa.eu/doi/10.2777/308407.

Foot, P. (1967). The problem of abortion and the doctrine of the double effect. *Oxford Review*, 5, 5–15.

Ghoshal, S., Mendhekar, R., Bruckman, A. (2020). Toward a grassroots culture of technology practice. *Proceedings of the ACM on Human-Computer Interaction*, 4(CSCW1), 1–28.

Hjalsted, A.W., Laurent, A., Marchman Andersen, M., Holm Olsen, K., Ryberg, M., Hauschild, M. (2021). Sharing the safe operating space: Exploring ethical allocation principles to operationalize the planetary boundaries and assess absolute sustainability at individual and industrial sector levels. *Journal of Industrial Ecology*, 25(1), 6–19. doi: 10.1111/jiec.13050.

Lasi, H., Fettke, P., Kemper, H.-G., Feld, T., Hoffmann, M. (2014). Industry 4.0. *Business & Information Systems Engineering*, 6(4), 239–242. doi: 10.1007/s12599-014-0334-4.

Latour, B. (2017). *Où atterrir ? Comment s'orienter en politique*. La Découverte, Paris.

McCauley, D.J. (2006). Selling out on nature. *Nature*, 443(7107), 27–28.

Meadows, D.H. (1972). *The Limits to Growth: A Report for the Club of Rome's Project on the Predicament of Mankind*. Universe Books, New York.

Metz, T. and Miller, S.C. (2016). Relational ethics. In *The International Encyclopedia of Ethics*, LaFollette, H. (ed.). Wiley-Blackwell, New York.

Minteer, B.A., Collins, J.P., Bird, S.J. (2008). Editors' overview: The emergence of ecological ethics. *Science and Engineering Ethics*, 14, 473–481. doi: 10.1007/s11948-008-9110-5.

Ribes, A., Boé, J., Qasmi, S., Dubuisson, B., Douville, H., Terray, L. (2022). An updated assessment of past and future warming over France based on a regional observational constraint. *Earth System Dynamics*, 13(4), 1397–1415. doi: 10.5194/esd-13-1397-2022.

Richardson, K., Steffen, W., Lucht, W., Bendtsen, J., Cornell, S.E., Donges, J.F, Markus Drüke, M., Fetzer, I., Bala, G., von Bloh, W. et al. (2023). Earth beyond six of nine planetary boundaries. *Science Advances*, 9(37) [Online]. Available at: eadh2458.org/10.1126/sciadv.adh2458.

Ricœur, P. (1984). Fondements de l'éthique. *Autres temps*, 3(1), 61–71. doi: 10.3406/chris.1984.956.

Seager, R., Ting, M., Held, I., Kushnir, Y., Lu, J., Vecchi, G., and Naik, N. (2007). Model projections of an imminent transition to a more arid climate in southwestern North America. *Science*, 316(5828), 1181–1184.

St. Clair, A.L. (2017). *Development Ethics*. Routledge, London. doi: 10.4324/9781315258003.

Steffen, W., Richardson, K., Rockström, J., Cornell, S.E., Fetzer, I., Bennett, E.M., Biggs, R., Carpenter, S.R., de Vries, W., Sörlin, S. et al. (2015). Planetary boundaries: Guiding human development on a changing planet. *Science*, 347(6223), 1259855. doi: 10.1126/science.1259855.

Trentesaux, D. and Caillaud, E. (2020). Ethical stakes of Industry 4.0. *IFAC-PapersOnLine*, 53(2), 17002–17007. doi: 10.1016/j.ifacol.2020.12.1486.

Van Der Weij, F., Steinert, S., Van De Poel, I., Alleblas, J., Melnyk, A., De Wildt, T. (2023). Value change and technological design. *IEEE Technology and Society Magazine*, 42(3), 25–32. doi: 10.1109/MTS.2023.3302406.

6

Operational Ethics in Industrial Systems of the Future: Methodological Elements

6.1. Introduction

As a result of advances in technologies, stemming from the digital world and the concept of Industry 4.0, a profound transformation of industrial systems is underway today. This transformation affects the design of these systems, their implementation and operation (Bidet-Mayer and Ciet 2016), as well as the specific features of the products they supply (Hennebert et al. 2019). Regarding their operation, industrial systems, most of which are partially automated, are becoming, through technologies such as AI (artificial intelligence) or IoT (Internet of Things), connected, intelligent, autonomous, capable of improving performance in terms of productivity, quality and deadlines, and of replacing, simplifying or relieving humans in the execution of certain tasks and the making of certain decisions, thereby increasing responsiveness and reducing the risk of errors (Vuksanović Herceg et al. 2020). The use of robotic systems (robots, cobots, exoskeletons) leads to technical performances superior to those that can be provided by human operators alone. In addition, these systems are enriched with data, ensuring the traceability of events.

The use of modern technologies in the operation of industrial systems is expanding, leading to an increasing number of new functionalities, most of which have yet to be imagined. In this context, beyond the largely improved technical dimensions, the developments linked to this use raise questions that

Chapter written by Damien TRENTESAUX, Lamia BERRAH and Karine SAMUEL.

can lead to ethical risks which are difficult to control (Rahanu et al. 2021). Such ethical risks can be identified at different levels (Figure 6.1):

– Human: through the new managerial roles allocated to humans, their potential replacement in productive mechanisms or those requiring decision-making, possible biases between their skills and the responsibilities assigned to them or the misuse of data generated during system operation.

– Company: in terms of its industrial system, its image, its know-how, the quality of life within it and even the consequences of the decisions made within it. If, in a routine, well-identified context in which actions are perfectly known, a socio-technical system can operate autonomously without major risk; this will not be the case in a non-routine, uncontrolled context, exposed to uncertainties due to the revolution brought about by the massive arrival of data and tools such as AI.

– Societal: society as a group of individuals and companies may see its humanist values transformed in favor of accelerated optimization of techno-centric performance to the detriment of human beings. The loss or transformation of professions and jobs is a cause for concern, as is the "uberization" of work and the emergence of micro-services that are not recognized as such. As a sign of this growing awareness, today's generation aspires to give meaning to their jobs and working lives (Peltier 2021; Gentina et al. 2022).

– Environment: through energy consumption and the rare earths required for computing, cybersecurity and data storage (Big Data, blockchain), for the operation of technological components and given the constraints linked to their production (scarcity of materials) and recycling.

To deal with these ethical risks and protect humans and the environment from the possible consequences, companies have equipped themselves with approaches and rules that they are constantly enriching and adapting to their context (circular economy (Gupta et al. 2021), Corporate Social Responsibility (CSR) (Agudelo et al. 2019), General Data Protection Regulation (GDPR), etc.). However, the answers provided by current frameworks and legislation remain very partial and evolve less quickly than technologies.

Furthermore, operational responses based on the concept of ethics, derived from moral philosophy, in the industrialization and operation of industrial systems, remain rare. This lack of a global vision and operational offer to meet the needs of companies is glaringly obvious. Decision-makers in charge of industrial systems performance management find themselves at a loss when faced with this situation.

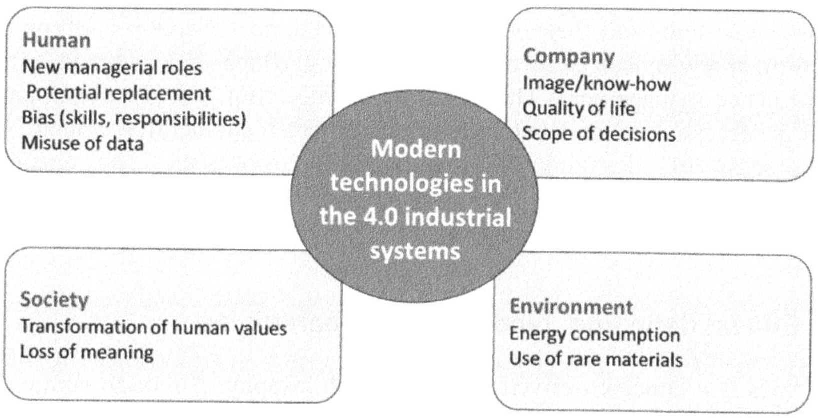

Figure 6.1. *Ethical risks associated with the use of modern technologies in the operation of 4.0 industrial systems*

With a multidisciplinary vision, the ideas presented in this chapter are based on two assumptions:

– The management of ethical risks during the operation of industrial systems, as part of the transition to "Factory 4.0", cannot be carried out independently of the requirements relating to the management and continuous improvement of the performance of these industrial systems; this management being the guarantor of the industrial viability of companies.

– The concept of industrial performance needs to be redefined to include an ethical dimension. The concept of industrial performance has been evolving since the first industrial revolutions. Initially focused on cost and effectiveness, it has been enriched to include other dimensions, such as efficiency in a lean context. By taking ethical risks into account, the challenge is to guarantee not only short-term, techno-centric performance, but also long-term performance, integrating the socio-technical dimension of industrial systems.

The aim of this chapter is to provide a few methodological elements that will enable us to delimit the contours of an operational integration of ethics in the performance management of 4.0 industrial systems, during their operation. To this end, section 6.2 presents some basic notions relating to the concept of ethics and its paradigms. After a brief introduction to the performance management of 4.0 industrial systems, section 6.3 reviews the state of the art regarding the consideration and application of ethics in industrial systems and their performance management. Section 6.4 proposes a few methodological elements for integrating ethical risks into industrial performance management. This is followed, in section 6.5, by a testimonial from an aeronautical and automotive equipment manufacturer, which is in the process of digitizing its manufacturing processes. The chapter's conclusion, presented in section 6.6, summarizes the main points made and outlines some of the study's outlooks.

6.2. Ethics: definition, typologies and paradigms

Ethics is a concept derived from moral philosophy. Although commonly understood, it is difficult to give it a universal definition and application.

Associated with societal expectations and values of morality and fairness (Morley et al. 2021), ethics has, for centuries and with many paradoxes at its core, been the subject of discussion in many fields such as science, philosophy and law. In this respect, "a good life, with and for others, in just institutions" (Ricœur 2015) can be seen as a definition that can convey, very simply, the semantics of the concept.

The convergence of the digital and physical worlds, where humans interact with complex artificial systems, means that a growing number of fields are concerned by ethics, beyond the traditional areas of application. The industrial systems of the future, examined in this chapter, are a perfect illustration of this. In this particular field of digital technology and AI, ethical behavior can concern two types of players: humans, on the one hand, in a traditional vision, and autonomous/intelligent systems, on the other hand (Bird and Spier 1995; Trentesaux and Rault 2017). The second type, not addressed in this study, refers to the concept of machine ethics, moral machines, moral robots, virtuous robots, etc. (Allen et al. 2005, 2006; Arkin et al. 2012).

Several philosophical currents consider the concept of ethics from different angles and have resulted in the construction of relatively different paradigms in their conception of ethics, such as deontology or the ethics of "duty" and consequentialism, including utilitarianism. The deontological paradigm is based on a principle of decision-making on the basis of immutable rules, while the utilitarian paradigm is based on a principle of decision-making on the basis of possible ethical consequences (Kant 1785; Prescient 2013; Bergmann et al. 2018). Another paradigm, the virtue paradigm, is based on the moral character, virtuous practices, rather than duties, rules or consequences of actions (Steen et al. 2021). As for the pragmatism paradigm, it advocates drawing inspiration from the reality of situations and is based on experience as well as the reasoning carried out by the person in a position to decide (Girel 2007). Table 6.1 provides an illustration of these different ethical paradigms, by considering a situation experienced in a company (L'Oréal éthique 2015), briefly described hereafter.

Situation: an operator working on a production line notices that one of the machines on the line is not operating normally, resulting in the production of faulty products. At the time of this observation, the line manager was unavailable and the supervisor did not react, even though the production schedule was very tight, the malfunctioning machine was in the middle of the production line and the quality department only checked the products before dispatching them. They have three options: stop the production line, inform the supervisor or do nothing.

Paradigm	**Deontology**	**Consequentialism**	**Virtue**	**Pragmatism**
Assessment of action according to the paradigm	Bad	Good	Good	Good/bad
Stopping the production line	Non-compliance with standards and rules defined in the job description	(+) Morality (+) Minimum production loss (+) Reduction in energy consumption (+) Waste reduction (–) Non-respect for hierarchy (risk of sanctions) (–) Production interruption cost (–) Date of intervention unknown (–) Non-mastering production delay	Respect for fundamental values: safeguarding production and loyalty to the company	If, according to culture and habits, stopping production is the best practice, the reaction is good; if not, it is bad

Paradigm	Deontology	Consequentialism	Virtue	Pragmatism
Informing the supervisor	Good	Good/bad	Good	Good/bad
	Compliance with the standards and rules defined in the job description	(+) Morality (+) Respect for hierarchy (+) Limited loss of production (+) Reduction in energy consumption (+) Date of intervention known (+) Mastering production delays (+) Waste reduction (–) Production interruption cost (–) Production of waste while waiting for the supervisor's reaction	Respect for fundamental values: safeguarding production and loyalty to the company	If, according to culture and habits, informing the supervisor is the best practice, the reaction is good; if not, it is bad
Doing nothing	Good	Bad	Bad	Good/bad
	Compliance with standards and rules defined in the job description	(–) Morality (–) Total production loss (–) Cost of defective products (–) Date of intervention unknown (–) Non-control of production delays (–) Energy consumption (–) Increased waste	Failure to respect fundamental values: loss of production and disloyalty to the company	If, according to culture and habit, doing nothing is the best practice, the reaction is good; if not, it is bad

Table 6.1. *Illustrations of some ethical paradigms (inspired by Mecheri 2021)*

Another aspect that concerns ethics is the way in which it is considered in the decision-making process. Following the example of sustainable development policies, two types of ethical consideration can be distinguished today: weak and strong.

Weakly taking ethics into account means considering ethics as a criterion that can be compromised in the interests of performance, whereas strongly taking ethics into account means forbidding any compromise. In this case, the ethical evaluation of a possible decision is carried out before any study of other criteria (similar to a lexicographical approach in multicriteria analysis) (Berrah et al. 2023).

Figure 6.2 summarizes some of the notions relating to the concept of ethics discussed in this section.

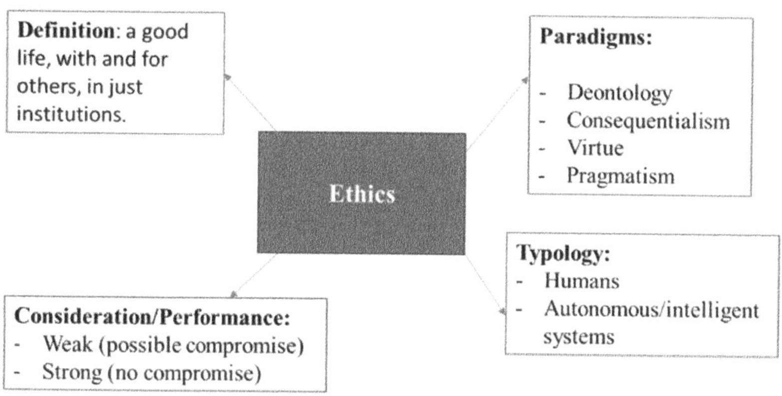

Figure 6.2. *Basic concepts of ethics*

6.3. Performance management for 4.0 industrial systems and its ethical risks

6.3.1. *Overview*

The overall aim of industrial performance management is to manage (all of the actions implemented) the achievement of the objectives assigned to the industrial system and the continuous improvement of the results obtained, on the basis of the means available (Bititci et al. 2016). Industrial objectives are traditionally associated with cost, quality and delivery criteria, to which the environmental criterion has been added more recently

(Jonsson and Rudberg 2014). Action plans can be defined in the sense of the four steps of the Deming wheel (Plan–Do–Check–Act). Performance management, in line with production management structures, covers the company's decision-making levels: strategic, tactical, operational and real time.

Moreover, as performance is a function of multiple criteria, its management is based on the premise that three conditions must be met in order to guarantee the company's long-term viability. These three conditions constitute the triangle (efficiency, effectiveness, efficacy) of performance. They can be formulated as follows (Gilbert et al. 1980) (Figure 6.3):

– system efficiency extended to activities peripheral to production;

– the effectiveness of the processes used to achieve objectives;

– the relevance of objectives in relation to available resources.

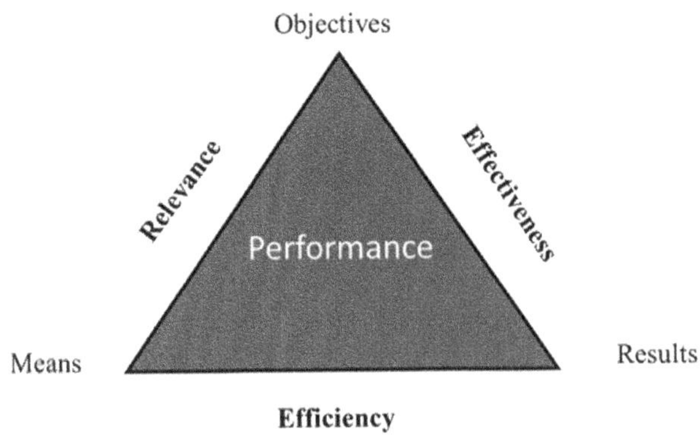

Figure 6.3. *The performance triangle (Gilbert et al. 1980)*

The integration of modern technologies is leading to new questions regarding the performance management of 4.0 industrial systems (Dalenogare et al. 2018). The digital transformation of this management is being studied (Cokins 2017), and intelligent decision support systems are being developed (Cardin et al. 2017). Maturity models for industrial systems are proposed (Schumacher et al. 2016), while the impact of technologies on the achievement of cost, quality and delivery objectives is analyzed (Büchi et al. 2020). In this stream of literature, the use of modern technologies remains an opportunity to optimize the industrial performance of companies and their supply chains, based on the enrichment of pre-existing management frameworks.

6.3.2. *State of the art on ethics in industrial systems of the future*

The ethical dimension of 4.0 industrial systems is not explicitly taken into account in performance management but is beginning to be addressed, as these systems are changing the way humans operate and interact (Radziwill 2018; Vakkuri et al. 2020). Ethical issues are discussed (Morley et al. 2021; Shayganmehr et al. 2021; Sidorenko et al. 2021), and their diversity, as well as their numerous and multidisciplinary impacts, are highlighted (Table 6.2) (Trentesaux and Caillaud 2020). However, the concept is delicate to grasp and raises a certain complexity (section 6.2). This may explain why ethics is still generally regarded as a non-functional requirement that will not add value to a company's operational processes, particularly when companies have short-term financial profitability as their sole goal.

Opportunities provided by modern technologies	Examples of consequences	Examples of ethical risks
Data traceability	Access to operator activity history	Evaluation and disclosure of operator performance
Smart control	Faster decision-making and shorter reaction times	Over-solicitation of operators Increased stress and fatigue
Smart decisions	Human replacement	Loss of skills, professions and know-how
Robotization (cobots)	Operation under non-standard conditions is not planned	Failure to anticipate human error
Logistics (voice picking)	Isolation of operators	De-motivation Depression
Data availability (Big Data/IoT)	Access to strategic company and human data	Cyber-attacks, disclosure of confidential data

Table 6.2. *Examples of ethical risks associated with the use of modern technologies in Industry 4.0*

Some studies are beginning to analyze ethics, technically speaking, in the form of risks incurred by the integration of AI into the 4.0 industrial systems (machine ethics, cyber ethics, etc.) (Yu et al. 2018; Trentesaux and Caillaud 2020). Without proposing a precise identification, these risks are considered to be managerial, organizational, operational, individual, social and technological (Casali and Perano 2021). Some authors distinguish between risks due to organizational and managerial transformations (De Cremer and

Moore 2020) and risks due to the transfer of decision-making to autonomous computing systems (Stahl 2021). However, some approaches to integrating these ethical risks are emerging. One approach is to advocate the development of a set of practices for specifying, according to its ethical conformity, any action involving interaction between humans and the system (Abràmoff et al. 2020; Trentesaux 2020). Along the same lines, "anti-patterns", referring to practices that should be avoided, are proposed (Vakkuri et al. 2020). The study of the scope of ethical risks, however, remains largely unexplored.

Studies concerning the ethical design and development of systems integrating AI are underway (Hoareau and Samuel 2020), advocating modular and iterative principles of ethical risk assessment (Vakkuri et al. 2021), as is reflection on ethical decision-making in business generally (Casali and Perano 2021). Several studies have begun to assess the consideration of ethical issues in industrial systems (Trentesaux et al. 2021; Ciobanu and Meşniţă 2022; Mezgár and Váncza 2022; Salamanca et al. 2022). These studies are still emerging to propose concrete solutions limiting ethical risks, but they suggest an integrated approach that systematically addresses the need for ethical risk assessment according to product lifecycle phases (from design to recycling) and decision-making level (from strategic to real time) (Jimenez et al. 2022; Leitão and Karnouskos 2022).

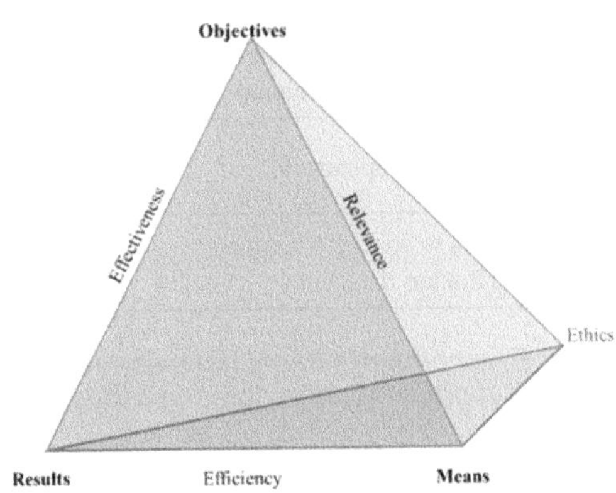

Figure 6.4. *The performance tetrahedron. For a color version of this figure, see: www.iste.co.uk/abel/ethics.zip*

Complementary research has been proposed on the need to extend the economic performance model to a sustainable model (Berrah et al. 2021a,

2021b). This research focused on the definition of a performance model that conceptually integrates the ethical dimension, without addressing the associated risks. This study argues that sustainable management and performance require an ethical vision of objectives, the use of resources and results. The triangle (efficiency, effectiveness, relevance) (section 6.2.1) can then be enriched by an additional dimension, inherent in the ethics that remain to be articulated. Three conditions of conformity, based on the respective notions of objectives, means and results, complete the conditions based on their association, two by two. It should be noted that this vision takes little account of ethics, since the latter is regarded as a condition to be met, in the same way as the other three performance conditions (section 6.2). Figure 6.4 shows this completed vision of performance, whose definition would evolve:

> Efficiency in the achievement of ethical objectives, in the efficient and ethical use of available means, subject to the relevance of these objectives and of the system in terms of the means used and the ethics of the results obtained.

In this context, Table 6.3 gives some examples of questions and illustrations of the link between ethics and the parameters (objectives, means, results) of performance as well as its conditions, conveyed respectively by the axes and planes of the tetrahedron (Berrah et al. 2021b).

	Examples of questions	**Illustrations of the link between ethical risk and performance**
Objectives	Are the objectives ethical?	Choosing an objective with negative social impact
Results	Are the results measured/obtained ethically?	Using the personal data of operators
Means	Are the means used/defined ethically?	Restricting the roles of operators
Relevance Plan (objectives, results, ethics)	Is the link between the objectives and results ethical?	Cyber-espionage Falsifying results

	Examples of questions	Illustrations of the link between ethical risk and performance
Efficiency Plan (means, results, ethics)	Is the link between the means and results ethical?	Replacing humans by AI (autonomous robots)
Effectiveness Plan (means, objectives, ethics)	Is the link between the means and objectives ethical?	Choosing objectives that are technically unattainable by the system

Table 6.3. *Examples of ethical and performance mapping within the tetrahedron (inspired by Berrah et al. 2021b)*

However, at present, despite growing awareness of the ethical issue (Hoekstra and Kaptein 2020; Borenstein and Howard 2021; Margherita and Braccini 2021; Raza 2022), no real operational and federating solutions are being proposed. Companies wishing to put ethics at the heart of their activities, in particular to meet the expectations of their managers, employees and the younger generations entering the job market, are currently at a loss (Jimenez et al. 2022).

They lack operational tools to help them manage, especially:

1) Identifying and managing the ethical risks inherent in future technological and organizational developments.

2) Analyzing the impact of the actions taken on both the ethics and the performance of their systems.

These observations are shared by researchers and industrialists, including NTN Europe, a bearing manufacturer and supplier to the automotive and aeronautical industries. The company, which is in the process of digitizing its industrial activities, has made its needs explicit in terms of taking ethical risks into account and is awaiting operational solutions.

An analysis of the responses provided by the literature, cross-referenced with these needs, highlighted a number of methodological elements presented in section 6.4 (Figure 6.5).

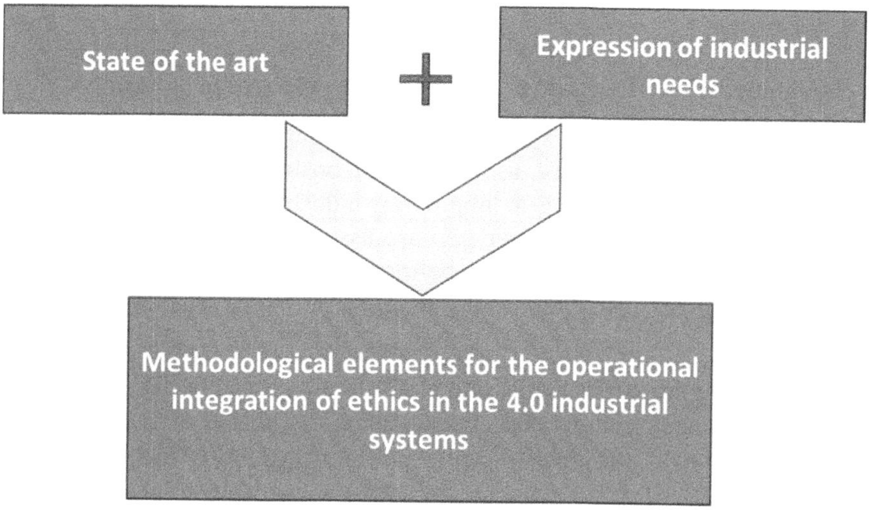

Figure 6.5. *Cross-section analysis*

6.4. Toward the operational integration of ethics in the 4.0 industrial systems

This section of the chapter presents the initial results of a study carried out on the operational integration of ethics into performance management, with regard to the operation of 4.0 industrial systems. The aim of this study is to develop an operational methodological tool that will enable those involved in the operation of 4.0 industrial systems to associate, in concrete terms, an ethical reflection and an analysis of its impact on performance with any action carried out within the framework of this management and in connection with the use of modern technologies.

The ultimate aim of these considerations is to provide ethical management support for industrial performance, in line with the regulatory frameworks in force within companies.

To this end, a first section (section 6.4.1) will be devoted to setting out the scope of the study. A second section (section 6.4.2) will be devoted to presenting the methodological elements required for the operational integration of ethics into performance management, in the context of operating 4.0 industrial systems.

6.4.1. *Scope*

Integrating ethics into industrial performance management means:

– Considering industrial systems in their operational phase and covering productive industrial activity, as well as the business processes associated with production, i.e. relating to improving industrial performance, quality, logistics, etc. The systems considered are assumed to be in the process of digitalizing their production and to be more or less autonomous depending on the intelligence integrated into them (e.g. using Machine Learning techniques).

– Mobilizing all departments and skills involved in the digitalization of industrial systems, i.e. general management, in charge of strategic and financial coherence; the industrial division, in charge of product realization and performance improvement; IT and information technologies, in charge of the development and maintenance of IT and digital devices integrated into systems; and human resources and CSR, in terms of employee recruitment and the impact on jobs.

6.4.2. *Methodological elements*

The concept of performance can be defined as "an exceptional, uncommon, optimal result. It is based on expectations that can be translated into objectives" (Boisvert 1995). Integrating ethics operationally into performance management first requires a definition of the notion of ethics as applied to industrial systems. This will be followed by an analysis of how ethics can be integrated and how the quest for industrial performance can evolve in the light of this integration.

6.4.2.1. *Integrating ethics into performance management*

The operational integration of ethics into performance management begins with an analysis of the constituent elements of ethics applied to engineering. The aim is to propose a definition and an approach appropriate to the operation of industrial systems. Operational integration implies an approach that "concretizes" the concept so that its principles can be applied. The operationalization of ethics can thus be achieved through a "risk management" approach. The result will be a methodological guide to help the people involved detect and manage ethical risks in the operation of industrial systems. Two steps are required: a preliminary step to identify ethical risks and a step to manage these risks (Figure 6.6).

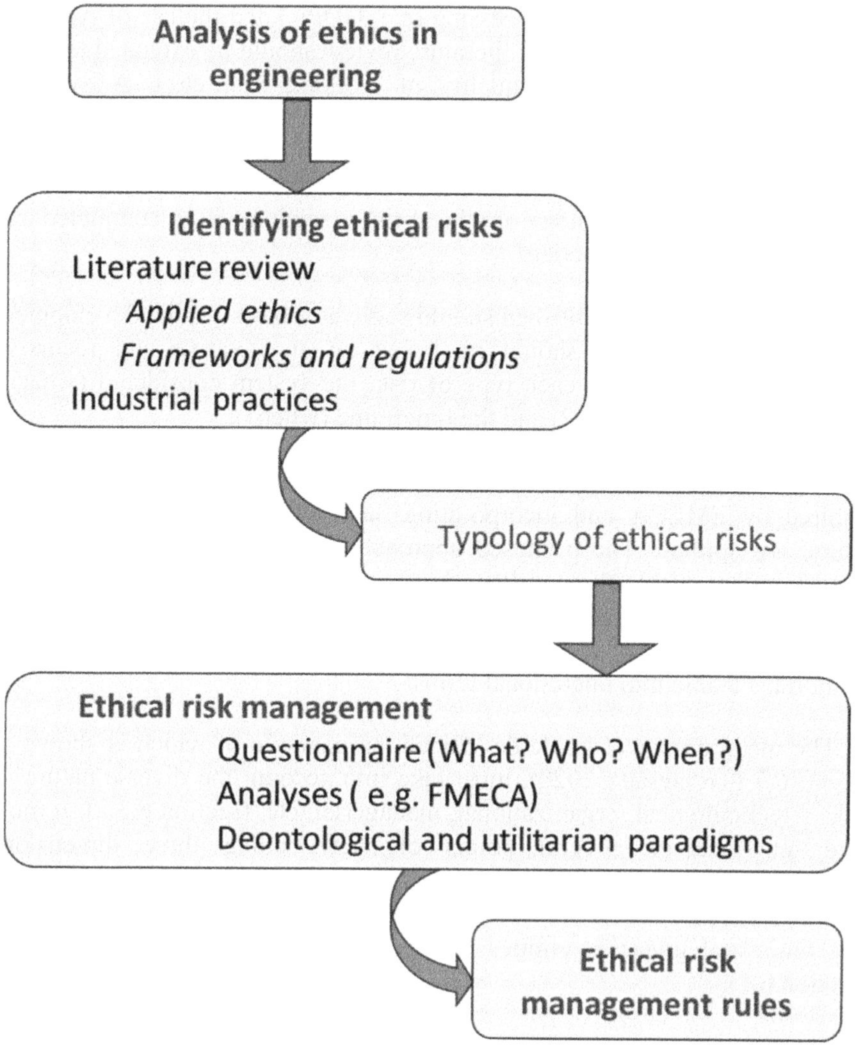

Figure 6.6. *Operational integration of ethics through a "risk management" approach*

The identification of ethical risks is based on a literature review in the field of ethics applied to several related fields (safety, ergonomics, etc.) as well as on the study of frameworks and recommendations associated with the consideration of ethics in relation to engineering. A focus should be placed on frameworks relating to data processing (e.g. GDPR) and the use of AI in the Factory of the Future field. The literature review should be extended to cover related topics (CSR, safety, quality of working life, etc.). A systemic decomposition of the systems studied makes it possible to identify couples (function, system implementing it); and for each, identify different ethical risks (Pacaux-Lemoine and Trentesaux 2019; Trentesaux 2020). The result of the study is a refined typology of ethical risks (section 6.2.2), completed and validated by industrial practice.

The risk typology established should serve as a basis for the development of questionnaires. This should be based on an iterative and recursive principle, specifying, for each type of risk, the system considered (what?), the entities impacted (who?) and the timeframe (when?).

Secondly, risk analysis methods – in particular, an impact study – inspired by FMECA and incorporating basic principles from operational safety, are applied. The proposed approach promotes the identification of properties that enable these risks to be managed according to deontological and utilitarian ethical paradigms (section 6.2), which are the most widely used in the field of ethics applied to engineering, since they have the merit of being translatable into operational terms.

The methodological guide developed, an example of which is shown in Figure 6.7 (Trentesaux 2020), must take into account the diverse nature of risks – technological, organizational, managerial, etc. (section 6.3.2). It must take into account several points of view, along three dimensions respectively: actors (management, production, IT, human resources, etc.) (section 6.4.1), decision-making levels (strategic, tactical, operational, real time) and impacted entities (human, company, society, environment) (section 6.1).

There are also important steps to consider: analyzing the mechanisms of interaction between the levels and accompanying the players involved in order to devise and implement solutions to manage these ethical risks and to assess their relevance. In addition, it is also necessary to question a wide panel of parties involved (operators, users, customers, suppliers, etc.) to assess the acceptability of these ethical risks, particularly over the long term. This will allow an accurate assessment to be made of the sustainability of decisions over a much wider horizon than that covered by the industrial processes studied (e.g. semesters or years).

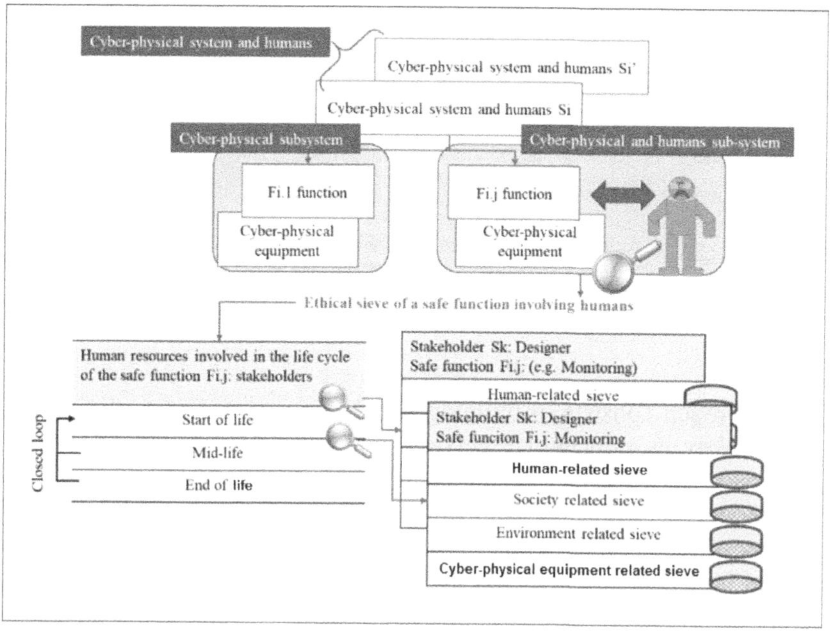

Figure 6.7. *Example of a methodological guide to managing ethical risks in the operation of 4.0 industrial systems (Trentesaux 2020). For a color version of this figure, see: www.iste.co.uk/abel/ethics.zip*

6.4.2.2. *Forcing change: the performance management model*

To integrate the ethical dimension and ensure that all management actions take this dimension into account as a matter of course, forces the evolution of the performance management model. This integration must lead to a management model whose role is both to continuously improve performance while taking into account the ethical dimension and to ensure that this consideration is geared toward optimizing performance. Consequently, the principles to be jointly considered in this management model are (Figure 6.8):

– managing the achievement of industrial system objectives and improving the results achieved;

– taking ethical risks into account when defining objectives and carrying out the corresponding actions;

– managing the ethical maturity of the industrial system;

– optimizing the impact of ethical approaches on performance.

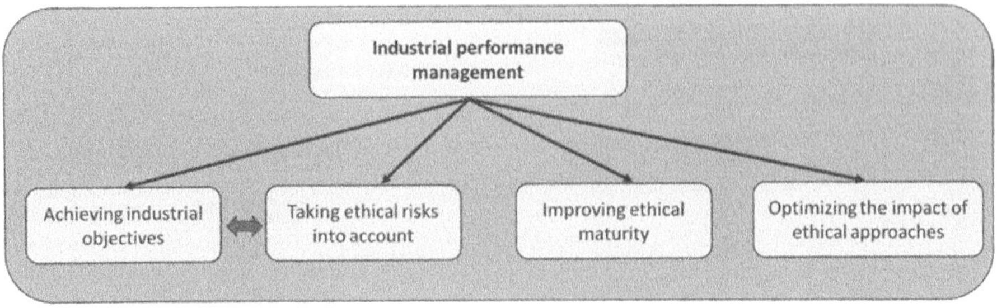

Figure 6.8. *The principles of ethical performance management*

The approach consists of building a reflection according to the proposed structuring, in its conceptual version, for example, on the basis of the performance tetrahedron presented above (Figure 6.4) if a "weak" consideration of ethics is adopted. Integrating ethics into performance management must begin with a state-of-the-art review of the frameworks suggested for managing and continuously improving the performance of the 4.0 industrial systems. Based on the analysis of this literature review, a performance management model should be developed to reflect the specificities of introducing modern technologies into industrial systems. Ethical, deontological or utilitarian rules, deduced from the risk management stage (section 6.4.2.1), enable adjustments to be made in the declaration of objectives and the use of means to prevent identified risks. These adjustments are developed using a systemic approach, enabling the deployment of performance parameters (objectives, means, results) in line with the four decision-making levels of industrial management (Figure 6.9).

Moreover, integrating ethical risk management into performance management can only be achieved through an iterative process, based on the continuous improvement of traditional performance criteria. Indicators relating to this integration should make it possible to assess, improve and sustain the ethical maturity of the industrial system, conveying the idea that ethics can be considered not just as a condition to be met but as a criterion to be improved (Berrah and Trentesaux 2020).

Since a company's viability depends on its industrial performance, a system must be put in place to analyze choices and evaluate ethical practices with regard to performance. This system must be accompanied by a practical demonstration that it is possible to improve performance by taking ethics into account. The integration of ethics into performance management is only effective once this proof has been established. Here too, an important step is to ask the various stakeholders about ethical practices, their relevance and their impact, in order to obtain their ownership and support.

The dashboard shown in Figure 6.10 summarizes the different types of performance indicators, which are useful for ethics-integrated performance management.

The conventional system of indicators based on the triptych cost–quality–delivery is enriched by indicators relating to ethics, identified sometimes as immutable rules, sometimes as a criterion whose performance can be improved.

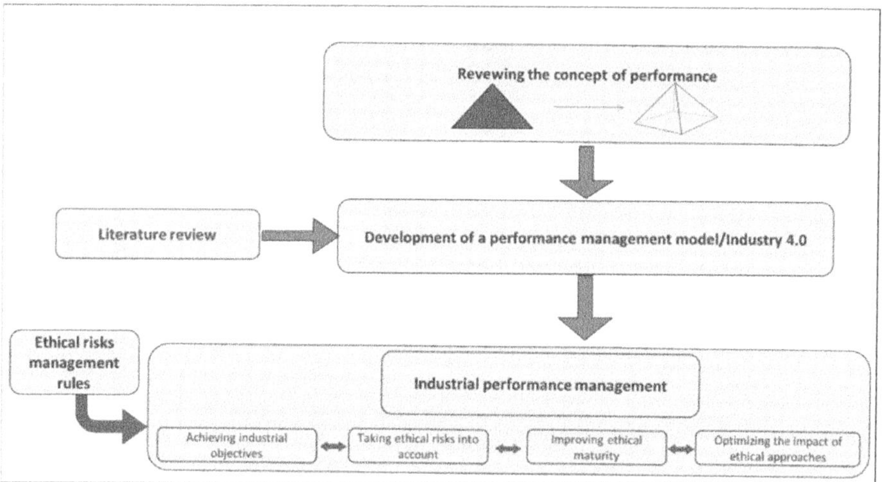

Figure 6.9. *Integrating ethics into performance management (the case of a "weak" consideration of ethics)*

6.5. Industrial testimony

NTN Europe, a subsidiary of the NTN Corporation, is one of the world's leading bearing designers, developers and manufacturers. With sales of €702.2 million in 2022, the company is active in the automotive, rail, renewable energies and aerospace markets.

NTN Europe employs approximately 6,500 people, mainly in Europe, and has 15 production sites, including seven in France.

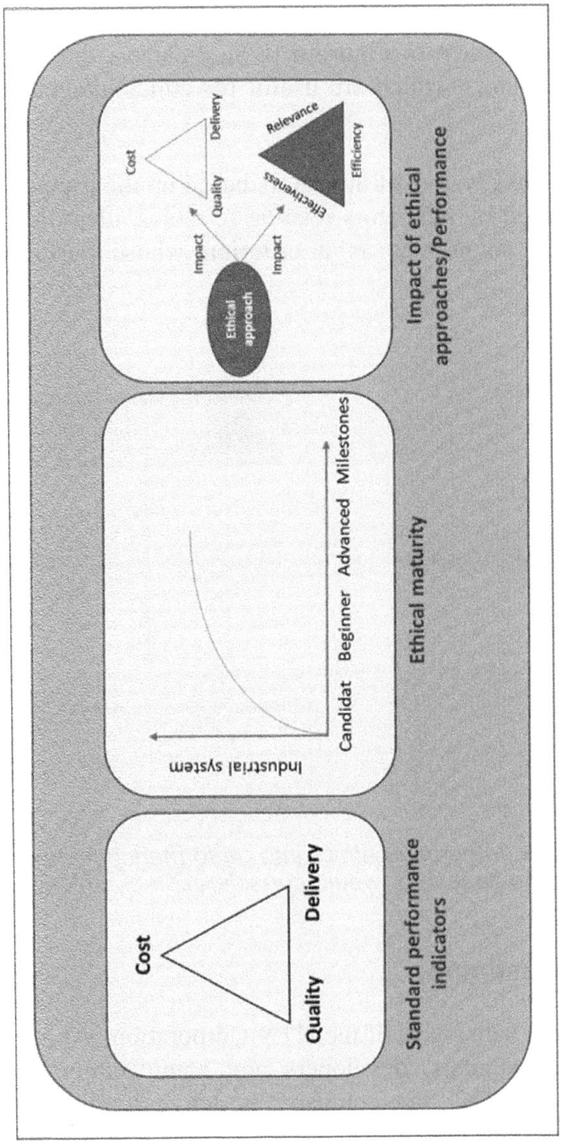

Figure 6.10. *The dashboard for ethical performance management*

Since 2015, the company's specialized aerospace site in particular has benefited from major investments to digitalize production, in line with the principles of Industry 4.0. As part of this, the "Digital Manufacturing" project has been implemented. This project prioritized the implementation of an MES (Manufacturing Execution System) solution to, on the one hand, rapidly meet customer expectations in terms of product-process traceability, and on the other hand, set up operational dashboards enabling the management of production stations (Berrah et al. 2021b).

The aeronautics site, intended as a model for all of the company's sites, has been studied and analyzed in order to deduce best practices and risks to be avoided from this experience. Through its Digital Transformation Committee (CTD), in charge of studying and validating projects linked to the digitalization of industrial processes, NTN Europe has drawn up an initial assessment confirming the idea that modern technologies optimize technical performance, while at the same time alerting the company to the ethical risks associated with the use of these technologies and the intensification of their use. The project continued, transforming the system and its use in depth, continuously improving performance, developing frugal and sustainable sourcing, making the company more agile, etc.

However, as these transformations have progressed, the company has become increasingly aware of the importance of the human dimension, which paradoxically appears to be essential for mastering the deployment and use of modern technologies. For example, the abandonment of low value-added tasks such as production data reporting, and the rise in expertise in terms of quality and flow management to support more autonomous management, are overturning the traditional role of production operators. It is now essential to master digital tools and to be partners in their development, in order to "customize" MESs to the needs of each workstation. The management structure is called into question by this autonomy – made possible by the availability of performance indicators directly updated by the information system on the workstations – without the intervention of intermediate levels such as team leaders. Production data, combined with sales, financial and human resources data, are increasingly being put to new uses (via augmented reality technologies, simulation, cloud computing, AI in a cyber-security context, etc.).

The questions raised by this digital transformation are manifold, and while the opportunities it offers are being discovered every day, the associated risks are also gradually coming to light. By way of illustration, Table 6.4 lists some of the ethical benefits and risks associated with the first stage of digitalization, the implementation of MESs and the two associated objectives, as well as some examples of the questions raised by manufacturers in this respect.

	Advantages	Ethical risks	Questions
Traceability	Reactivity	Traceability of human activity	Is it desirable to optimize traceability for products and processes (over 90%), when there is a risk that traceability will be measured for humans?
	Matching equipment manufacturers' requirements	Competition between human operators	How can we prevent the data tracking products and processes from being used to assess human performance and added value?
	Shorter response times	Human operator replacement	Under the pretext of technocentric, short-termist performance, should humans be replaced by AI?
Production station control	Reactivity	Loss of skills	Is it fair to replace humans in their activities without offering them new ones, in line with their skills?
	Autonomy	Liability incurred Isolation Pressure	Is it fair to ask humans to make autonomous/isolated decisions in unknown situations without prior training?

Table 6.4. *Examples of benefits and risks associated with the implementation of MESs at NTN Europe*

With this in mind, NTN Europe has decided, in line with its CSR policy, to go beyond this awareness-raising stage. NTN Europe is convinced of the urgent need to put in place a system that will enable the ethical dimension to be taken into account in the operational management of the industrial system. This means revisiting its performance management model, in which objectives are regularly revised upward, results are analyzed with this in mind, and resources are allocated according to the results and the new values to be achieved. The aim is twofold:

– Questions concerning ethical risks must be systematized, enabling all risks to be covered, at all levels and with regard to all of the people involved.

– Performance management must integrate identified risks into its statement of objectives and choice of associated actions and resources, at all decision-making levels.

The process of operational integration of ethics into corporate performance management is underway, in line with the methodological elements presented throughout this chapter. By way of illustration, and following the logic of Table 6.3, Table 6.5 identifies the different axes of the performance tetrahedron (efficiency, relevance, effectiveness, ethics) (Figure 6.4), corresponding to the above questions, and associates examples of actions to limit ethical risks with them.

Correspondence (ethics, performance parameters, questioning)	Questions	Suggested actions
Results Axis (results, ethics)	Is it desirable to optimize traceability on products and processes (over 90%) when there is a risk of seeing this traceability measured for humans?	Use simulation models with multi-criteria impact to validate objectives.
Efficiency Plan (means, results, ethics)	How can we prevent the data tracking products and processes from being used to assess human performance and added value?	– Consult operators in advance of any potential use of their data. – Conduct a posteriori checks on the use of operator data. – Guide any assessment of human performance based on technical performance.

Correspondence (ethics, performance parameters, questioning)	Questions	Suggested actions
Efficacy Plan (means, results, ethics)	Is it fair to replace humans in their activities without offering them new ones, in line with their skills?	– Rethink the missions assigned to operators. – Formalize new job description sheets.
Effectiveness Plan (means, objectives, ethics)	Is it fair to ask humans to make autonomous/isolated decisions in unknown situations without prior training?	– Define new responsibilities within a less hierarchical, more coordinated management structure. – Define a support protocol for operators, to complement the supervision screens associated with their missions.

Table 6.5. *Correspondence (ethics, performance) and examples of actions taken to manage ethical risks at NTN Europe*

6.6. Conclusion

Despite a growing awareness of the ethical issues associated with the use of modern technologies in 4.0 industrial systems, and the urgent need to address them, companies – including NTN Europe, a partner in this study – are keen to put ethics at the heart of their activities. This is particularly the case when it comes to meeting the respective expectations of their managers, employees and the younger generations entering the job market, who are waiting for answers to these issues. Indeed, although ethics concerns all players and intervenes at all levels, the frameworks applied in companies and the work proposed in the literature only partially respond to its integration. This integration remains only partially considered in the practices and culture of companies and in the work of the academic community.

Based on this observation and the need for a systematic procedure, combining ethical practices and operational tools to help manage ethical risks in the performance management of 4.0 industrial systems, this chapter has sought to draw up some methodological elements concerning this integration. These elements concern a definition of ethics applied to industrial systems, the identification and management of ethical risks and, finally, the revision of the performance management model to incorporate these risks.

The methodological elements put forward should lead to the creation of practical, robust mechanisms underpinning the systematic inclusion of ethics in the fundamentals of industrial performance. This will then no longer be synonymous only with technocentric, short-termist performance, but also with sustainable performance guaranteeing the viability and longevity of the company.

6.7. Acknowledgements

This chapter was written as part of the ANR ETHICS40 project (ANR-23-CE10-0014), whose members are LAMIH/UPHF, LISTIC/USMB, CERAG/UGA and industrial partner NTN Europe. The authors would like to thank the ANR for its support.

6.8. References

Abràmoff, M.D., Tobey, D., Char, D.S. (2020). Lessons learned about autonomous AI: Finding a safe, efficacious, and ethical path through the development process. *American Journal of Ophthalmology*, 214, 134–142.

Agudelo, M.A.L., Jóhannsdóttir, L., Davídsdóttir, B. (2019). A literature review of the history and evolution of corporate social responsibility. *International Journal of Corporate Social Responsibility*, 4(1), 1–23.

Allen, C., Smit, I., Wallach, W. (2005). Artificial morality: Top-down, bottom-up, and hybrid approaches. *Ethics and Information Technology*, 7, 149–155.

Allen, C., Wallach, W., Smit, I. (2006). Why machine ethics? *IEEE Intelligent Systems*, 21, 12–17.

Arkin, R.C., Ulam, P., Wagner, A.R. (2012). Moral decision making in autonomous systems: Enforcement, moral emotions, dignity, trust, and deception. *Proceedings of the IEEE*, 100(3), 571–589.

Bergmann, L.T., Schlicht, L., Meixner, C., König, P., Pipa, G., Boshammer, S., Stephan, A. (2018). Autonomous vehicles require socio-political acceptance – An empirical and philosophical perspective on the problem of moral decision making. *Frontiers in Behavioral Neuroscience*, 12(31), 13–25.

Berrah, L. and Trentesaux, D. (2020). Decision-making in future industrial systems: Is ethics a new performance indicator? In *Service Oriented, Holonic and Multi-Agent Manufacturing Systems for Industry of the Future: Proceedings of SOHOMA 2020*, Borangiu, T., Trentesaux, D., Leitão, P., Cardin, O., Lamouri, S. (eds). Springer, Cham, 231–245.

Berrah, L., Cliville, V., Trentesaux, D., Chapel, C. (2021a). Industrial performance: An evolution incorporating ethics in the context of industry 4.0. *Sustainability*, 13(16), 9209.

Berrah, L., Cliville, V., Trentesaux, D., Chapel, C. (2021b). Performance industrielle : une évolution intégrant l'éthique dans le contexte de l'Industrie 4.0. In *Congrès international CIGI QUALITA 2021*, Grenoble.

Berrah, L., Trentesaux, D., Jimenez, J.F. (2023). Ethics in performance management of future industrial systems: Weak and strong views. In *Service Oriented, Holonic and Multi-Agent Manufacturing Systems for Industry of the Future: Proceedings of SOHOMA 2023*, Borangiu, T., Trentesaux, D., Leitão, P., Cardin, O., Lamouri, S. (eds). Springer, Cham.

Bidet-Mayer, T. and Ciet, N. (2016). *L'industrie du futur : une compétition mondiale*. La Fabrique de l'Industrie, Paris.

Bird, S.J. and Spier, R. (1995). Welcome to science and engineering ethics. *Science and Engineering Ethics*, 1, 2–4.

Bititci, U., Cocca, P., Ates, A. (2016). Impact of visual performance management systems on the performance management practices of organisations. *International Journal of Production Research*, 54(6), 1571–1593.

Boisvert, H. (1995). Comprendre, mesurer et gérer la productivité, la comptabilité par activités. In *Congrès international de génie industriel de Montréal. La productivité dans un monde sans frontières*, 835–844.

Borenstein, J. and Howard, A. (2021). Emerging challenges in AI and the need for AI ethics education. *AI and Ethics*, 1(1), 61–65.

Büchi, G., Cugno, M., Castagnoli, R. (2020). Smart factory performance and Industry 4.0. *Technological Forecasting and Social Change*, 150, 119790.

Cardin, O., Trentesaux, D., Thomas, A., Castagna, P., Berger, T., Bril Elhaouzi, H. (2017). Coupling predictive scheduling and reactive control in manufacturing hybrid control architectures: State of the art and future challenges. *Journal of Intelligent Manufacturing*, 28(7), 1503–1517.

Casali, G.L. and Perano, M. (2021). Forty years of research on factors influencing ethical decision making: Establishing a future research agenda. *Journal of Business Research*, 132, 614–630.

Ciobanu, A.C. and Meşniţă, G. (2022). AI ethics for industry 5.0 – From principles to practice. In *Workshop of I-ESA*, Valencia, 22.

Cokins, G. (2017). Enterprise performance management (EPM) and the digital revolution. *Performance Improvement*, 56(4), 14–19.

Dalenogare, L.S., Benitez, G.B., Ayala, N.F., Frank, A.G. (2018). The expected contribution of Industry 4.0 technologies for industrial performance. *International Journal of Production Economics*, 204, 383–394.

De Cremer, D. and Moore, C. (2020). Toward a better understanding of behavioral ethics in the workplace. *Annual Review of Organizational Psychology and Organizational Behavior*, 7, 369–393.

Gentina, É., Pauwels-Delassus, V., Leclercq-Vandelannoitte, A. (2022). Infidèles, zappeurs et slasheurs ? Les Z et l'émergence d'une nouvelle forme de fidélité employeur. *Revue de gestion des ressources humaines*, 125, 55–71. doi: 10.3917/grhu.125.0055.

Gilbert, G.R., Collins, R.W., Brenner, R. (1980). Age and leadership effectiveness: From the perceptions of the follower. *Human Resource Management*, 29(2), 187–196.

Girel, M. (2007). Pragmatisme et Éducation morale : philosophie et conduite de la vie chez Peirce, James et Dewey. *L'art du comprendre, SERAPHIS - Société d'etudes et de recherches d'anthropologie*, 16, 49–79.

Gupta, H., Kumar, A., Wasan, P. (2021). Industry 4.0, cleaner production, and circular economy: An integrative framework for evaluating ethical and sustainable business performance of manufacturing organizations. *Journal of Cleaner Production*, 295, 126253.

Hennebert M.A., Cayrat C., Morissette L. (2019). Transformation des PME manufacturières : entre promesses et réalités de l'industrie 4.0. *Gestion*, 44(3), 86–89.

Hoareau, E. and Samuel, K. (2020). Discrimination and fairness in Big Data analytics. In *Conférence AIM*, Atlanta.

Hoekstra, A. and Kaptein, M. (2020). Ethics management: A pluralistic and dynamic perspective. In *Global Corruption and Ethics Management: Translating Theory into Action*, Jurkiewicz, C.L. (ed.). Rowman & Littlefield, Lanham, 109–118.

Jimenez, J.F., Berrah, L., Trentesaux, D., Chapel, C. (2022). Towards the ethical awareness integration on industrial performance management systems. *IFAC-PapersOnLine*, 55(10), 3232–3237.

Jonsson, H. and Rudberg, M. (2014). Performance measurement for production systems in construction. Article [Online]. Available at: http://urn.kb.se/resolve?urn=urn:nbn:se:liu:diva-105991 [Accessed 25 February 2023].

Kant, E. (1785). *Fondements de la métaphysique des mœurs*. E. Kant, Königsberg.

Leitão, P. and Karnouskos, S. (2022). The emergence of ethics engineering in industrial cyber-physical systems. In *2022 IEEE 5th International Conference on Industrial Cyber-Physical Systems (ICPS)*, Coventry, 1–6.

L'Oréal éthique (2015). Charte éthique : l'éthique au quotidien. Article [Online]. Available at: https://www.loreal.com/-/media/project/loreal/brand-sites/corp/master/lcorp/2-group/news-and-documentation/publications/code-of-ethics/codeofethicsfrench.pdf [Accessed 13 January 2021].

Margherita, E.G. and Braccini, A.M. (2021). Managing industry 4.0 automation for fair ethical business development: A single case study. *Technological Forecasting and Social Change*, 172, 121048.

Mecheri, C. (2021). Ethique et Industrie 4.0 : définition et témoignage industriel. Master's Thesis, INP Grenoble.

Mezgár, I. and Váncza, J. (2022). From ethics to standards – A path via responsible AI to cyber-physical production systems. *Annual Reviews in Control*, 53, 391–404.

Morahan, M. (2015). Ethics in management. *IEEE Engineering Management Review*, 43, 23–25.

Morley, J., Kinsey, L., Elhalal, A., Garcia, F., Ziosi, M., Floridi, L. (2021). Operationalising AI ethics: Barriers, enablers, and next steps. *AI & Society*, 1–13.

Pacaux-Lemoine, M.P. and Trentesaux, D. (2019). Ethical risks of human–machine symbiosis in Industry 4.0: Insights from the human–machine cooperation approach. *IFAC-PapersOnLine*, 52(19), 19–24.

Peltier, J. (2021). Les jeunes et l'entreprise. Report, Fondation Jean-Jaurès [Online]. Available at: https://www.jean-jaures.org/publication/les-jeunes-et-lentreprise/ [Accessed 13 February 2022].

Prescient (2013). Privacy and emerging fields of science and technology: Towards a common framework for privacy and ethical assessment. Report [Online]. Available at: https://cordis.europa.eu/project/id/244779/reporting [Accessed 5 March 2015].

Radziwill, N.M. (2018). The fourth industrial revolution. *The Quality Management Journal*, 25(2), 108–109.

Rahanu, H., Georgiadou, E., Siakas, K., Ross, M., Berki, E. (2021). Ethical issues invoked by Industry 4.0. In *European Conference on Software Process Improvement*. Springer, Cham, 589–606.

Raza, S.A. (2022). A paradigm shift to ethical decision-making – Incorporating systemic epistemology into complex socio-technical decision support systems research. *Journal of Decision Systems*, 32(1), 177–200.

Ricœur, P. (2015). *Soi-même comme un autre*. Éditions du Seuil, Paris.

Salamanca, C.T., Berrah, L., David, P., Trentesaux, D. (2022). Integration of ethical issues in the 4.0 transition of internal logistics operations. In *Service Oriented, Holonic and Multi-Agent Manufacturing Systems for Industry of the Future: Proceedings of SOHOMA 2022*, Borangiu, T., Trentesaux, D., Leitão, P., Cardin, O., Lamouri, S. (eds). Springer, Cham, 304–316.

Schumacher, A., Erol, S., Sihn, W. (2016). A maturity model for assessing Industry 4.0 readiness and maturity of manufacturing enterprises. *Procedia Cirp*, 52, 161–166.

Shayganmehr, M., Kumar, A., Garza-Reyes, J.A., Moktadir, M.A. (2021). Industry 4.0 enablers for a cleaner production and circular economy within the context of business ethics: A study in a developing country. *Journal of Cleaner Production*, 281, 125280.

Sidorenko, E.L., Khisamova, Z.I., Monastyrsky, U.E. (2021). The main ethical risks of using artificial intelligence in business. In *Current Achievements, Challenges and Digital Chances of Knowledge Based Economy*, Ashmarina, S.I. and Mantulenko, V.V. (eds). Springer, Cham, 423–429.

Stahl, B.C. (2021). Ethical issues of AI. *Artificial Intelligence for a Better Future*, 35.

Steen, M., Sand, M., van de Poel, I.R. (2021). Virtue ethics for responsible innovation. *Business and Professional Ethics Journal*, 40(2), 243–268. doi: 10.5840/bpej2021319108.

Trentesaux, D. (2020). Ensuring ethics of cyber-physical and human systems: A guideline. In *International Workshop on Service Orientation in Holonic and Multi-Agent Manufacturing Systems for Industry of the Future: Proceedings of SOHOMA 2020*, Borangiu, T., Trentesaux, D., Leitão, P., Cardin, O., Lamouri, S. (eds). Springer, Cham, 223–233.

Trentesaux, D. and Caillaud, E. (2020). Ethical stakes of Industry 4.0. *IFAC-PapersOnLine*, 53(2), 17002–17007.

Trentesaux, D. and Rault, R. (2017). Designing ethical cyber-physical industrial systems. *IFAC-PapersOnLine*, 14934–14939.

Trentesaux, D., Caillaud, E., Rault, R. (2021). A framework fostering the consideration of ethics during the design of industrial cyber-physical systems. In *Service Oriented, Holonic and Multi-Agent Manufacturing Systems for Industry of the Future: Proceedings of SOHOMA 2021*, Borangiu, T., Trentesaux, D., Leitão, P., Cardin, O., Lamouri, S. (eds). Springer, Cham, 349–362.

Vakkuri, V., Kemell, K.K., Kultanen, J., Abrahamsson, P. (2020). The current state of industrial practice in artificial intelligence ethics. *IEEE Software*, 37(4), 50–57.

Vakkuri, V., Kemell, K.K., Jantunen, M., Halme, E., Abrahamsson, P. (2021). ECCOLA-A method for implementing ethically aligned AI systems. *Journal of Systems and Software*, 182, 111067.

Vuksanović Herceg, I., Kuč, V., Mijušković, V.M., Herceg, T. (2020). Challenges and driving forces for Industry 4.0 implementation. *Sustainability*, 12(10), 4208.

Yu, H., Shen, Z., Miao, C., Leung, C., Lesser, V.R., Yang, Q. (2018). Building ethics into artificial intelligence. *arXiv preprint*, 1812.0295.

7

AI for Industry: Transforming the Daily Lives of Maintenance Operators

In a highly constrained industrial environment, AI is gradually moving into an unexpected field: that of computer assistance for maintenance. In the following, we will discuss how an innovation can germinate little by little, the conditions of its acceptance and the dialogical processes in which it is involved. It is the fruit of several years of industrial cooperation and innovation.

7.1. Genesis of this innovation

Computer assistance for maintenance has long been a key area for AI. That is: expert systems (and, more specifically, fault diagnosis), event memorization and retrieval, and trend interpretation for predictive maintenance. AI focuses on the exploitation of large masses of data, or on "specialized", targeted expert knowledge, depending on the era, research fields or technological opportunities: hybrid AI has yet to be developed in this field.

Our innovation combines expert knowledge and the latest AI techniques. It is a real case study and the fruit of a dynamic R&D program involving several industrial partners: EDF R&D, FRAMATOME, SPIE Nucléaire and TECHNICATOME, Boost Conseil and ASSYSTEM. The demonstration was done by SPIX Industry.

Chapter written by Anne DOURGNON, Eunika MERCIER LAURENT and Alain ANTOINE.

Its history is part of a panorama of successful projects, some of which are cited in Mercier-Laurent (2011). These projects have the following:

– an initial phase of observation and understanding of the situation, the players involved and the project's expectations;

– a good understanding of field expertise (i.e. industrial maintenance: procedures, operators, operational context), taking KM (Knowledge Management) requirements into account (know-how is contextualized, references are shared, implicit knowledge is expressed). AI technologies and voice technologies are well known;

– the gradual discovery of needs, through experimentation, successive trial and error, as it is possible to make mistakes, readjust, etc. (Needs Discovery (Mercier-Laurent 2007));

– the synergy and dynamism of the people involved in the project, with everyone contributing to the success of the project.

Balancing the components of the "Innovation Ecosystem" is, in fact, the sine qua non of success, along with recognition of each participant, whether in terms of listening, involvement or valuing. The user is integrated into the innovation process, as advocated by Amidon (1997), which is related to Knowledge Innovation (similar ideas can be found in Xtreme Programming[1] and Design Thinking).

The pragmatic approach (CEREFIGE 2023) involves a wide range of very different professions with a common goal. It allows us to explore new paths while others are abandoned, thus paving the way for innovation. The pragmatic approach, which comes from management sciences, aims to bring together practitioners and academics in an investigative process to define the problem (problem setting) that is disrupting the course of the activity. The process involves all the stakeholders (abductive methods, problem solving) (Dourgnon et al. 1996; Avenier 2018).

This approach focuses on formal and informal discussion forums, including those involving operational staff with their more or less implicit business knowledge. This kind of research is a long-term process, and in this case, it covers several chapters. Now, we open the first chapter of this story.

1 See: http://www.extremeprogramming.org/.

7.2. Background of this innovation

As we may imagine, this is the story of a complex industrial environment where every material, object and action is part of a codified nomenclature. Every action scrupulously follows a precise sequence. This is also the story of cooperation between tradespeople: work is often done in pairs, where one works and the other checks and completes. Hours go by, one after the other. The environment is noisy, the weight of the documents is quite considerable, the attention is constant. Actions are guided by scrupulous compliance with procedures and a commitment to good practice. Shared vigilance and experience mean that everyone has a keen eye for "the little thing" that goes wrong, the rag lying around, the missing screw or the oil stain glistening on the floor.

Industrial maintenance, whether preventive or curative, scheduled or not scheduled, is a long sequence of checks and actions, as well as of diagnoses. Diagnoses are deductive: from a cause, we deduce consequences; inductive: from consequences, we go back to causes; abductive: from symptoms or situations, we infer possible causes (Dourgnon et al. 1996).

The language is coded in a reference system specific to the field. However, maintenance operators and the other stakeholders involved do not use these codes indefinitely. They also like to use a more natural, colorful language, and we can understand them!

Imagine two operators in charge of specific equipment. In the preparatory phase, as well as throughout their work, they apply procedures, fill in forms, take notes in their notebooks, discuss similar situations where machines have malfunctioned and come up with ideas.

7.2.1. *A low-key innovation*

Certain memories resurface: didn't this machine have a similar fault in another place, at another time? Didn't a colleague tell me to do that "small thing" at that precise moment?

Hazards abound in this well-ordered world: I have forgotten to take out my garbage bag, a screw is stuck, and I cannot get it loose, etc. These are all unprecedented situations in which we talk to each other, i.e. to humans! Face-to-face with a colleague, remotely by audio and, more rarely, by video. No non-human interaction was planned or even envisaged. We are referring to dialogical interactions (Mourey 2018), of course, not to computerized interactions – more or less sophisticated – or "paper" interactions with ubiquitous documentation.

There are already a lot of machines in these environments, and adding artificiality may not be a good idea. So, the question of dialogue with an artificial being has never been raised. And yet, the environment is already quite "robotized". The operators use "secure communication": each response from an actor is duly repeated by the pair, then confirmed to minimize the risk of error. It is indeed artificial, in the sense that there is nothing natural about it. In fact, we refer to it as *communication*, not *dialogue*. This mode of communication is documented in a small memo, very well done (it is obvious that the experiment took place long ago!), didactic but mandatory in its application.

Observation of these dialogue modes inspired me to propose a dialogue with a virtual assistant capable of dealing with unexpected situations. This assistant would be able to "reason" by analogy, requiring the "memories", the feedback of colleagues.

All the partners involved in this part of our collaborative R&D project ConnexITy (EDF 2023), namely EDF R&D, FRAMATOME, SPIE Nucléaire and TECHNICATOME, were keen to experiment within this collaborative framework. From the outset, the teams concerned – maintenance operators and trainers – were involved in the project. This was a great opportunity.

The partners in this experiment have the following skills: artificial intelligence (EDF and FRAMATOME), ergonomics (idem), "programming" and organization of maintenance (EDF and FRAMATOME), operational maintenance (SPIE Nucléaire), training in maintenance operations (SPIE nucléaire), digitization of maintenance operations (TECHNICATOME), augmented reality (EDF and FRAMATOME) and Data Science (EDF, Boost Conseil, ASSYSTEM).

7.3. The naysayers

Nevertheless, things were not quite that simple. In March 2018, we organized an exchange meeting with 18 people (EDF, SPIE Nucléaire,

FRAMATOME, TECHNICATOME, ASSYSTEM, BOOST Conseil, DEDALE). A video demonstration was included in the program.

The demonstration filmed a "dialogue" between a technician and a voice assistant. The voice assistant took the initiative, and the technician responded as best they could to the assistant's questions. The "dialogue" suffered from two issues: an overly artificial standard voice, accentuated by the video, and the unpleasant impression that the technician was "enslaved" to the voice assistant. This impression was heightened by the fact that the participants in the meeting were not involved in the scene but were merely actors in the background.

The following extract from the audience's reactions reflects moderate enthusiasm:

– "not really thrilled";

– "not convinced";

– "not sure it's suitable";

– "beware of the robotization of human beings";

– "I can't imagine operators talking to a machine";

– "mistrust";

– "for training, not for the field";

– "doubts about the value";

– "what about teamwork?";

– "little relevance";

– "will it save time?".

These reactions are all the more understandable given the highly constrained working environment. Take, for example, the tool inventory, which is mandatory before any work is carried out. This inventory is exhaustive: all tools are listed, and the expiry date of their calibration certificate or compliance with regulations is checked. The sequence is therefore tedious, as everything is read and confirmed in secure communication. If, on top of this, a robot-controlled inventory is imposed, it is easy to understand the reluctance and even rejection of those involved.

With the help of ergonomists, we reworked the dialogue mode by switching postures. The operator now has the upper hand. They chose the order in which the inventory is taken. This latitude is small but essential. The human grabs the tool in front of them – a torque wrench, a screwdriver – then specifies its characteristics and quality. Then, they move on to the next, etc. In addition to freedom in the order in which tools are listed, there is also the freedom of language. In the event of ambiguity, the voice assistant suggests that the operator check.

This simple example illustrates the new paradigm. The operator carries out the inventory that the voice assistant confirms, and not the other way around. The environment is already very constrained, so let us avoid constraining it even more!

7.4. Dealing with hazards

Luckily, the ConnexLab Digital Innovation Laboratory is an operational laboratory that puts ideas to good use. This Lab is dedicated to the nuclear industry and is part of EDF Lab campus in Paris Saclay (Marcel Boiteux Campus). When I joined the project at the end of 2017, a very credible demonstrator had been produced, with a life-size reproduction of the power plant environment: a 3D copy of a pump, with its control box and cable, on the floor grating, with access protected by chains and signs, and the photo of a power plant room in the background. To reinforce the illusion and validate the concepts in the field, the demonstrations were carried out by real operators in white overalls, equipped with all the necessary representative tools.

In this age of the "remote", it seems anachronistic to assert that being all on the spot, in Saclay's ConnexLab, was decisive. In this Lab, the operators tell and relive – what they believe to be – their *real* lives. At first glance, the work of maintenance operators is governed by procedures. But these operators have eyes and ears, they see and hear above the ambient noise. A rag lying around, a screw falling to the floor, an unusual noise? So, many hazards need to be dealt with without deviating from procedures. In the implacable sequentiality of procedures, micro-events disrupt the supposedly linear course of activity.

Taking these hazards into account was therefore a priority. François Palaci, an ergonomic research engineer at EDF R&D, happily proposed the idea of a *Digital Concierge*. This savvy concierge, always ready to listen, would respond to solicitations and may even anticipate them. We put this idea into practice: during the inventory prior to the pump seal change operation, the Digital Concierge advises the operator to bring a waste bag (to collect the used seal).

7.5. A decisive demonstration

Six months later came the "Electric Days" in October 2018. This was a major three-day exhibition of innovations in the field, held in the vast hall of the Cité des Sciences at La Villette, Paris.

Thanks to development by SimSoft Industry (now SPIX Industry), we were able to offer an immersive demonstration "as if you were there". The operator interacted with the voice assistant via a microphone attached to their headset. The pre-inventory of tooling, the maintenance operation itself, then the inventory at the end of the operation: everything was carried out in an almost routine manner, in strict compliance with procedures. The sequence seemed natural, thanks to the ergonomists! In doing so, we lifted the taboo on the use of voice assistants in power plants.

Figure 7.1. *Stand demonstration. For a color version of this figure, see www.iste.co.uk/abel/ethics.zip*

This entirely "wired" demonstration, with no other ambition than to remove this taboo, led to subsequent developments at EDF, and work has continued in the rest of the ConnexITy project.

This innovation in usage was made possible by bringing together the views of several professions (AI, ergonomics, voice and language processing, maintenance and maintenance training).

7.6. The keys to success

The collaborative framework of the experiment avoided the pitfalls of bad vocal experiences, which can quickly become irritating. Putting the people directly concerned into the situation was a determining factor. Dialogue is natural, and no one is "stuck" in a sequential sequence of voice commands with no way out. It must always be possible to ask questions to our *vocal companion*, without deviating from procedures: "Is there a wiring problem on this valve box?" (to be asked in a more or less polished form).

Recopying sequential procedural operation in a voice assistant is doomed to failure and rejection. We need to "*de-sequentialize*", to bring life as it is into the power plant. For this, we need the cooperation of ergonomists. We also need to take the time to explain the unspoken aspects of the operators' specialties, in a way they can understand. Best to remind the operator that, with this valve, the housing seal maintenance is not the same as with the previous one. It is also a good idea to point out prohibited wiring. Operators should be able to ask: "Why?". Sharing experience also helps us to memorize: "don't forget to take a waste bag".

The voice assistant is a companion, empathetic, cautious, attentive, focused. It is a communicator, a very smart robot, almost a confidant, to whom you could tell your discoveries and observations, just to replace the little logbook. The debriefing at the end would be much easier (it could be textual or vocal). This is a good time to talk about everything that happened, and it is worth sharing.

Creating innovative work groups, such as ConnexLab, with a laboratory that replicates a power plant, is very effective. This type of collective limits the effects of disconnection between the field and analysts. It fosters both perspective-taking and cross-fertilization. Acquiring knowledge is then easier, for better understanding and identification of the type of information to be collected. The more learning is updated and adapted, the more "alive" the robot becomes. New questions may arise. We could even go a step further and consider equipment as companions with a voice: "What type of valve are you?"; "I'm an electrically operated valve with manual release".

This dialogical process would allow a joint construction of an excellent quality Knowledge Base, which would evolve over time. Moreover, the response would be adjusted according to the interlocutor:

– either dialogical: exchanges are discursive, and the listener is also a bit of an actor;

– or monological: the speaker tells a story.

Learning through dialogue is not the same as "transmitting knowledge", which is why it is so difficult. And it is so much easier to give presentations with slides. Here, it is a real-life situation, with a continuous recording of knowledge.

7.7. Overcoming obstacles

Technology is not an obstacle here. It exists and is already omnipresent in the domestic environment. It must, of course, be adapted to the industrial environment, which has its own language, as well as a sustained ambient noise. But the art of understanding the problem in its technological and human context, and of choosing, combining and maintaining technologies over time, is a difficult one.

Another challenge is to make the most of all thc participants, and to create and maintain an overall dynamic. This requires dialogue, common references and a shared vocabulary. This is why the idea of Knowledge-based AI (ontologies or other ad hoc knowledge models, developed together as part of an innovation process with users (Mercier-Laurent 2020)) flourished and gave rise to intense production, before dying out because it was not taken up and integrated into the tools. In the current situation, contextual knowledge is not integrated into traditional chatbots.

Finally, taking into account the complexity of real-life situations implies a systemic approach, favoring the abstraction/generalization of concrete cases in a global analysis. We need to work on complex real-life situations, combining different levels (professions and players, equipment and systems, activities and procedures, safety and security with their regulatory framework, events and hazards, past, present and future). This is the price to pay for modularity, genericity and reusability (Newel 1982; Chandrasekaran 1983; Clancey 1985).

7.8. Outlook

Numerous perspectives are open and some are already underway. These include the thorny subject of learning from experience, which has been tackled with varying degrees of success: using data analysis methods (Lannoy and Procaccia 1994), case-based reasoning (Auriol 1995), natural language processing and, more recently, generative AI[2].

Despite today's highly constrained format, there is still a certain amount of freedom, with the possibility of proposing different paths as the dialogue progresses. There is now a new way of learning from experience: on the one hand, "tell me what you did" (storytelling) and, on the other, given the difficulty of finding appropriate tools (not too silent or too talkative), the possibility of an open dialogue. Why not a tool intelligent enough to fill in the gaps itself? Knowledge could be acquired in real time, with the possibility of checking and querying similar experiences along the way. This would allow us to take a step back as we know that the experience of colleagues can save precious time!

Today, the time between the commissioning of power plants and the end of their operation is long, very long. This inevitably leads to semantic shifts (Dourgnon and Antoine 2022): people no longer understand each other, even though they are talking about the same system. This is all the more problematic as experience is capitalized on for future use, even years later. This effect is exacerbated by the multiplicity of players belonging to different structures, and by the lack of collaboration. In fact, a KM approach involves several stakeholders with a common goal in mind. Fourth-generation AI, combining the advantages of symbolic and connectionist AI, could provide part of the answer (Mercier-Laurent 2021).

As for generative AI, now perceived as a magic wand, it is only in its infancy. The art of using it, particularly in a complex industrial environment, has yet to be learned (by asking generative AI the right questions and "injecting" the user's knowledge in the dialogue).

2 At IMDR in particular. See: https://www.imdr.eu.

Can you imagine asking an algorithm to combine expert knowledge to "invent" the procedure to be applied? On the one hand, every step of the reasoning or procedure to be followed is now deterministic (procedures are described in exhaustive manuals). On the other hand, in this field, the trained eye of operators enables them to appreciate the approach to be followed. Know-how is always contextual. Generative AI is not yet able to understand the particularities of context, so it remains an appendix, to be explored independently. Some knowledge will always remain in the heads of experts (tacit knowledge). Nevertheless, in the near future, the use of generative AI on private databases could yield good results. This remains to be explored.

7.9. Acknowledgments

We would like to thank Aminata Mbengue and Jean Brangé (Boost Conseil), François Palaci, Stéphane Chassaigne, Benoît Levesque, Fabien Leray and Guillaume Terrasse (EDF R&D), Jean-Bernard Thevenon (FRAMATOME), Choukri Trabelsi, Gilles Chareyre and Karim Touaouza (SPIE Nucléaire) and Hubert Guillermain (TECHNICATOME).

7.10. References

Amidon, D. (1997). *The Innovation Strategy for the Knowledge Economy*. Butterworth Heinemann, Newton.

Auriol, E. (1995). Intégration d'approches symboliques pour le raisonnement à partir d'exemples : l'induction et le raisonnement par cas dans le cadre du diagnostic technique. PhD Thesis, Université de Paris 9, Paris.

Avenier, M.-J. (2018). La stratégie "chemin faisant" revisitée 20 ans après. In *Stratégie organisationnelle par le dialogue*, Fabbe-Costes, N. and Gialdini, L. (eds). Economica, Paris, 43–52.

CEREFIGE (2023). Approche pragmatiste des organisations [Online]. Available at: https://cerefige.univ-lorraine.fr/ressources-approche-pragmatiste-des-organisations/ [Accessed 12 September 2023].

Chandrasekaran, B. (1983). Towards a taxonomy of problem solving types. *AI Magazine*, 4(1), 9.

Clancey, W.J. (1985). Heuristic classification. *Artificial Intelligence*, 27, 289–350.

Dourgnon, A. and Antoine, A. (2022). Glissements sémantiques et Intelligence artificielle. *L'information grammaticale*, 172, 29–36.

Dourgnon-Hanoune, A., Porcheron, M., Ricard, B. (1996), Méthodes d'intelligence artificielle pour le diagnostic. *Journées franco-allemandes sur la mécanique et IA : les applications*, Paris, 1–9.

EDF (2023). Le ConnexLab, Laboratoire d'Innovations Numériques de la filière nucléaire fête ses 4 ans ! [Online]. Available at: https://www.edf.fr/groupe-edf/inventer-lavenir-de-lenergie/rd-un-savoir-faire-mondial/toutes-les-actualites-de-la-rd/le-connexlab-laboratoire-dinnovations-numeriques-de-la-filiere-nucleaire-fete-ses-4-ans [Accessed 17 June 2023].

Lannoy, A. and Procaccia, H. (1994). *Méthodes avancées d'analyse des bases de données du retour d'expérience industriel*. EDF, Paris.

Mercier-Laurent, E. (2007). Rôle de l'ordinateur dans le processus global de l'innovation à partir des connaissances. HDR Thesis, Université Lyon 3, Lyon [Online]. Available at: http://emlkmi.free.fr/fichiers/hdr-eunika.pdf [Accessed 15 September 2023].

Mercier-Laurent, E. (2011). *Les écosystèmes de l'innovation*. Hermes-Lavoisier, Paris.

Mercier-Laurent, E. (2020). The future of AI and AI for the future. In *Unimagined Futures – ICT Opportunities and Challenges*, Strous, L., Johnson, R., Grier, D.A., Swade, D. (eds). Springer, Cham.

Mercier-Laurent, E. (2021). Greening and smarting IT – Case of digital transformation. In *Artificial Intelligence for Knowledge Management, Energy and Sustainability*, Mercier-Laurent, E. and Kayakutlu, G. (eds). Springer, Cham, 637.

Mourey, D. (2018). Coordination et coopération des supply chains : un processus dialogique, créatif et résistible qui s'accomplit chemin faisant. *Revue Française de Gestion*, 44, 125–141. doi: 10.3166/rfg.2019.00295.

Newel, A. (1982). The knowledge level. *Artificial Intelligence*, 18, 87–127.

Rousseau, F. (2015) Touchez vos idées. Fédérer par les objets 3D [Online]. Available at: https://vimeo.com/113017326 [Accessed 8 March 2023].

Conclusion

C.1. From ethics to responsibility

The digital transition of our economic, environmental and social ecosystem is in full swing. As part of its Horizon Europe research and innovation program, the European Commission has launched the "Twin Transition" challenge, which aims to harmonize the digital and ecological transitions in an era of global warming. This challenge is the consequence of an economic and societal model underpinned by connectivity to increasingly extensive and influential information systems, which has sometimes led to deregulations (or risks of deregulation) of the societal and natural ecosystems, as it is primarily focused on profit generation. The deregulation (or risk of deregulation) is sometimes generated by the artificial intelligence (AI) systems themselves, or sometimes the impacts. Here are just a few examples:

– the risks associated with generative AI (e.g. ChatGPT, Bing, Gemini, etc.) in terms of misinformation, identity theft and intellectual property;

– the dissemination of false information, which can undermine the trust, quality and value of AI systems and their results;

– infringement of intellectual property rights, which can undermine the innovation, competitiveness and creativity of AI developers and users;

– vulnerability to cybersecurity threats, which can compromise the reliability, robustness and security of AI systems and their data;

Conclusion written by Hedi KARRAY.

– lack of data confidentiality, which can expose the personal and sensitive information of AI users and stakeholders to unauthorized or malicious access;

– biases in AI algorithms, which often reflect historical biases in training data, remain a major challenge.

These societal and natural ecosystem deregulation risks represent a major challenge (Mikalef et al. 2022). They point to the responsibility of AI to adopt approaches that help regulate this ecosystem. As these AI-based systems contribute to the digital transition, it is necessary to consolidate the notion of responsibility in their design.

The notion of responsible AI (RAI) refers to the practice of designing, developing and deploying AI systems that adhere to ethical principles and values, such as fairness, accountability, transparency and human dignity, and can therefore be trusted (Dignum 2017). The notion of responsibility in AI is not limited solely to the notion of moral ethics (studied in philosophy and more generally in the humanities and social sciences). It extends to a notion of applied ethics that comes under technically defined and sometimes even regulated practices, principles and rules (e.g. RGPD) (Shneiderman 2021; Zhu et al. 2022).

C.2. Principles and challenges behind responsible AI

For AI systems to be considered responsible, they must comply with a number of principles (Arrieta et al. 2020; Trocin et al. 2023):

– *Trust*: this refers to the ability to understand, explain and justify the operation, results and impacts of AI systems, as well as ensuring their compliance with ethical and legal standards. Trust also involves reducing bias and discrimination in data and algorithms, and promoting transparency and accountability among AI players.

– *Privacy*: this concerns the protection of personal and sensitive data collected, processed and shared by AI systems, as well as respect for the consent and rights of individuals. Privacy also involves preventing data leakage, theft and misuse, and implementing mechanisms for data encryption, anonymization and minimization.

– *Safety*: this involves the prevention and detection of attacks, intrusions and manipulations aimed at compromising the integrity, availability and performance of AI systems, as well as harming users and third parties. Safety also involves strengthening the robustness, resilience and reliability of AI systems, and developing verification, validation and testing methods.

– *Fairness*: this means ensuring that AI systems treat everyone fairly and avoid affecting groups of people in similar situations differently. For example, when AI systems provide recommendations on medical treatment, loan applications or employment, they should make the same suggestions to all of those with similar symptoms, financial circumstances or professional qualifications. Fairness also means reducing bias and discrimination in data and algorithms, and promoting transparency and accountability among AI players.

– *Inclusion*: this means ensuring that AI systems meet the needs and expectations of all potential users, taking into account their cultural, social, linguistic, physical and cognitive diversity. For example, when AI systems offer translation, speech recognition or text-to-speech services, they should be able to handle a variety of languages, accents, dialects and modes of expression. Inclusion also means encouraging the participation and consultation of users and stakeholders in the design, deployment and use of AI systems.

– *Reliability*: this means ensuring that AI systems operate at expected levels of performance, even in the presence of uncertainty or danger. Reliability also involves preventing and detecting errors, failures and malfunctions in AI systems, and correcting or mitigating them.

– *Robustness*: this involves enhancing the ability of AI systems to withstand or overcome adverse conditions, including digital security risks. Robustness also involves developing methods for verifying, validating and testing AI systems, and making them adaptable to changes in context or environment.

– *Safety*: this means ensuring that these systems do not cause unintentional damage to users or the environment. AI systems are increasingly complex, autonomous and interconnected, making them difficult to control, predict and understand. In addition, AI systems can have significant impacts on society, the economy and the environment with uncontrollable scenarios. This can include global systemic risks such as nuclear war and cyberwarfare due to the use of AI, as well as dangers linked to self-enhancing AI systems with their emerging uncontrollable goals.

– *Interpretability*: this is the ability to understand, explain and justify the operation, results and impacts of AI systems, as well as ensuring their compliance with ethical and legal standards. Interpretability also involves providing relevant, easy-to-understand information to people affected by AI systems, so that they can challenge or accept their decisions.

– *Transparency*: this means disclosing and communicating information about AI systems, so that people who interact with them can know when, how and why they are being used. Transparency also means making AI systems accessible and verifiable by independent parties, and respecting the rights and expectations of users and stakeholders.

– *Control*: this involves mastering and regulating AI systems, so that they act in accordance with human intentions and values, and do not exceed the limits set by designers, operators or regulators. Control also involves anticipating and managing the potential risks associated with AI systems, and putting in place mechanisms for correction, repair and deactivation.

– *Accountability and liability*: this is the obligation to account for the actions, decisions and impacts of AI systems, as well as the ability to assume the consequences and repair any damage. Accountability also implies defining and distributing the roles and obligations of AI players, such as designers, operators, users and regulators.

– *Governance*: this refers to the set of rules, standards, processes and institutions that frame and guide the development, deployment and use of AI systems, as well as stakeholder participation and representation. Governance also involves promoting all of the values and principles of responsible AI.

C.3. Responsible AI: a threat or an opportunity?

The goal of responsible AI is to provide systems that are fair and beneficial to people, society and the environment. From a societal and environmental perspective, responsible AI is an opportunity to reduce the risks and costs of AI, such as compliance, devaluation and trade-offs. It will ensure that AI systems comply with laws and regulations, mitigate potential harm and balance the interests of different stakeholders, namely (Ghallab 2019):

– improving applications in healthcare, education, industry and the environment;

– reducing inequalities and achieving greater inclusiveness;

– protecting humans from harmful applications such as emotional dependency;

– eliminating and combating prejudice: sexist, ethnic, racial;

– minimizing the risks of a hybrid workforce;

– improving a human-centered human–machine partnership for task completion;

– fighting conspiracy theories and misinformation through transparency;

– creating AI systems that are reliable, beneficial and aligned with human values;

– creating an open AI culture.

From an economic point of view, the potential economic impact of AI is enormous and could generate a great deal of profit (Renieris et al. 2023). Overall, AI could contribute up to $15.7 trillion to the global economy by 2030 (Rao 2017). According to studies (Purdy and Daugherty 2016), by 2035, AI-based tools could contribute to increasing business profitability by an average of 38%. Indeed, AI tools give small- and medium-sized enterprises (SMEs) the opportunity to innovate, as they can better predict customer behavior and prices, and anticipate changes in demand (Kergroach and Bianchini 2021). Also, these tools could help SMEs to increase their productivity, for example, by refocusing activities on higher value-added functions, or by reducing costs. Such systems could also help SMEs in particular to overcome administrative and financial bottlenecks and increase their responsiveness (Kergroach and Bianchini 2021). According to studies, responsible AI could increase this impact by 15–40% (Chui et al. 2023).

Many companies are beginning to understand that responsible AI is not a brake or a threat to profit, but rather an opportunity. At least 10% of the AI budgets of 80% of companies will be committed to complying with regulations that primarily tackle notions related to responsibility from 2024 onwards. Regulatory pressure generates a large potential market opportunity for private equity and venture capital investors to fund start-ups (Accenture 2002).

C.4. Responsible AI challenges

While responsible AI offers significant opportunities, a number of challenges and obstacles stand in the way of its progress. Resolving these issues is crucial to ensuring the ethical development and deployment of AI technologies. Some of the main challenges include:

– *Lack of common norms, standards and frameworks*: there is neither a consensus nor a clear and consistent definition of what responsible AI means and how to measure and guarantee it. Indeed, countries, regions, disciplines and stakeholders may have different ethical principles, values and objectives for AI systems. As a result, international collaboration and coordination are very difficult to achieve in order to reach consensus on international standards and regulations.

– *Lack of technical and organizational capacity*: organizations (especially SMEs) lack the expertise, resources and support needed to adopt and implement responsible AI systems.

– *Lack of diverse and multidisciplinary stakeholders*: most AI systems are designed and developed on an ad hoc basis by a (small) homogeneous group of people, without sufficient input and feedback from diverse and multidisciplinary stakeholders. This can lead to biased, unfair and irresponsible AI systems that harm or exclude certain people.

– *Lack of alignment with humanistic values and goals*: most AI systems are focused on profit, efficiency or performance, without considering the potential trade-offs and risks to human values and goals.

– *Lack of respect for data ownership and consent to data use*: without clear regulations, it can be difficult to know who owns user data, whether it is the individual user, the platform collecting it, or both. This can lead to misuse or exploitation of personal data without proper consent.

In addition to these challenges, there are a number of technical barriers that need to be overcome in order to build responsible AI systems. These include:

– *Explicability and transparency*: many AI algorithms, especially those based on complex deep learning models, are often considered "black boxes" with limited explicability. This means that the system itself does not understand why it has obtained a result or performed an action. In addition, the terms of use and privacy policies of AI systems can be complex and not very user-friendly, leading to "consent fatigue".

– *Managing large quantities of data*: striking a balance between exploiting data for AI development and protecting individuals' right to privacy is a complex challenge. In addition to ensuring data accuracy, implementing the right to be forgotten and other data-related rights can pose technical challenges. It should also be noted that the historical biases present in the training data of self-learning AI systems remain a major challenge.

– *Rapid technological progress*: AI models and techniques are advancing very rapidly and can outpace the development of software infrastructures for responsible AI, leading to gaps in the response to emerging ethical concerns.

– *Complexity of autonomous systems*: in the field of robotics and autonomous systems, ethical advances and challenges linked to decision-making, responsibility and risks of misuse are becoming more complex.

C.5. An ecosystem for responsible AI

Addressing these challenges and barriers requires a collaborative effort from researchers, policymakers, digital industry leaders and the wider community. Research, legal and societal discussions, and proactive measures underway (the European AI ACT) are essential to advance responsible AI and minimize the risks associated with AI systems. This progress will only be possible through cooperation and collaboration within an innovation ecosystem, supported by a network of actors and activities, that promotes the ethical development and use of responsible AI (Deshpande and Sharp 2022). It includes researchers, developers, users, regulators, policymakers, civil society and other stakeholders involved in the creation, implementation and governance of AI systems that adhere to ethical principles and values.

Research and innovation players

– *Research institutions and universities*: researchers explore ethical considerations, bias mitigation techniques and the transparency of AI algorithms. They contribute to the theoretical foundations and practical applications of responsible AI.

– *Industry initiatives and consortia*: several industry groups and consortia bring together companies, experts and organizations to collaborate on defining standards, best practices and frameworks for responsible AI.

– *Open source communities*: open source projects focused on responsible AI, such as *TensorFlow's Fairness Indicators and IBM's AI Fairness 360*, foster collaboration and the development of tools that promote transparency, fairness and responsibility in AI.

AI system developers

– *Start-ups and innovation hubs*: start-ups drive innovation in the field of responsible AI, developing new tools, algorithms and approaches to address ethical challenges. Innovation hubs provide a platform for these start-ups to collaborate, receive support and commercialize responsible AI solutions.

– *Technology providers*: *technology companies and AI technology providers invest in responsible AI research and development* (Accenture 2002).

– *Consulting firms*: *consulting firms specializing in AI ethics and responsible AI practices help companies meet ethical challenges.*

– The SHS and ethics community: *AI ethics experts and opinion leaders* – social sciences and humanities experts and AI ethics opinion leaders contribute to the responsible AI ecosystem by sharing ideas, participating in discussions and influencing the direction of ethical considerations in AI development and deployment.

Regulatory and social organizations

– *Governmental and regulatory organizations*: contribute by developing and enforcing policies and regulations to ensure ethical use, protect user privacy and address the societal impact of AI technologies.

– *Ethics and standard organizations*: organizations focused on AI ethical considerations and standards, such as the *AI Ethics Global Network* and the *IEEE Ethics in Action Committee*, which help define guidelines and standards for responsible AI.

– *Nongovernmental organizations*: NGOs dedicated to technology ethics, such as the *AI Now Institute*, play a role in promoting responsible AI practices, conducting research and engaging with policymakers.

– *Civil society*: civil society is essential for responsible AI. Forums, public debates and awareness campaigns help to inform the public about AI-related issues, gather diverse viewpoints and ensure that AI technologies align with societal values.

C.5.1. *Actions for responsible AI*

The responsible AI ecosystem is already active and has set up and continues to initiate actions to strengthen and support the transformation and transition of AI systems towards responsible AI.

Research avenues explored (Dignum 2019; Wang et al. 2020; Lu et al. 2023):

– *Neuro-symbolic (hybrid) AI*: a type of AI that combines neural network-based learning (e.g. deep learning) with symbolic knowledge representation and logical reasoning (e.g. ontologies).

– *Explainable AI*: a type of AI that can provide meaningful and intuitive explanations for the behavior and results of AI systems, for example, via feature attribution, counterfactual analysis and causal inference.

– *Algorithmic fairness techniques*: algorithms that actively detect and mitigate biases in AI models, such as reweighting of training data, adversarial training and fairness-conscious machine learning.

– *Federated learning*: approaches for training models on decentralized devices or servers without exchanging raw data. This helps protect user confidentiality.

C.5.2. *Policy measures: initiatives and regulations*

The Presidency of the European Commission has announced the launch of a new initiative in 2023 to make European supercomputers available to innovative European AI start-ups to train their reliable AI models. The commission also announced the "GenAI4EU" initiative, which aims to support the development of new use cases and emerging applications in Europe's fourteen industrial ecosystems. In 2024, an amendment to the *EuroHPC* regulation was established to create AI factories.

The European Union is also making advances on the legal framework related to AI, positioning it as a pioneer in the world with the *DATA Act* and *AI Act*. In November 2023, the Council of the EU adopted a new regulation on harmonized rules on access to and fair use of data (DATA Act). In December 2023, the EU reached agreement on the world's first comprehensive law on AI, which will support the development, deployment and adoption of reliable and responsible AI.

C.5.3. *Technical progress*

A technological upheaval began in November 2022 with a new type of AI system unknown to the general public, called generative AI with the introduction of ChatGPT by OpenAI. Since then, according to NBC, interest in AI has accelerated exponentially in the technology sector.

Responsible AI has become a priority for many companies, and will become more important over the next five years[1]. According to Gartner, by 2025, 70% of organizations will have operationalized their AI architectures due to the rapid maturity of AI orchestration initiatives.

C.5.4. *Public awareness and education*

According to the European Consumer Organization's AI survey (2020), more than half of Europeans believe that companies are using AI to manipulate consumer decisions, while 60% of respondents in some countries believe that AI is leading to greater abuse of personal data (BEUC 2020).

Raising awareness of the risks of AI and popularizing its issues among the general public will increase the consciousness of users (consumers of AI). They will then demand a rapid transition to responsible and ethical AI systems.

C.6. References

Accenture (2002). From AI compliance to competitive advantage: Becoming responsible by design. Report, Accenture, Dublin.

Agarwal, S. and Mishra, S. (2021). *Responsible AI*. Springer, Cham.

Arrieta, A.B., Díaz-Rodríguez, N., Del Ser, J., Bennetot, A., Tabik, S., Barbado, A., Herrera, F. (2020). Explainable Artificial Intelligence (XAI): Concepts, taxonomies, opportunities and challenges toward responsible AI. *Information Fusion*, 58, 82–115.

BEUC (2020). Artificial Intelligence: What consumers say. Report, BEUC, Brussels.

Chui, M., Hazan, E., Roberts, R., Singla, A., Smaje, K., Sukharevsky, A., Zemmel, R. (2023). *The Economic Potential of Generative AI The Next Productivity Frontier*. McKinsey & Company, London.

Deshpande, A. and Sharp, H. (2022). Responsible AI systems: Who are the stakeholders? In *Proceedings of the 2022 AAAI/ACM Conference on AI, Ethics, and Society*, 227–236. ACM, New York.

1 See Venturebeat (2020): https://venturebeat.com/ai/how-people-are-using-ai-to-detect-and-fight-the-coronavirus/.

Dignum, V. (2017). Responsible artificial intelligence: designing AI for human values. PhD Thesis, Delft University of Technology, Delft.

Dignum, V. (2019). *Responsible Artificial Intelligence: How to Develop and Use AI in a Responsible Way*. Springer, Cham.

Ghallab, M. (2019). Responsible AI: Requirements and challenges. *AI Perspectives*, 1(1), 1–7.

Kergroach, S. and Bianchini, M.M. (2021). *The Digital Transformation of SMEs*. OECD Publishing, Paris.

Lu, Q., Zhu, L., Xu, X., Whittle, J. (2023). Responsible-AI-by-design: A pattern collection for designing responsible AI systems. *IEEE Software*, 40(3), 63–71.

Mikalef, P., Conboy, K., Lundström, J.E., Popovič, A. (2022). Thinking responsibly about responsible AI and 'The dark side' of AI. *European Journal of Information Systems*, 31(3), 257–268.

Purdy, M. and Daugherty, P. (2016). Why artificial intelligence is the future of growth. Remarks at AI now: The social and economic implications of artificial intelligence technologies in the near term. Report, Accenture, Dublin.

Rao, A.S. and Verweij, G. (2017). Sizing the prize: What's the real value of AI for your business and how can you capitalise? Report, PWC, London.

Renieris, E.M., Kiron, D., Mills, S. (2023). Building robust RAI programs as third-party AI tools proliferate. MIT Sloan Management Review, MIT, Cambridge.

Shneiderman, B. (2021). Responsible AI: Bridging from ethics to practice. *Communications of the ACM*, 64(8), 32–35.

Trocin, C., Mikalef, P., Papamitsiou, Z., Conboy, K. (2023). Responsible AI for digital health: A synthesis and a research agenda. *Information Systems Frontiers*, 25(6), 2139–2157.

Wang, Y., Xiong, M., Olya, H. (2020). Toward an understanding of responsible artificial intelligence practices. In *Proceedings of the 53rd Hawaii International Conference on System Sciences. Hawaii International Conference on System Sciences (HICSS)*, 4962–4971. University of Sheffield, Sheffield.

Zhu, L., Xu, X., Lu, Q., Governatori, G., Whittle, J. (2022). AI and ethics – Operationalizing responsible AI. In *Humanity Driven AI: Productivity, Well-being, Sustainability and Partnership*, Chen, F. and Zhou, J. (eds). Springer, Cham.

List of Authors

Marie-Hélène ABEL
Heudiasyc, CNRS
Université de technologie
Compiègne
France

Alain ANTOINE
Université de Lorraine
Nancy
France

Bruno BACHIMONT
Costech
Université de technologie
Compiègne
France

Lamia BERRAH
LISTIC
Université Savoie-Mont-Blanc
Annecy
France

Grégory BONNET
MAD-GREYC
Normandie Université
Caen
France

Nadjet BOURDACHE
MAD-GREYC
Normandie Université
Caen
France

Emmanuel CAILLAUD
CNAM
Paris
France

Anne DOURGNON
EDF R&D
Chatou
France

Jean-Gabriel GANASCIA
CNRS
Sorbonne Université
Paris
France

Lou GRIMAL
Université de Chambéry
France

Hedi KARRAY
Université de Technologie
Tarbes
France

Nada MATTA
LIST3N
Université de technologie
Troyes
France

Eunika MERCIER LAURENT
Université de Reims
Champagne-Ardenne
France

Alain MILLE
LIRIS, CNRS
INSA
Lyon
France

Abdel-Illah MOUADDIB
MAD-GREYC
Normandie Université
Caen
France

Inès SAAD
MIS
Université de Picardie Jules Verne
Amiens
France

Karine SAMUEL
CERAG
INP-Grenoble
France

Florence SÈDES
IRIT, CNRS
Université de Toulouse
France

Mihail STOJANOVSKI
MAD-GREYC
Normandie Université
Caen
France

Damien TRENTESAUX
LAMIH
Université Polytechnique
Hauts-de-France
Lille
France

Index

I, M

N, O

P, Q

R, S

T, U

V, W

Other titles from

ISTE

in

Information Systems, Web and Pervasive Computing

2025

STOCKINGER Peter
The Art of Communication: Semiotic Foundations and Strategic using Applications

2024

ALBAN Daniel, EYNAUD Philippe, RICHET Jean-Loup, VITARI Claudio
Information Systems Management: Governance, Urbanization and Alignment – 2nd edition

PINET François, BATTON-HUBERT Mireille, DESJARDIN Eric
Geographical Data Imperfection 2: Use Cases

SEDKAOUI Soraya
Automated Data Analytics: Combining Human Creativity and AI Power using ChatGPT

2023

POMEROL Jean-Charles
Action in Uncertainty: Expertise, Decision and Crisis Management

REVEST Valérie, LIOTARD Isabelle
Digital Transformation and Public Policies: Current Issues

2022

ACCART Jean-Philippe
Library Transformation Strategies

BEN REBAH Hassen, BOUKTHIR Hafedh, CHÉDEBOIS Antoine
Website Design and Development with HTML5 and CSS3

BOADA Martí, LAZARO Antonio, GIRBAU David, VILLARINO Ramón
Battery-less NFC Sensors for the Internet of Things

BRÉZILLON Patrick, TURNER Roy M.
Modeling and Use of Context in Action

CHAMOUX Jean-Pierre
The Digital Era 3: Customs and Practices

KARAM Elie
General Contractor Business Model for Smart Cities: Fundamentals and Techniques

LAURENT Sébastien-Yves
Conflicts, Crimes and Regulations in Cyberspace
(Cybersecurity Set – Volume 2)

2021

EL ASSAD Safwan, BARBA Dominique
Digital Communications 1: Fundamentals and Techniques
Digital Communications 2: Directed and Practical Work

GAUDIN Thierry, MAUREL Marie-Christine, POMEROL Jean-Charles
Chance, Calculation and Life

LE DEUFF Olivier
Hyperdocumentation
(Intellectual Technologies Set – Volume 9)

PÉLISSIER Maud
Cultural Commons in the Digital Ecosystem
(Intellectual Technologies Set – Volume 8)

2020

CLIQUET Gérard, with the collaboration of BARAY Jérôme
Location-Based Marketing: Geomarketing and Geolocation

DE FRÉMINVILLE Marie
Cybersecurity and Decision Makers: Data Security and Digital Trust

GEORGE Éric
Digitalization of Society and Socio-political Issues 2: Digital, Information and Research

HELALI Saida
Systems and Network Infrastructure Integration

LOISEAU Hugo, VENTRE Daniel, ADEN Hartmut
Cybersecurity in Humanities and Social Sciences: A Research Methods Approach (Cybersecurity Set – Volume 1)

SEDKAOUI Soraya, KHELFAOUI Mounia
Sharing Economy and Big Data Analytics

SCHMITT Églantine
Big Data: An Art of Decision Making
(Intellectual Technologies Set – Volume 7)

2019

ALBAN Daniel, EYNAUD Philippe, MALAURENT Julien, RICHET Jean-Loup, VITARI Claudio
Information Systems Management: Governance, Urbanization and Alignment

AUGEY Dominique, with the collaboration of ALCARAZ Marina
Digital Information Ecosystems: Smart Press

BATTON-HUBERT Mireille, DESJARDIN Eric, PINET François
Geographic Data Imperfection 1: From Theory to Applications

BRIQUET-DUHAZÉ Sophie, TURCOTTE Catherine
From Reading-Writing Research to Practice

BROCHARD Luigi, KAMATH Vinod, CORBALAN Julita, HOLLAND Scott, MITTELBACH Walter, OTT Michael
Energy-Efficient Computing and Data Centers

CHAMOUX Jean-Pierre
The Digital Era 2: Political Economy Revisited

COCHARD Gérard-Michel
Introduction to Stochastic Processes and Simulation

DUONG Véronique
SEO Management: Methods and Techniques to Achieve Success

GAUCHEREL Cédric, GOUYON Pierre-Henri, DESSALLES Jean-Louis
Information, The Hidden Side of Life

GEORGE Éric
Digitalization of Society and Socio-political Issues 1: Digital, Communication and Culture

GHLALA Riadh
Analytic SQL in SQL Server 2014/2016

JANIER Mathilde, SAINT-DIZIER Patrick
Argument Mining: Linguistic Foundations

SOURIS Marc
Epidemiology and Geography: Principles, Methods and Tools of Spatial Analysis

TOUNSI Wiem
Cyber-Vigilance and Digital Trust: Cyber Security in the Era of Cloud Computing and IoT

2018

ARDUIN Pierre-Emmanuel
Insider Threats
(Advances in Information Systems Set – Volume 10)

CARMÈS Maryse
Digital Organizations Manufacturing: Scripts, Performativity and Semiopolitics
(Intellectual Technologies Set – Volume 5)

CARRÉ Dominique, VIDAL Geneviève
Hyperconnectivity: Economical, Social and Environmental Challenges
(Computing and Connected Society Set – Volume 3)

CHAMOUX Jean-Pierre
The Digital Era 1: Big Data Stakes

DOUAY Nicolas
Urban Planning in the Digital Age
(Intellectual Technologies Set – Volume 6)

FABRE Renaud, BENSOUSSAN Alain
The Digital Factory for Knowledge: Production and Validation of Scientific Results

GAUDIN Thierry, LACROIX Dominique, MAUREL Marie-Christine, POMEROL Jean-Charles
Life Sciences, Information Sciences

GAYARD Laurent
Darknet: Geopolitics and Uses
(Computing and Connected Society Set – Volume 2)

IAFRATE Fernando
Artificial Intelligence and Big Data: The Birth of a New Intelligence
(Advances in Information Systems Set – Volume 8)

LE DEUFF Olivier
Digital Humanities: History and Development
(Intellectual Technologies Set – Volume 4)

MANDRAN Nadine
Traceable Human Experiment Design Research: Theoretical Model and Practical Guide
(Advances in Information Systems Set – Volume 9)

PIVERT Olivier
NoSQL Data Models: Trends and Challenges

ROCHET Claude
Smart Cities: Reality or Fiction

SALEH Imad, AMMI, Mehdi, SZONIECKY Samuel
Challenges of the Internet of Things: Technology, Use, Ethics
(Digital Tools and Uses Set – Volume 7)

SAUVAGNARGUES Sophie
Decision-making in Crisis Situations: Research and Innovation for Optimal Training

SEDKAOUI Soraya
Data Analytics and Big Data

SZONIECKY Samuel
Ecosystems Knowledge: Modeling and Analysis Method for Information and Communication
(Digital Tools and Uses Set – Volume 6)

2017

BOUHAÏ Nasreddine, SALEH Imad
Internet of Things: Evolutions and Innovations
(Digital Tools and Uses Set – Volume 4)

DUONG Véronique
Baidu SEO: Challenges and Intricacies of Marketing in China

LESAS Anne-Marie, MIRANDA Serge
The Art and Science of NFC Programming
(Intellectual Technologies Set – Volume 3)

LIEM André
Prospective Ergonomics
(Human-Machine Interaction Set – Volume 4)

MARSAULT Xavier
Eco-generative Design for Early Stages of Architecture
(Architecture and Computer Science Set – Volume 1)

REYES-GARCIA Everardo
The Image-Interface: Graphical Supports for Visual Information
(Digital Tools and Uses Set – Volume 3)

REYES-GARCIA Everardo, BOUHAÏ Nasreddine
Designing Interactive Hypermedia Systems
(Digital Tools and Uses Set – Volume 2)

SAÏD Karim, BAHRI KORBI Fadia
Asymmetric Alliances and Information Systems:Issues and Prospects
(Advances in Information Systems Set – Volume 7)

SZONIECKY Samuel, BOUHAÏ Nasreddine
Collective Intelligence and Digital Archives: Towards Knowledge Ecosystems
(Digital Tools and Uses Set – Volume 1)

2016

BEN CHOUIKHA Mona
Organizational Design for Knowledge Management

BERTOLO David
Interactions on Digital Tablets in the Context of 3D Geometry Learning
(Human-Machine Interaction Set – Volume 2)

BOUVARD Patricia, SUZANNE Hervé
Collective Intelligence Development in Business

EL FALLAH SEGHROUCHNI Amal, ISHIKAWA Fuyuki, HÉRAULT Laurent, TOKUDA Hideyuki
Enablers for Smart Cities

FABRE Renaud, in collaboration with MESSERSCHMIDT-MARIET Quentin, HOLVOET Margot
New Challenges for Knowledge

GAUDIELLO Ilaria, ZIBETTI Elisabetta
Learning Robotics, with Robotics, by Robotics
(Human-Machine Interaction Set – Volume 3)

HENROTIN Joseph
The Art of War in the Network Age
(Intellectual Technologies Set – Volume 1)

KITAJIMA Munéo
Memory and Action Selection in Human–Machine Interaction
(Human–Machine Interaction Set – Volume 1)

LAGRAÑA Fernando
E-mail and Behavioral Changes: Uses and Misuses of Electronic Communications

LEIGNEL Jean-Louis, UNGARO Thierry, STAAR Adrien
Digital Transformation
(Advances in Information Systems Set – Volume 6)

MONINO Jean-Louis, SEDKAOUI Soraya
Big Data, Open Data and Data Development
(Smart Innovation Set – Volume 3)

NOYER Jean-Max
Transformation of Collective Intelligences
(Intellectual Technologies Set – Volume 2)

VENTRE Daniel
Information Warfare – 2nd edition

VITALIS André
The Uncertain Digital Revolution
(Computing and Connected Society Set – Volume 1)

2015

ARDUIN Pierre-Emmanuel, GRUNDSTEIN Michel, ROSENTHAL-SABROUX Camille
Information and Knowledge System
(Advances in Information Systems Set – Volume 2)

BÉRANGER Jérôme
Medical Information Systems Ethics

BRONNER Gérald
Belief and Misbelief Asymmetry on the Internet

IAFRATE Fernando
From Big Data to Smart Data
(Advances in Information Systems Set – Volume 1)

KRICHEN Saoussen, BEN JOUIDA Sihem
Supply Chain Management and its Applications in Computer Science

NEGRE Elsa
Information and Recommender Systems
(Advances in Information Systems Set – Volume 4)

POMEROL Jean-Charles, EPELBOIN Yves, THOURY Claire
MOOCs

SAAD Inès, ROSENTHAL-SABROUX Camille, GARGOURI Faïez
Information Systems for Knowledge Management

SALLES Maryse
Decision-Making and the Information System
(Advances in Information Systems Set – Volume 3)

SAMARA Tarek
ERP and Information Systems: Integration or Disintegration
(Advances in Information Systems Set – Volume 5)

2014

DINET Jérôme
Information Retrieval in Digital Environments

DUBÉ Jean, LEGROS Diègo
Spatial Econometrics Using Microdata

HÉNO Raphaële, CHANDELIER Laure
3D Modeling of Buildings: Outstanding Sites

KEMBELLEC Gérald, CHARTRON Ghislaine, SALEH Imad
Recommender Systems

MATHIAN Hélène, SANDERS Lena
Spatio-temporal Approaches: Geographic Objects and Change Process

PLANTIN Jean-Christophe
Participatory Mapping

RIGO Michel
Formal Languages, Automata and Numeration Systems 1: Introduction to Combinatorics on Words
Formal Languages, Automata and Numeration Systems 2: Applications to Recognizability and Decidability

TORRES-MORENO Juan-Manuel
Automatic Text Summarization

VENTRE Daniel
Chinese Cybersecurity and Defense

2013

BERNIK Igor
Cybercrime and Cyberwarfare

CAPET Philippe, DELAVALLADE Thomas
Information Evaluation

LEBRATY Jean-Fabrice, LOBRE-LEBRATY Katia
Crowdsourcing: One Step Beyond

SALLABERRY Christian
Geographical Information Retrieval in Textual Corpora

TURENNE Nicolas
Knowledge Needs and Information Extraction: Towards an Artificial Consciousness

2012

BUCHER Bénédicte, LE BER Florence
Innovative Software Development in GIS

GAUSSIER Eric, YVON François
Textual Information Access

STOCKINGER Peter
Audiovisual Archives: Digital Text and Discourse Analysis

VENTRE Daniel
Cyber Conflict

2011

BANOS Arnaud, THÉVENIN Thomas
Geographical Information and Urban Transport Systems

DAUPHINÉ André
Fractal Geography

LEMBERGER Pirmin, MOREL Mederic
Managing Complexity of Information Systems

STOCKINGER Peter
Introduction to Audiovisual Archives

STOCKINGER Peter
Digital Audiovisual Archives

VENTRE Daniel
Cyberwar and Information Warfare

2010

BONNET Pierre
Enterprise Data Governance

BRUNET Roger
Sustainable Geography

BUFFET Olivier, SIGAUD Olivier
Markov Decision Processes in Artificial Intelligence

CARREGA Pierre
Geographical Information and Climatology

CAUVIN Colette, ESCOBAR Francisco, SERRADJ Aziz
Thematic Cartography – 3-volume series
Thematic Cartography and Transformations – Volume 1
Cartography and the Impact of the Quantitative Revolution – Volume 2
New Approaches in Thematic Cartography – Volume 3

LANGLOIS Patrice
Simulation of Complex Systems in GIS

MATHIS Philippe
Graphs and Networks – 2nd edition

THERIAULT Marius, DES ROSIERS François
Modeling Urban Dynamics

2009

BONNET Pierre, DETAVERNIER Jean-Michel, VAUQUIER Dominique
Sustainable IT Architecture: the Progressive Way of Overhauling Information Systems with SOA

PAPY Fabrice
Information Science

RIVARD François, ABOU HARB Georges, MERET Philippe
The Transverse Information System

ROCHE Stéphane, CARON Claude
Organizational Facets of GIS

VENTRE Daniel
Information Warfare

2008

BRUGNOT Gérard
Spatial Management of Risks

FINKE Gerd
Operations Research and Networks

GUERMOND Yves
Modeling Process in Geography

KANEVSKI Michael
Advanced Mapping of Environmental Data

MANOUVRIER Bernard, LAURENT Ménard
Application Integration: EAI, B2B, BPM and SOA

PAPY Fabrice
Digital Libraries

2007

DOBESCH Hartwig, DUMOLARD Pierre, DYRAS Izabela
Spatial Interpolation for Climate Data

SANDERS Lena
Models in Spatial Analysis

2006

CLIQUET Gérard
Geomarketing

CORNIOU Jean-Pierre
Looking Back and Going Forward in IT

DEVILLERS Rodolphe, JEANSOULIN Robert
Fundamentals of Spatial Data Quality

Printed and bound by CPI Group (UK) Ltd, Croydon, CR0 4YY
13/09/2026
14961048-0003